# The Spirit of the Laws in Mozambique

JUAN OBARRIO is assistant professor of anthropology at Johns Hopkins University.

The University of Chicago Press, Chicago 60637
The University of Chicago Press, Ltd., London
© 2014 by The University of Chicago
All rights reserved. Published 2014.
Printed in the United States of America

23 22 21 20 19 18 17 16 15 14     1 2 3 4 5

ISBN-13: 978-0-226-15372-8 (cloth)
ISBN-13: 978-0-226-15386-5 (paper)
ISBN-13: 978-0-226-15405-3 (e-book)
DOI: 10.7208/chicago/9780226154053.001.0001

Library of Congress Cataloging-in-Publication Data

Obarrio, Juan, author.
    The spirit of the laws in Mozambique / Juan Obarrio.
        pages   cm
    Includes bibliographical references and index.
    ISBN 978-0-226-15372-8 (cloth : alk. paper)—ISBN 978-0-226-15386-5
(pbk. : alk. paper)—ISBN 978-0-226-15405-3 (e-book)  1. Mozambique—Politics
and government—1994–  2. Citizenship—Mozambique.  3. Ethnology—
Mozambique.   I. Title.
    DT3389.O34 2014
    349.679—dc23
                                                                2014004077

♾ This paper meets the requirements of ANSI/NISO Z39.48-1992 (Permanence of Paper).

FOR VALERIA

# Contents

# Introduction

## *The Spirit of the Laws*

### Context

"We made a terrible mistake." This statement was made by Mozambican politicians, academics, and development experts linked to the ruling party in reference to the history and the present of the "customary." I encountered versions of it sporadically during my preliminary visits to the country in 2000 and more concretely and more often during the initial months of my fieldwork a few years later.

In the winter of 2004 Mozambique found itself poised before the law, summoned by the courts of an emerging order of global capital and international jurisprudence.[1] What was the spirit of this law?

International actors speaking the intricate language of the juridical promoted once again "modernization" and "development"[2] through social planning, leading toward the "rule of law" and "structural adjustment." Within this national process, shaped by transnational vectors, multiple political agents coalesced and collided in complex articulations. Some types of authorities, such as local institutions of "popular justice," located within a liminal juridical space, were vanishing, while others, such as chiefs, were returning, enjoying entitlements granted by a new dispensation of "recognition." This broad juridical reform of the state revealed profound fractures within the national territory and its political imaginations. Already at the beginning of my study of the reform, I encountered decisive paradoxes.

I was inquiring about questions related to the field of the political and to the postconflict transition between very different regimes, as part of a research framework that included the crucial question of the status of tradition within modern democracy. Yet the statement on mistakes regarding the customary referred the conversation time and again back to the question of customary law and authorities in a manner that denoted, first, a historical centrality that I had somewhat downplayed and, second, a multiplicity of political meanings of "custom" that my research framework or my political views had not fully accommodated until then. This book attempts to make sense of that centrality and of the historical transformations of various senses of indigeneity within contemporary African democracy.

This book addresses transformations of the state form under neoliberal reforms in Africa from the viewpoint of the dilemmas of citizenship and custom. The following study of a specific place at a key moment in time aims to shed light on the meaning of the return, or perhaps redemption, of the historical past in the present. Each chapter of this book explores a different angle on local, everyday material entanglements between the temporalities of the state and the customary, while the conclusion addresses the meaning of the customary for political questions of life and death.

I originally conceived the fieldwork project on which this book is based around the year 2000 in order to explore empirically, from the vantage point of an African post-Socialist and postconflict situation, the contemporary form of the postcolonial state. I focused on two main theoretical issues offered by the Mozambican case: first, the status of the state as the alleged main locus of politics and, second, the relation of continuity between war and the political. In Mozambique, the field of indigeneity occupied a central place within both the civil war and the postconflict transition to liberal democracy.

Mozambique constituted a key place to study these dimensions of the political. The singular experience of an African version of Socialism—Leninist avant-gardism, Maoist collectivization, Ujamaa-type villagization, centralist developmentalism, ban on custom, and construction of a new subjectivity of the citizen—added different and profound dimensions to questions regarding the political, the law, and citizenship rights. Mozambique's history since the late 1960s, encompassing colonialism, underground armed struggle, Socialism, civil war, and liberal democracy, opened up multiple perspectives on the question of politics understood as a continuation of armed conflict, as well as on issues of reconciliation and justice. The timing of my research underscored a crucial fact that the post-Socialist condition made evident: the renewed centrality of the customary and the local within neoliberal reforms driven by global actors.

My first research trip to Mozambique took place in 2000, at about the time that the Mozambican state reversed a ban on the customary that had been in place since independence in 1975, passing a juridico-political reform that recognized "traditional authorities," reincorporating them into the fields of local governance and development. During my preliminary research trips, I worked from a political and epistemic perspective that placed the customary—chiefs, norms, ritual—at a relevant yet marginal level of analysis. As a cluster of legacies from precolonial and colonial times, it could be seen as fostering some of the pitfalls and deficits of post-colonial democracy.

My subsequent long fieldwork proved some of my initial presuppositions wrong and located the issue of the customary, and with it the issues of democracy, emancipation and inclusion, at a very different dimension of analysis. Conversations with elite politicians and foreign experts, and their assertions about locality, indigeneity, and rights, disclosed for me the centrality that custom held for the political future of the nation-state and its multiple potential meanings both for various factions within the "state" and also for different sectors of rural and periurban populations.

During my initial research in Maputo, the capital of Mozambique, I surveyed contradictory remarks made by state officers, consultants, judges, and lawyers and abandoned my own initial self-deception with regard to aspects of political processes (such as preliminary thoughts about the overarching hegemony of donor agencies) and the straightforward utilitarian meaning of reforms with respect to the juridical and political status of locality. I then immersed myself in the history and currency of logics of sovereignty that were being transformed at the level of the nation-state, first, in the context of an analysis of the urban milieus and central state and, later, as a deep study of rural and periurban localities and populations.

I encountered what Mozambican political actors referred to by many different names and misnomers that refer to precolonial, colonial, or post-colonial political regimes. These new turns of phrase or revived, older, ritualized sayings referred to something akin to the force of the historicity of the customary, as a kind of resilience that has multiple, changing senses.

Obviously, there were deep disjunctions between the idealized views of foreign and national politicians in the capital and the materiality of local processes in rural regions. These differences and misunderstandings have crucial effects on the design and implementation of new laws and policies and reproduce a mirror effect that maintains a distance between the imagined "state" and "customary."

As I engaged in my fieldwork on the local state in northern rural areas, far from the capital, speaking with local officials, rural peasants, and periurban dwellers, I observed dynamics of the customary related to ritual norms and kinship that were quite distant from the "postdevelopmentalist" instrumental views of officials of the ruling party and donor agencies. It took me years of reflection, discussion, and rewriting on what I observed at work in northern localities, in terms of law, custom, rights, norms, kinship, ritual, and the body, to arrive at the version of those processes and the view of the state that I present in this book.

While political actors in the capital affirmed, from the perspective of macrolegal reform, that the customary held key import for the potential of democracy, my fieldwork both confirmed this significance and contradicted it. "We made a terrible mistake," affirmed the development agents and reformists when explaining the reasons behind the new program of recognition of custom. Exploring various paradoxical angles of this statement, I arrived at a perspective that is quite different from the rationale for the (neo)liberalization of the state. In the following chapters I study entwinements of law and custom that shape state and citizenship in unforeseen, nondemocratic ways and yet seem to hold potential for emancipation. Let us anticipate some of the facts reviewed in the book.

Around 2003–4 in Maputo, a seemingly infinite number of cases, files, and records were precariously lodged, waiting for a sentence forever delayed, overflowing the offices and hallways of official courts. In the obscure corridors of the ministries, a constant rush of people and a proliferation of forms, reports, project proposals, and drafts of laws were the signs of an ongoing juridical reform that aimed at transforming the very basis of a state transitioning from long decades of bureaucratic colonial fascism and Afro-Socialism.[3] At the very same time, far away up north, in a rural district or in the periphery of a small town, the enactment of laws was deferred, and juridical reform of institutions and norms was unevenly implemented.

The ruptures of temporalities and social modalities that separated the south from the center and north of the country generated a time lag of historical anachronisms and social disruption, affecting the status of juridico-political authorities addressed by the reform of the central state. Chiefs, former state officers, and local tribunals either reemerged or vanished at different velocities, calibrated by the speed of juridical reform. The imposition of jurisdictional power seemed broken, or at least deferred.

In the villages and in the periurban neighborhoods, various "traditions" deployed the sovereignty of other norms, speaking the language of another type of law. After a ban of nearly thirty years, "custom" was again at stake in the former "People's Tribunals,"[4] which were still at work despite having been removed from the state system by the new Constitution of the democratic transition. Customs reemerged as well in the rural "customary courts" of chiefs, who were being granted official recognition by the same ongoing juridical reform of the central state.[5]

In these two forms of community tribunal of the Mozambican north, citizens found themselves amid the perils and potentialities of an age emerging out of the violence of the war and moving toward uncertain transformations of the nature of sovereignty. At stake were the very identity and contemporary fate of the individual—the citizen, the subject—entangled within the webs of the law's sovereignty, being shaped by a constant recombination of various juridical regimes and historical narratives. Let us consider some of the features of the systemic political transition, as seen through the prism of the locality.

Customary authorities who had recently regained state recognition of their authority solved conflicts in rural districts, often competing for political power, legitimacy, and legal jurisdiction with other chiefs, as well as with structures remaining from a previous political era. In semiurban areas, the former Socialist secretaries as well as the old People's Tribunals were still at work, mingling oral traditions and written registers, customary law and state codes. Relabeled "community courts," they base their legitimacy on invocations to ideologies and iconographies from the previous party-state system, even though they are no longer considered to be part of the state.

The recent trajectories of these juridico-political institutions posed the question of the difficult reconstitution of sociality within entangled processes of war, violence, and democracy, which highlighted the force that founds that law, evident in local customary norms and authorities that were proposed by the state and donors as a key component in the democratization and decentralization process. The question of the force of law, or the legitimate and legal monopoly on violence, is related both to official state law and to the local norms that are juridically "recognized," thus unsettling received, clear, hierarchical distinctions between "top-down" and "bottom-up" views on the state and the local. War and conflict, or legal violence, are axes that show how the "state" and its local other are mutually reproduced. The issue of war vis-à-vis the political, the way in which armed conflict shapes the contours of democracy, posed several questions that are explored in the following chapters. For instance, how are polities reconstructed after devastating periods of death and destruction? How does internal armed conflict affect the notion of a single nation-state and its reformulation after the ceasefire? What was the substance that held together this society and the multiple communities that formed it? In the absence of formal official reconciliation, given the nature of the democratic peace process shared by two former enemy armies, what mechanisms reconstituted sociality at the level of the local?

## Argument

The broad reform of the state taking place at the time of my field research in 2003–4 presented the problem of the centrality of the law in contemporary political transitions. This condition posed several questions that I sought to answer empirically through my fieldwork: Why is the field of the juridical so central within neoliberal politico-economic reform? How is the political judicialized as political struggles become claims on recognition of legal rights? More specifically, how are these global processes experienced from the singular vantage point of contemporary Africa?

This book presents an ethnographic exploration of the current status of the "spirit of the laws" in an African postcolony, studying how legal reform is reshaping both the central-state apparatus and the locality, transforming dynamics of governance and citizenship. It analyzes the predicament of state sovereignty in contemporary Africa through the study of the confluence and struggle of multiple jurisdictions.

My main argument is that despite the wave of democratization and liberalization that has occurred over the last two decades, currently the African state juridically enforces a type of restricted citizenship, linked to the reappraisal of precolonial customary formations. I substantiate this claim through the study of a broad legal reform that produces a renewed essentialization of allegedly purist "traditions." These reified customs, which include remains of violence and authoritarianism, had already been profoundly reshaped by modern colonial and early postcolonial state governance. This book's specific contribution is to illustrate how, beyond the mere dichotomy of modernist citizenship and colonial subjecthood, a new form of "customary citizenship" emerges, blending national belonging, official rights, and local norms and claims, encompassing vast sectors of the population within a process of inclusive exclusion.

This ethnography focuses on one particular case study as an example of this broader and varied political condition, through a historical and ethnographic analysis of the place and scope of the realm of the customary in Mozambique. The customary played a key role in colonial governance (1890–1975) and the devastating civil war (1977–92) and, marking the specificity of the Mozambican case, was banned by the FRELIMO (Frente de Libertação de Moçambique; Mozambican Liberation Front) party-state system for twenty-five years (1975–2000). The recognition of locality and customary law and authorities by the FRELIMO regime during the democratic transition thus constitutes a historically significant political intervention.

The study of trajectories of the customary within recent postcolonial history leads to the analysis of the crucial role that this field has played within recent neoliberal reforms. Throughout the continent, researchers have described instances of the entwinement of "modernity" and "tradition," as well as the complex, imbricated topographies of legal pluralisms. This book, however, analyzes the juridical fate of the customary in the unique and paradoxical context of the entwinement of custom and former Socialist state institutions that had the explicit task of opposing and obliterating tradition during the previous decades.

Mozambique has been hailed as a success story by political analysts as well as by the international community of donors, who have supported the juridical reform of the state that has been ongoing since the end of the civil war and the transition from Socialism in the mid-1990s. Positive accomplishments have been identified in several key areas, such as post-conflict democratic transition and the honoring of the peace accords; post-Socialist reform of the state apparatus; liberalization of the centralized, planned economy and partial privatization of the public sector; as well as broad policies of deregulation and decentralization of governance and democratization of local state structures, including, crucially, the recognition of formerly banned customs and traditional authority.

The imaginary of the law, chosen as the main template for the transformation of the logic of governance (from Socialism to liberal democracy) and for the reconstruction of a devastated society (from international law to custom), recalled the early modern, enlightened program of the spirit of the laws. Juridical reforms were based on latter-day Enlightenment principles of social improvement and scientific observation and recast the limpid logic of norms as the foundation of sovereignty. The law constitutes the ideological framework for the definition of state sovereignty, through the legal inclusion or exclusion of its alleged other (markets, international community, the customary). Agents of governance currently deploy the law as a spirit of the times: an elusive, both rational and magical formula for the reform of the social.

The spirit of the laws is an image-concept that has constituted the kernel of state sovereignty since early modern times, from its inception in Europe to its dislocated implementation in colonies (and postcolonies) such as Mozambique. In the following chapters, I describe its contemporary unfolding as an attempt to juridically demarcate fields of alterity, to restrain the theologies of local political authority, the magicality of spirits, and the violence of the customary and its present juridical form as community. Through formulaic rhetoric, theatrical performance, and fetishism, the "spirit" of the laws reveals the magicality of the mythological genealogies of the state itself. It discloses ritualized political imaginations that conjure through coups, strokes, and sleights of hands, through texts and speeches of law and jurisdiction, a bounded, rational entity holding the "legal monopoly on violence."

Focusing on the question of citizenship, the ethnography of the law presented in this book reveals pronounced ambiguities or sheer failures in the process of juridical reform. Extensive fieldwork in the Mozambican central and local states, encompassing institutional settings, transnational influences on government, and various conceptions of the state's scope and practice have led to this critical study of transformations of citizenship that offers different conclusions from those presented by the state and donors.

This study gathers narratives from ordinary citizens and from state officials working in the upper and lower echelons of the administration in the capital and in a northern province, as well as from historical and documentary sources. These local perspectives offer the foundation for an analysis of the reason of the state and its art of government within the entanglements of multiple apparatuses, examining the activities of various state agencies in search of legitimacy. This ethnographic perspective led to a critical appraisal of the analytical categories of central and local and their alleged connections.

This case study aims to contribute to the broader literature on the anthropology of the state from the viewpoint of the specificity of African contexts. It focuses on the singular features of a post-Socialist state undergoing a profound juridical reform as it transitions to democracy within a post–civil war condition. More specifically, the book studies the contours and scope of a state immersed in a broad process of neoliberal reconstruction, understood as a juridico-economic program of deeply regulated deregulation aimed at the privatization of the economy, decentralization of governance, and reconstitution of the subjectivity of the citizen. It shows the way in which the post-Socialist condition is a particular version of the African postcolony, in which neoliberal deregulation has not produced a blanket, all-encompassing transformation. Rather, aspects of previous regimes of governance—colonial, Socialist—remain entangled within the current dispensation. The ethnographic lens for understanding this process was to examine the amalgamation of the fields of law and justice, and the place of custom within them, as expressed through juridical reform.

The study of the juridical reform of the state promoted by international donors, which provided funds that amounted to half the national budget, disclosed the ambiguous centrality of the law within the democratic transition from Socialism and civil war to the civil state of liberal democracy. What was the thrust of this "spirit" of the law? How did it articulate with other spirits, other forces, other local norms? What was its jurisdiction?

The fieldwork at the local level yielded other questions on the juridical. How is sociality produced through a quasi-metaphysical kernel, or spirit, of the law in official or customary courts and in rituals of conflict resolution? What is the foundation of this law, its "force"? What is the fundamental difference between the structures of the law and the aspiration for justice? Is sovereignty founded solely upon violence, as a straightforward reading of continuities between war and politics might have it? Or are other forces of life, of survival, and of a shared living-with the other located at the foundation of political community? What is the space of "custom" entrenched within this "law"?

Whereas transformations such as those occurring in Mozambique over the last two decades can be grouped under the general, if imprecise, label of neoliberal processes, they show crucial variations within the far-reaching category of neoliberalism. While some generic features are identifiable with this political and economic formation, such as policies of deregulation, privatization, decentralization, and so on, singular cases provide different angles, and African states in particular show striking particularities. This book studies one instance of this: the privatization of a state apparatus that nevertheless retains key features of a previous centralized political regime in terms of socioeconomic development, population management, and legal rights. The argument moves on to show the centrality of the customary and indigeneity for the politico-economic privatization and decentralization of the state.

The law is a privileged, yet relatively understudied, prism through which to study the most salient singularities of African cases. Classical liberal theory presents the realm of the juridical as the foundation of state sovereignty, and its current iteration as neoliberalism also operates on the basis of a striking prevalence of the law—or, more precisely, a legal discourse shaped by the hegemonic logic of the market—as the organizing principle of society.

Deployed against the grain of its origins in Enlightenment thought, the spirit of the laws is a useful concept for studying modernist ideas of state and citizenship rights. It sheds light on the trajectories of Western discourse, ritual, and ideology as they became adapted in the colony and were later transformed in postcolonial times. A current round of juridical and moral reform, conducted under the auspices of neoliberal postmodernization, endows the concept with new heuristic purchase.

The Enlightenment's spirit of the laws carried a promise of emancipation, yet its implementation in the colony obviously took the form of racial segregation and social discrimination rather than universal legal rights. A postcolony such as Mozambique, in the decade of the 2000s, exemplified the difficult paradox of reinstating the logic of the law within a new incarnation of the early modern perspective on the juridical foundation of sovereignty, now under the form of a neoliberal transition from socialism to a restricted, economic conception of the "rule of law." The following chapters offer an ethnographic study of this process defined here under the concept of the "state of structural adjustment," which is a strategic situation of power, a temporal condition and assemblage of private and public sovereigns amalgamated by the spirit of the law, its spectral magicality, and its institutional materiality.

Whereas democracy, transparency, and the scope of rights in Africa were not key concerns for national elites and the international community during the Cold War, the contemporary global obsession with the rule of law and its variations across the postcolonial world merits an ethnographic study from the perspective of an anthropology of justice that denaturalizes it and places it in historical context. In particular, the ways in which concurrent regimes of subjectification and subjecthood shape the democratic monad, the postcolonial citizen, provide a crucial locus for studying the current predicament and potential of the state in Africa. Hence, this ethnography of the state focuses on a history of the present of citizenship. It traces the question of the customary as the state's other, the space that the (colonial and postcolonial) state has used as a tool to fashion itself, from the construction of locality as the realm of indigeneity to its contemporary version as "community."

## Structure and Main Concepts

The book is divided into two parts. The first part of the book studies the recent juridical reform of governance, within a history of relations between the state and the customary. The second part illustrates how, at the level of the local state, former Socialist authorities and institutions amalgamate law, custom, neoliberal norms, and previous Socialist forms in a novel form of local governance whose meaning and range exceed the mere "return" of colonial governmentality.

Thus, the first part studies the "central" state in the capital city, illustrating the process of legal reform of the state produced through the joint work of transnational donor agencies and national state units. The second part studies the "local" state in a northern periurban district, focusing on law and justice through an ethnography of a peculiar institution: the former Socialist People's Tribunals, still at work in rural and periurban areas.

An anthropology of law and justice is extremely relevant for the study of the contemporary neoliberal emphasis on the realm of the juridical as a key space of state reform. A focus on the law reveals key aspects of the African postcolonial condition that remain understudied, within processes of transition affecting both governance and subjectivities. In this context, the category of "jurisdiction" appears as a main locus to study the potentials and pitfalls of sovereignty in the postcolony. The contemporary African state is here studied as a labyrinthine entanglement of multiple, competing jurisdictions, underscoring the crucial role that the demarcation of locality plays within current processes of governance in the subcontinent.

Intervening in current debates on the nature of African postcolonial governance, the book develops two main concepts: the state of structural adjustment and customary citizenship. At the level of the nation-state and central institutions of governance in the capital, the analysis centers on the state of structural adjustment as an entanglement of post-Socialist national state units and transnational donor agencies, an amalgam of private and public forms of sovereignty that exerts governance and shapes the reform of the state apparatus. The book studies the way in which the logic of the state of structural adjustment does not grant full citizenship rights to its population but rather enforces (in periurban and rural areas) a localized form of political belonging and national attachment defined here as "customary citizenship." The latter part of the book provides concrete examples of this condition in local institutions of governance, legal rights, and access to justice.

The state's recent politics of recognition produces a locally inflected form of national belonging, enacted through a detour marked by the subjection to "custom" and traditional authority and by a process of subjectification strongly shaped by kinship and adscriptions to locality. This book traces ethnographically the historical production of this condition through legal codification, illustrating the political contours of customary citizenship in the current work of former Socialist structures of governance at the local level, the "dynamizing groups," or party-state units that enacted executive and judicial powers. Following questions of law and citizenship within these institutions, the ethnography focuses on the former People's Tribunals. These courts are still at work in the north of the country, despite having been excluded from the official judiciary system through constitutional reform. These institutions, which had been explicitly implemented by the postrevolutionary state to oppose custom ("obscurantism") and the authority of traditional chieftaincies, at the time of my fieldwork in the mid-2000s still enforced a mixture of official law, former Socialist normativity, customary law, and kinship rules.

In Mozambique the realm of the customary is deeply embedded within the histories of colonialism, socialism, and various periods of warfare. Therefore, the contemporary reappraisal and recognition of custom, and its embrace even within local, former Socialist institutions, can be interpreted as an implicit national policy of "truth and reconciliation." Customary citizenship thus plays a central role in the state form that has been produced by the postconflict democratic transition and its neoliberal economic reforms.

The argument of the book moves from history and socioeconomic analysis to ethnography, and from the study of the "central" state and the scene of the development industry and legal reform to the space of locality and its sites of legal authority and dispensation of justice. The empirical analysis of postcolonial politics leads to a conceptualization of the state as a field of forces rather than as an apparatus. It appears as an assemblage that evokes the original etymological meaning of the state as "status," or condition.

This conceptualization is sustained, in the following chapters, by an ethnographic and historical analysis that demonstrates the ruptures, discontinuities, and fissures within the alleged unity—administrative, juridical, territorial—of the state. From the perspective of law, the analysis of jurisdiction reveals the impossibility for this kind of state to fully demarcate and encompass a locality, that is, to impose sovereignty on jurisdictional districts. The modernist spirit of the laws has to negotiate its power and scope with myriad other local spirits and normativities. This leads to a state that cannot be conceptualized in terms of scale. Rather, the ethnography in the following chapters shows that it is a "state of things," an assemblage of various agencies where different temporalities, memories, and imaginaries coalesce.

The chapters that follow provide an empirical analysis of a post-Socialist state of structural adjustment and customary citizenship from the interconnected perspectives of the nation's capital and a northern locality. The genealogy of the state form provides the context for the ethnography of a local "minor state," formed by institutions such as the Bureau of the Neighborhood Secretary and the community court. This raises the question of the law understood also as historiography, which is studied ethnographically here through detailed observation of how current juridical reforms amount to a rewriting of national history, through accounts of the relations between the state and the customary.

The next chapters examine the political and juridical contours of a locality, focusing on questions of law and citizenship rights. They explore ethnographically the ways in which the local state and, in particular, the community court are spaces where public and private spheres coalesce around the figure of the citizen, as individuals perform aspects of subjectivity and a public use of reason related to the enactment of citizenship rights. The ethnography analyzes overlapping regimes of subjectification that mingle at the community court and produce a "customary citizen," molded by the state's normativity as well as by tradition and kinship.

I will now briefly outline the contents of each chapter, to show how they present singular, different aspects of the history and present form of the state, as well as of the key space of the customary within the political.

Chapter 1 sets the sociohistorical context for the ethnographic case study of instances of law and justice, locating the book's main arguments on the state, citizenship, and law in relation to a discussion of trends in analyzing the state form in general and in Africa in particular.

Chapter 2 provides a general historical introduction to the state in Mozambique. It studies the juridical construction of the customary as a technology of governance anchored in a political economy. The history of the state viewed from the perspective of the legal distinction between citizen and subject provides a genealogy of current forms of customary citizenship. The trajectory of custom is traced through the transition between colonial and postcolonial regimes, marked by war and conflict, and the deployment by the current post-Socialist state of a politics of "recognition" of the customary as a central feature of a process toward economic liberalization and democratic "rule of law." The juridical reform deployed by the state and international agencies can thus be seen as a historiography that redefines the scope of the state and the shape of the local. The historical analysis shows the conundrums involved in the transition from the colonial realm of the customary to the postcolonial, neoliberal space of the community.

Chapter 3 elaborates on the contours of the state within the neoliberal condition, presenting an ethnographic study of the capital city in terms of the scenes and agents of development and the settings of the juridical reform of justice and the local customary. This political space is conceptualized as the state of structural adjustment, as an assemblage of public and private, national and foreign agents. The chapter examines key debates on citizenship in contemporary Africa, offering a succinct definition of "customary citizenship." As a bridge between the study of the central state in Maputo and of the local state in the north of the country, the final sections explore questions of jurisdiction over space and time as a critique of the alleged sovereign territorialization enacted by the state.

Chapter 4, the first chapter of part 2, situates the previous study of the central state and juridical reform in the capital in relation to a locality in a northern province. Studying everyday politics and access to justice, it analyzes the local not as a matter of scale but rather as textures and modalities. This chapter presents the institutions of a "minor state," which enforces an ambiguous sovereignty, having been constitutionally excluded from the state apparatus. The study of the community courts allows us to observe the current juridical foundations of the state from a local perspective. In the context of regional politics, the ethnography analyzes issues of justice from the perspectives of the lives and labor of Socialist state officials, as well as the legal and material infrastructures that sustain the work of the courts. The limits of the law's reach are revealed through the operations of community courts that struggle for jurisdiction among contesting forces in a periurban neighborhood. The daily procedures of the courts show how jurisdiction fails to demarcate a precise territory or faithfully enact the state's judgments and decisions. Commands emanating from the capital, designed to circumscribe the space and time of locality, are disrupted, displaying the limits of the attempted refoundation of the law throughout postcolonial history.

Chapter 5 studies the local state's attempts at securing legitimacy in the locality through a staged ritualization of its sovereignty. The chapter explores the poetics and politics of the enactment of jurisdiction. It discusses the theatricality involved in the blending of customary law, kinship norms, and official law by the community court. Studying jurisdiction as the voice of the law, it focuses on a counterpoint of rhetoric and gesture deployed between the judges and the litigants. This ceremony of justice illuminates two main issues: first, the elusive kernel of the law's power of commandment and, second, the central role of temporality in the force of law.

Chapters 6 and 7 provide ethnographic descriptions of the citizen-subject and case studies that illustrate an emergent customary citizenship through excerpts of cases and detailed observations from a community court. Chapter 6 focuses on issues of corporeality and relatedness that form the jurisdiction of kinship. It studies how customary law is enforced in conjunction with official state law. Chapter 7 concentrates on citizenship and civility by focusing on the figure of the postcolonial citizen-subject, who is shaped by both law and custom. It studies entitlements and rights of belonging within various local and national spheres.

The conclusion revisits the question of the spirit of the laws in terms of juridical conceptions of the state and how they are lived in the registers of the ordinary and the local. It offers a reflection on postcolonial citizenship in Africa as a coalescence of vectors of inclusion and exclusion, which at the same time constitutes a field of demand and action for a crucial politics of life.

# PART I

# Mozambique: Before the Law

In 2004, in Mozambique's capital, a juridical reform of the state with future, uncertain results was unfolding. In the rural northern provinces, men and women were being called daily before the law and judged by the local apparatus of justice according to an articulation of official state norms and a newfound "tradition." Daily, community courts, chiefs, churches, mosques, and party cells engaged in a struggle over jurisdiction. This dissemination of norms—and the attempt to conjugate them under the aegis of rational planning—questions the nature of the law's command in the postcolony. A space is opened up for an inquiry into the specific perspective that African forms of governance offer on the uncanny blending of rationality and disorder underlying the bureaucracies that deploy the force of law. Both localities, southern capital city and northern rural district, were entangled within a double bind, a back-and-forth movement influenced by foreign actors and forces.

Mozambique presented a sociopolitical landscape that showed deep disjunctions between regions in terms of political allegiance, economic development, infrastructures, and cultural formation, which interrupted the actual enactment of the law. The absolutely compromised legitimacy of jurisdiction illustrates the predicament of sovereignty in the postcolony, as the reemergence of "custom" and its entanglements with the law produce a multiplicity of political vectors. This proliferation does not weaken state sovereignty, appearing rather as a technology of governance within local spaces of contention about the meaning of national citizenship.

The spatial and temporal discontinuities between different areas of the country separate the spaces of the inception of the law and the spaces of its alleged enforcement. The disjunctures are both territorial and historical. Trends from the past appeared to return, slightly transformed. The arbitrary logic of colonial power still seems to permeate aspects of the force of law that structured postcolonial politics[1]—for instance, in the key role that locality and custom have been granted in the new legal programs.

This juridico-political reorganization of sociality produced definitive impacts in the realm of citizenship. The legal reform of the post-Socialist state generated an individual citizen torn between the call of unfathomable laws and the apparent absurdity of recurrent political alterations, constantly mixing various disparate systems of norms. "Tradition" appeared to be a bedrock of certainty both for agents of governance and for members of the local communities placed under their uncertain jurisdiction. Unexpectedly, given the country's recent political history, "custom" was once again reformatting local senses of citizenship and national belonging.

The nature of the law's sovereignty was undergoing profound transformations marked by the demise of political regimes and the end of a devastating internal armed struggle. The post-Socialist and the neoliberal juridico-political regimes seemed to blur under the auspices of transnational forms of capital and power that present features analogous to those of the previous colonial regime. In this context, former Socialist elites were intricately linked to foreign donor agencies in a continuous "state of structural adjustment."

At the same time facets of the previous one-party regime persisted. The "civil society" sought by transnational donors appeared to be but a cluster of institutions cut off from the state apparatus itself. Sovereignty was dispersed, as the commands generated by the central state were distorted at the moment of their implementation in the localities, according to the needs and designs of elites or local imaginations of power.

These seemingly neocolonial modalities of power operate through entanglements of private and public political sovereignties and economic agencies. The law occupies center stage in these processes in the form of a juridical reform propelled by transnational financial capital and a nascent global juridical infrastructure, which links in new ways international law and global courts with the normative spaces of locality. The discourses on law and development are, as in late colonial times, the principal tools for transforming political sovereignty and economic extraction, as a new iteration of primitive accumulation.

Those processes involved a new reconfiguration of the juridical foundation of sovereignty. This implied a broad economic and political reshaping of a nation-state through the law, mandated by a global discourse on governance, in which the rule of law and the law of value—economic and political liberalization—go hand in hand in the salvaging progression that allegedly leads every particular to a universal democratic stage.

And yet, this hypostasis of the law[2] contradicts its own foundations and petitions of principle. As the following chapters demonstrate, abstract juridical distinctions between state and society, private and public, or foreign and national become blurred when confronted with actual political conditions on the ground.

This was the juridico-political landscape in the mid-2000s when Mozambique, immersed in a democratic transition, was situated before the law and the legal status of sovereignty as the prerogative of the state was increasingly denied by new forms of global governance and conditionality represented by donor agencies, corporations, and nongovernmental organizations (NGOs). The formula "before the law" entails two related senses, one spatial and the other temporal. Both meanings are crucial to an interpretation of postcolonial politics in terms of legacies from colonial and precolonial social formations expressed in current domains of law and custom.

First, "before" in a spatial sense depicts a situation of being summoned to a court of law, be it international, national, penal, civil, or even customary. Second, "before" in a temporal sense can imply systems of normativity that were in place prior to the sovereignty of the rule of law. It alludes to the status of social order and norm previous to any written codification. In the context of contemporary African politics, this can be associated with the reappraisal of "custom" and precolonial norms and the way in which "traditional culture" blends with legal forms and is presented as a panacea for a current institutional impasse or a transition from the disorder of armed conflict to the prescribed accountability of modern democratic regimes.[3] Both meanings, spatial and temporal, crisscross within the contemporary Mozambican context, as transnational agencies and capital attempt to refashion the state through the social engineering of locality, by means of programs to reconstitute life through an articulation with the law.

## State of the Art

This analysis of the Mozambican case study engages current debates on the anthropology of the state from the specific viewpoint of literature on the state and citizenship in the African postcolonial condition. The

Mozambican state has undergone dramatic transformations in the span of a few decades. Between the late 1970s and the early 2000s this nation-state went from late colonialism to Socialism, then from civil war to liberal democracy, and also experienced deep changes in its juridical and economic regimes. Earlier on, in the nineteenth century, the territory that today is known as Mozambique—the end result of a diplomatic-military ultimatum given by Great Britain to Portugal—had been allocated to several distinct concessionary companies before becoming a proper colonial territory in the mid-1940s. These historical nuances allow a case like Mozambique to illuminate conundrums that belong to the general theory of the state.

The historical passage from a territory ruled by different concessionary corporations to a colony and, later on, from a People's republic to a liberal democratic state calls into question the juridico-political unity of a nation-state. What legal frameworks legitimize its identification as the same nation-state? Does the foundation on a constitution or the recognition by international law suffice to establish the historical continuity of the state apparatus?

The chapters that follow explore, from the perspective of law and justice, key questions about the sovereignty of the state form in contemporary Africa. What is the nature of a state whose budget is mainly composed of foreign aid? What is the relation between executive and legislative powers when legislation is proposed and funded by donor agencies and drafted by foreign consultants? What is the territorial authority of a state whose jurisdictional power is contested at the level of the locality? What is its scope if crucial state functions—regarding customs, taxes, or territorial security and control—are delegated to private corporations? What are its boundaries if local traditional chiefs perform duties as officially recognized "assistants" of the local state and if supposedly nonexistent, former local units are still recognized by local populations as legitimate government?

In the last couple of decades, exploring similar questions, an extremely rich bibliography in legal and political anthropology has criticized, de-reified, and deconstructed the concept of the state, putting in question the certainty of its center and the magic of its margins. Two main lines of inquiry can be identified within that broad corpus, which have influenced the approach presented here. One line focuses on regulation and governmentality; the other focuses on imagination and magicality. Let us observe how these analytic trends illuminate the study of the African state and the specific Mozambican case.

The first trend sheds light on the nature of the state as a field of multiple units, agencies, and modalities of regulation and focuses on practices of contract and control. The emphasis is placed on "governmentality" as an ideologized practice of power, which works through the production of "effects," creating and enhancing the state's alleged limits, hierarchy, or territoriality. These studies analyze the state's self-fashioning vis-à-vis its other, as well as surveillance and control of "nonstate" sectors, whether market, civil society, political society, or various communities.[4]

With regard to Africa, studies employing this approach focus on the structure of postcolonial governmentality from the point of view of citizenship. This type of analysis is centered on normative categories regarding juridical institutions and the structure of the state apparatus. It takes the presence of a unified state apparatus for granted, placing locality within a restricted "cultural" space separated from the sphere of the political. This trend studies postcolonial African state formations in terms of legacies from colonial regimes, emphasizing in particular the place of the customary as a crucial locus of colonial governance that still determines the form of contemporary citizenship.

This trend focuses on the question of the bifurcated structure that the postcolonial African state inherited from colonial regimes. This decentralized form pivots on the distinctions between the central state and the local state, on the one hand, and between urban citizens and rural subjects, on the other. The emphasis is on the relation between citizenship and its opposite, subjecthood, and on the central place of the customary in transitions from colonial to postcolonial rule. A methodological distinction between culture and law leads to a differentiation between cultural rights and official legal rights.

The perspective that I take shows how customary norms and official law actually function as parallel realms of normativity, with state law also being a localized, performed construct. Hence, I avoid the dialectical binary between citizenship and subjecthood. On the one hand, the following chapters study the question of subjectification (and subjectivity) as a means to observe critical nuances in the citizen/subject distinction. On the other, they demonstrate that what is being demanded, contested, and granted at present is a form of citizenship that blends aspects of customary norms and legal rights, here defined as "customary citizenship."

The second trend in much of contemporary legal and political anthropology studies social imaginaries of the political and ways in which the state is perceived in everyday, localized contexts. It focuses on practices of collective memory and imagination, studying symbol and ritual to emphasize the performativity at stake in the establishment of the state's legitimacy. These studies engage the idea of the state as a multiple assemblage of institutions, or a field of forces, within a conception of the political as a strategic formation of confronting vectors. These studies examine state sovereignty while criticizing the alleged territorial and institutional unity of a single state apparatus.

Some of these works focus on the idea of the state as a mask or a fetish, emphasizing the "magicality" of state formations and an unstable constitutive link between violence and rationality. They illustrate how the legality and legitimacy of the state are reinforced by means of imagination and performance. This anthropology equates the concrete substance of the state with the materiality of memory, signs, and images.[5]

In relation to this perspective, a trend in the study of the African state focuses on imaginaries of power and ritualization of state sovereignty. It observes postcolonial governance as textured cultural forms ingrained in formations of state power, studying them in terms of the "grotesque," the "banality of power," and "conviviality between rulers and governed." This trend, focused on governmentality and the specific "historicity of the state in Africa"[6] provides a useful framework to study disparate state agencies immersed within a field of strategic forces. Centrally, this trend proposes the key notion of the "rhizome state," which describes the African state apparatus as entwined with a subterranean array of clientelistic social networks. This trend also presents the notion of African governmentality as a "politics of the belly," a form of governance that combines imaginaries of consumption and bodily function with private profiting from public office and the occult action of invisible forces.

The notion of the state as a mask or fetish can be operationalized in the African context as a condition in which the state apparatus appears as the central locus of political power, while it occludes a political field formed by a multiplicity of local actors and vectors (e.g., the customary). This condition is readily observed in the locality, as the ultimate laboratory of governance and definitive test of sovereignty. The African state partly founds its legitimacy, vis-à-vis local population and international community, on its recognition of the customary and tradition. Governance, in this postcolonial context of slippery meanings and elusive imaginations, means that the state fetish in its turn fetishizes the customary as true tradition. The state reproduces through official discourse and legislation the implicit magicality present in the realm of customary ritual and norm. This articulation of the modern state apparatus with the customary reinforces the sense of a mask covering the fetishization of an apparatus as sole central-ized locus of power.

Some conceptions proposed by this trend pave the way for a recu-peration of the original sense of the category of the state as a status or condition, which the following chapters study as the state of structural ad-justment operating today in Africa.


## The Spirit of the Laws

The question of the spirit of the laws bridges the motifs of the two afore-mentioned trends in analysis of the state: the magicality implied by the spirit and the institutionality embedded in the law. The spirit of the laws of current neoliberal reforms articulates the ritual imagination of the state and its practices of governance. Through the juridical reproduction of the customary ("community") the state harnesses aspects of the alleged magi-cality of the "natural" state of tradition, its customs, and its rights.

Although the two lines of inquiry on the state pursue separate paths, this book offers a contribution by connecting aspects of their different ap-proaches. The focus on governmentality and the focus on performance or magicality are suitable for studying local instances in which an imaginary of the customary—its discourse, ritual, authority—is deployed as part of a ritualization of the spectacle of state power through the quotidian work of institutions of justice. The book explores postcolonial governmentality as a discourse and "art of government" or performativity of power through localized strategies linking institutional apparatuses. It does this through a study of questions of law and justice, which provide a specific angle on the theatricality of state sovereignty and the legitimization of its sovereignty, allegedly grounded on the juridical. The emphasis on an ethnography of locality and of the context of the minor state to study questions pertaining to the nation-state and citizenship is motivated by the fact that it is pre-cisely at the level of the local that the sovereignty of the modernist spirit of the law and its jurisdiction are contested through the encounter with other spirits, other norms, and other voices.

Some aspects of the two lines of inquiry overlap. Both allow for a per-spective on the state as a loose set of agencies and pave the way for a conception of the state as a relation.[7] The approach pursued in this book focuses on the jurisdiction of legal agencies and their blending of violence and reason as the fundamental relation that defines the state apparatus.

The import of this approach lies in the fact that whereas classical liberal theory locates the foundation of sovereignty in the juridical realm, the force of law constitutes the key entry point for a critical study of the principles and pitfalls of the liberal democratic state.

From the perspective of the local, and as a distillate from those theoretical debates, my ethnographic research led to revisiting the primordial meaning of the concept of the state in its etymological origin as *status*. This concept referred to the situation of the prince's estate and power, as the condition in which a sovereign finds himself. The category evolved, moving from force to law, from conveying a person's state to representing the state as a (legal) person or individual subject. The historically original notion of the state as a temporal condition and the instability of its political identity throughout remarkable historical transformations show the central role of questions of temporality within juridico-political postcolonial formations, which must supplement the usual spatial analysis of a state's territoriality.

The ethnographic study of the Mozambican state as a semipublic/semiprivatized sovereign institution did not lead to a conceptualization of the state as an apparatus with bounded demarcations, be they clear territorial or institutional borders. The consistency and boundaries of the state apparatus—from the mingling with transnational and private entities at the "macro" level to the blurred borders vis-à-vis the customary at the "micro" level—revealed themselves as quite imprecise. The ethnography unveiled the state as a condition, as a state of things.

The two trends of analysis of the state hold opposite views on issues of state structure, governance, and historical developments of state and citizenry, and their different perspectives on the question of civil society in Africa hold particular interest for this study.

## The State as Relation

Mozambique presents a remarkable paradox within global schemes of governance. A post–Cold War, post-Socialist, postconflict democratic transition driven by the international community has generated an official recognition of traditions that had been berated as "obscurantist" by the same political elites who had been in power since independence and has authorized the return of "traditional authorities" previously banned by the Socialist regime for being an instrument of colonialism. This singular case of slightly exaggerated contours speaks of the resilience and renewed power of the customary throughout postcolonial Africa and its centrality within current processes of governance and recognition of rights. The specific political contours of the customary and its key role in schemes of colonial and postcolonial governance are perhaps the only strictly "African" characteristics of the political in the continent. Yet they have not been a central feature in most analyses of the neoliberal moment in Africa, in which the local customary has been crucially recoded as community.

In the context of the vast recent literature on the state and citizenship in Africa, the next few chapters focus on the crucial relevance of locality for the current status of sovereignty in the continent, in terms of both the central state's self-fashioning by means of the construction of locality and perspectives on that state projected from the realm of the local. The centrality that the demarcation of the local holds within global political processes acquires specific contours in Africa, in terms of regional identity, ethnicity, and local responses to nation building. Among coalescing vectors of state governance, conflict, autochthony claims, demands on land and resources, and regional identity formations, the regulation of the local is, today as it was during late colonial times, the main locus around which governance is shaped. This situation is not just framed by the state programs. Since the end of the Cold War, international donors have also emphasized the question of locality in their recommendations and programming.

While the perspective from the locality sheds insight on practices of governance, the ethnography demonstrates that state sovereignty should not be studied according to its own claims, as a matter of scale. Rather, the local is presented here as a modality, as a matter of textures and entangled temporalities. The focus of the next chapters is on the detailed study of a "minor" state, an assemblage of authorities acting at the local level, performatively enacting questions of history and memory in order to constantly rebuild their legitimacy in difficult times marked by deep political transformations.

From the perspective of dynamics of law and aspirations to justice, the following historical and ethnographic chapters study imaginations of the state collectively constructed and disputed by members of "local communities" and state officers. The relevance of this case study lies in its analysis of a region that has historically been marked by distrust of, if not outright opposition to, the state apparatus, through local tactics of political ritual and violence. In the mid-2000s, when I carried out my fieldwork, the province analyzed here was the only one in which the RENAMO (Re-sistência Nacional Moçambicana; Mozambican National Resistance) op-position governed three out of five local districts.

The politico-economic passage from Socialism to democracy produces an expanded crisis of legitimacy of the state's institutionality and perfor-mativity, weakening the state's control over sectors of the population. In that context, legitimacy vis-à-vis both the international community of donors and the national population is constantly reconstructed through performances—rhetoric, gestures, symbols—that become ingrained in institutional forms. At both the level of the central state apparatus and the level of the locality, one of the central aspects of this performativity is the question of the customary.

In the capital city, Maputo, the national elites reproduce the idea of the customary, developing policies that recognize the "community" and that respond to conditionality from foreign donors. These policies also conceptually generate a certain population, which is granted a degree of national citizenship merged with elements of local belonging and custom-ary entitlements. The reproduction of the customary as a distinctive Af-rican element of the nation-state reverses, in the new democratic era, key normativity emanating from the Socialist period. This process develops alongside the reproduction of a differentiated realm of "customary citi-zenship," which has valuable political and economic consequences for the two process of liberalization of the state and the economy, which work in tandem within the overarching frame of the juridical reform.

The two modes of performativity, institutional and theatrical or ritual, are also enacted at the level of the locality. Thus, the minor state is ana-lyzed in the latter part of this text as the site where the citizens of the locality encounter the work of the state on an everyday basis, through both its dynamics of institutional governance and its practices of rhetoric and theatricality aimed at carrying out that work in a legitimate manner. The struggle to impose sovereignty in the locality, in the midst of multiple vectors of power—local, national, transnational—demonstrates that the state is not a single unified object or apparatus. The state is not a mask ei-ther, as posited by the critique of sovereignty as anchored in the law—that is, the state as the disguised visage of a singular sovereign subject, or legal person. The field of segmentary political formations shows that one of the main ways to understand the state is to conceive of it as a relation. This relation can be called jurisdiction.

Jurisdiction is a category that links the cleavages of the central and the local state, thus providing a key entry point to study the question of sovereignty in the African postcolony. Jurisdiction is a useful heuristic tool to approach questions of both territoriality and temporality. The objective of demarcation and rule over a local space also implies the calibration and control of multiple time frames that, as do so many other juridico-political schemes, crowd the locality.

The proliferation of overlapping jurisdictions is neither commended here as "legal pluralism" nor merely criticized for its apparent resemblance to colonial governmentality. The empirical terrain shows that there might be some specific postcolonial or post-Socialist key significance, in terms of governance of the local, in the silent toleration or even active promotion of a disorderly dissemination of legal schemes.

The "state of structural adjustment" recalibrates the temporal and spatial scope of state and locality. As the law establishes its jurisdiction upon time, history itself becomes the object of development, and the official narrative on the nation-state's recent past is rewritten. The ethnographic chapters that follow demonstrate how the state constitutes a malleable, temporal condition, a historically determined field of forces and imaginaries, or a state of things.

The African postcolony represents a maze of competing jurisdictions, which interrupts the dialectical and totalizing reason of the state. In Mozambique the trajectory of jurisdiction is saturated with the temporalities of historical difference. Articulations of law and violence have produced various overlapping legal regimes and competing sovereignties. Locality has been fragmented and reconstituted in multiple ways by the application of force, between legitimacy and legality. "Community" has been redefined through various temporal and spatial vectors, a shattered space that has given way to a proliferation of authorities and layer upon layer of norms, amid politics of suspicion and surveillance, hope and deception.

The concept of jurisdiction implies the practice of both voicing the law and establishing a legitimate, correct sentence, according to the two meanings of "right." Jurisdiction is the truthful pronouncing of a sentence, within a circumscription and the saturation of an enclosed territory by a legitimate voice. Sovereignty, as a transcendent, totalizing principle, must nonetheless always be enacted through its minor key, or jurisdiction. Yet an analysis of the effects of the law in quotidian settings in the African postcolony almost never finds that fullness of voice, that stentorian sovereignty that might suffuse the space of the local.

The necessary passage through the local interrupts the alleged sovereignty of the juridical. The abstraction of a legitimate speech is not imposed on a territory; rather, something more akin to the materiality of systems of writing competes and struggles in the locality. The opposition between different local authorities and customs, among them the state's own traditions, shows the deferral of the enforcement of the law, as blurred signatures and inchoate calligraphies disperse in multiple situations and locations.

In Mozambique, the struggle to impose jurisdiction is not defined merely by the competition and competence of courts of law. While the disjunctures and articulations between customary courts, community courts, and official district tribunals are crucial, opposite vectors of political authority intervene in a war of positions. Jurisdiction is a constantly unfolding battlefield between various authorities: customary chiefs, former Socialist agents, official state judges and prosecutors, religious leaders, the police. It is a space of different overlapping legal or normative regimes and violence, associated with various historical epochs. Each of those authorities and regimes understands the practice of jurisdiction in a different manner. Some among them might even claim jurisdiction over invisible realms, informed by other spirits and laws.

In the postcolony, fragments from a shattered national totality that never fully existed proliferate as scattered pieces carrying various historical legacies. They tend toward a future of unpredictable forms. The disseminating histories of local territories unsettle any fixed sense of political sovereignty or legal jurisdiction. Thus, the legitimate speech of a nation-state deploying its sovereign law as a historical narrative is interrupted. The legal fiction of jurisdiction as the expression of an original voice fails the test of the locality, of its textured history and its entangled everyday politics as continuation of war. Jurisdiction cannot be imposed by the postcolonial central state without negotiation and articulation with multiple local life-worlds and temporalities. Jurisdiction is not the voice of the law but a dialect; it is but the locally inflected accent of an alleged, original national language. While supposedly emanating from a central, national source of speech and presented by legal developmentalist programming as being inscribed in the register of the official national language, the political struggles at the level of the local show that jurisdiction is always pronounced, in the last instance, in the vernacular.

This localized jurisdiction produces a specific inflection on national belonging. The perspective advanced in this book observes singular forms of citizenship being enacted in terrains of access to justice and in relation to the question of civility. Fundamentally, the book tackles the question of how the customary has been equated with local civil society in recent reformist and developmentalist discourse and how it is being related to official law and rights within an emergent form of citizenship. "Customary citizenship," deployed by the state of structural adjustment in relation to a nascent civil society, constitutes a key element in the study of a specific type of state, understood as a contingent, unstable political condition. The next two chapters describe the historical trajectory and present dynamics of this state of structural adjustment and the key place that customary citizenship holds within it.

# CHAPTER TWO

# Law as History

Mozambique, which gained independence from Portugal in 1975, began its transition from Socialism in the late 1980s, with the abandonment of a Marxist-Leninist platform by the party-state system incarnated by FRELIMO (Mozambican Liberation Front) and the subsequent adoption of structural adjustment programs that sought to liberalize the centrally planned economy.[1] In 1992, an internationally engineered peace agreement put an end to a devastating civil war between the government and the South African– and United States–backed guerrillas of RENAMO (Mozambican National Resistance). This Cold War exercise of struggle by proxy left 1 million casualties, 1.7 million refugees, and 3.2 million internally displaced persons out of a population of  million. The economy and infrastructure were almost totally destroyed, with losses being estimated at $20 billion. This context of war and a Socialist political system of centralized administration are the immediate historical precedents of the current liberal democratic regime, which consists of a multiparty system—FRELIMO and RENAMO account for almost 90 percent of the vote—that held its fourth presidential election in October 2009. In this transitional process, FRELIMO has carried out an almost unheard-of feat: a former Marxist party has managed to remain in power through four general elections following the demise of the Socialist bloc and the end of the Cold War.

The transition to democracy and rule of law was hailed as a successful process of national reconciliation and politico-economic opening. In reality, a very complex network of juridical and political processes, at both the macrolevel and more localized scales, suggests that the transition has not gone all that smoothly. Instead, not only do the dynamics of the previous regime remain, albeit under a new façade, but also certain features that originated in colonial and even precolonial times have returned with new strength, adapted to the current novel conditions.

Central to this transition was the implementation of a major legal reform, shaped and funded by foreign development agencies, that encompassed both the formal justice system and several instantiations of "informal" or "customary" law. The reform, however, took place within a field of contention and negotiation and thus did not follow a linear path. Rather, the process has produced a series of legal amalgams and contradictory political juxtapositions, in which new spirits of the laws emerge from within the broad regime of "development," revealing the ambiguities of the dual processes of state and market reform and the ways in which postmodern global governance, in a neo-imperialist way, produces the return of juridical regimes linked to colonial rule and its legacies of violence.

The background of this reform is symptomatic of the predicament of the current democratic regime, which is conditioned to a large extent by foreign aid and structural adjustment. The two main politico-economic processes in Mozambique's democratic transition are deeply interrelated. These consist of (a) the attempt to secure the democratic transition and the rule of law, by reforming state structures; and (b) a process of consolidation of the transition from a Socialist planned economy to a liberalized capitalist market economy. Both processes of reform are intricately connected. The transformation of the country's legal structures and justice system not only is required to consolidate the transition both from Socialism and from previous colonial juridico-political structures but is also a central aspect of a liberalization process of "opening" the economy to global capitalism. Mozambique is still in 2012 considered to be among the fifteen poorest countries in the world, and roughly 60 percent of its state budget amounts to foreign aid. These aid funds, which have shifted from humanitarian emergency aid in the immediate postwar period to the current developmentalist aid, include both loans and grants. Moreover, Mozambique, which has a very reduced industrial sector, presents one of the world's lowest rates of urbanization. While Portuguese capital dominates the banking system, out of ten mega-industrial projects, seven originate in South African investment and the other three indirectly serve South African trade.

In the first half of the 2000s, when fieldwork for this book was conducted, the country's economy was growing at an average annual rate of 8 percent. But the high growth rates were due to very concentrated enclaves of production and extraction that themselves reproduce structures from the past. Colonial administrative patterns and economic spaces of production and trade still persist today. The three current "development corridors" that crisscross the country in the northern, central, and southern regions reproduce the main economic passages designed at the beginning of the twentieth century by the colonial state economy and the private interests of neighboring countries. The current liberalization of the economy involves not only the promotion of foreign investment but also an ongoing process of "primitive accumulation" that aims at creating a national bourgeoisie or private sector, which basically will evolve from the political structures that have administered the state sector since independence. The process involves shifting the country's legal framework toward the privatization of the state sector and deregulation of markets.

Through an analysis of the World Bank's reports on Mozambique, interviews with aid officers and legal experts, as well as participation in seminars on the reform of the justice sector held by foreign agencies, it becomes clear that the Bretton Woods institutions and the rest of the donor community have emphasized legal reform as the main axis of state/administrative reform. Among the conditions attached to the disbursement of loans and aid money to Mozambique, new legislation and the reform of old codes are a central issue. World Bank documentation includes explicit conditions regarding justice reform as a requirement for the country's eligibility for debt reduction programs. The rationale behind these conditions is a neoliberal ideology, which argues that a liberal-capitalist reform of the justice system is crucial for the process of economic opening (related to structural adjustment policies of privatization, deregulation of investment and flow of capital), which will subsequently bring socioeconomic "development" and "poverty alleviation." This discourse presents justice as a "service" provided by the state to individual citizens, who are depicted as customers and consumers.

The juridical regime is crucially imbricated with the economy, to the point that it becomes impossible to separate these two spheres, which according to liberal doctrine are distinct. The historical, political, and economic sources of the "poverty" that is to be "alleviated" are never examined in the aseptic juridical discourse of the development reports, where misery and hunger are depicted as almost natural facts. The vicious circle of debt that deepens the misery is not acknowledged and will only be enhanced by most of the programs that propel a further enlargement of the country's debt.

"Development" is an assemblage of regulating schemes that are allegedly aimed at guiding a society up a linear scale of political and economic evolution, toward the full unfolding of capitalism's potential. Development constitutes a juridical regime in two senses. In the first sense, the law is the main framework for development, functioning indeed as a general political economy, as evidenced in the legal reform that has reshaped the Mozambican state in the last decade. In the second sense, the law itself is the "object of development," as illustrated in particular by the creation of a series of legal instruments that (re)construct the concepts of community and jurisdiction. These documents are politico-juridical development exercises, aimed at regulating political authority and the delivery of "justice" at the local level, at enhancing some kind of agricultural development, and at mustering local resources and political structures to undertake major infrastructural works.

Who is entitled to write the letter of the laws? A complex set of tracks channels the distribution of commands, as well as the flow of resources and investments. Within this network, remainders of state sovereignty mingle with a series of governmental practices exercised by an elusive, yet all-too-material entity, the "international community," a collection of units from the Bretton Woods institutions and agencies from various donor nation-states. At times, the figure that emerges is that of a latter-day protectorate, a conjunction of private and public interests reminiscent of aspects of colonial governmentality. It is an entity that could be labeled the "state of structural adjustment."

The Mozambican juridical sphere is itself a multilayered pastiche of various legal and regulatory regimes, combined with various normativities, sedimented throughout colonial and postcolonial history. The current "system" of legality and conflict resolution is a mosaic of overlapping political structures and legal regimes, resembling one of the Chinese encyclopedias famously "uncovered" by Borges. A manifold array of "informal" mechanisms of conflict resolution (chiefs, religious structures, kinship) mingles with aspects of Roman law, colonial codes, Socialist normativity, Western constitutionalism, and common law, constituting an extremely complex infrastructure in a landscape of political fragmentation and juridical difference. The apparatus of justice appears divided de facto between a formal state system and a largely majoritarian informal system, which encompasses many overlapping entities, some of which are located under the ambiguous concept of "the customary." Examples of the weak, so-called formal state system of justice and the largely majoritarian informal system of conflict resolution include official courts, customary chieftaincy courts, "community courts" (the former revolutionary

People's Tribunals), churches, mosques, former Socialist structures such as "dynamizing groups" (*grupos dinamizador*) and party-state cells, FRELIMO and RENAMO structures, associations of neighbors, networks of relatives, and even foreign and national NGOs.

De jure, several juridical regimes coexist, superimposed upon each other. The main legal frame in the country continues to be Portuguese law, even in those cases where the codes enforced today in Mozambique have already been superseded, reformed, or dropped in the former metropolis, as is the case, for example, with the Mozambican civil code. Roman law was the narrative language of the independent autonomous state, the one that guided its political orientation and its modalities of colonizing the social, including the strongly centralized mode of government reminiscent of Portuguese colonialism. But that writing was covered by a new one: Socialist legal dispositions regarding customary laws and authorities, the establishment of communal villages, the movement and control of populations, the rationing of food, price controls, and the nationalization of business. Although aimed at erasing much of the colonial regime ("destroy the colonial state apparatus" were Samora Machel's words of order), the revolutionary state nevertheless kept the essence of a previous juridical order. Most of the state apparatus from the colonial regime was maintained, albeit with a few key transformations, motivated by the incorporation of Marxist-Leninist forms of political organization. A crucial change was the dismantling of the whole system of "customary authority" that had been shaped and used by the Portuguese in their own version of the British system of indirect rule and French Indigénat, as will be discussed below.[2] The process was a complex and subtle one. In some regions local chiefs maintained shares of power through relatives who had high ranks in the new local Socialist party cells and structures. Sometimes the chiefs occupied those positions themselves, at least until 1979.[3] The legal reforms undertaken in the mid-2000s aimed at transforming this state of affairs, modifying the relations between its elements through new legislation on community courts, district tribunals, customary authority, and land. They revealed the fragmentary, transient condition of a nation-state understood as a situation: a state of things.

## General Economy[4]

Current forms of government resonate strongly with historical trajectories and past modalities of power. Over the several hundred years of

Portuguese presence, the space of the colony underwent profound, violent transformations. The later period of colonial modernization in the twentieth century was founded on new legal engineering, which aimed to transform the political landscape of locality through a new juridical regime. The Indigenato, a Portuguese version of indirect rule, dramatically transformed local structures of power while forcing vast sectors of the population into a modernized, stylized form of slavery: corvée labor. This particular juridical regime constitutes a key precedent for current processes of local governance and citizenship.

From the second half of the nineteenth century until 1942, the loose occupation of the territory by the Portuguese state produced an uneven political and administrative landscape crowded with private concessionary companies, colonial units, and fragments of local kingdoms.[5] The Colonial Act adopted in Lisbon in 1930 marked the end of the private sovereignty of concessionary corporations and the commencement of an expanded policy of developmentalism with regard to services and infrastructures, railways, transport, and agro-industry.

The progressive consolidation of the colonial state can be observed through the study of the management of the native population and the framing of citizenship issues in terms of the evolution of labor legislation and the shaping and policing of the "customary."[6] The colonial regime operated upon a highly contested social terrain marked by external local opposition and its own shortcomings due to lack of economic and political resources. The contours and reach of colonial rule were very uneven, marked by a disjuncture between its own petitions of principles and political discourse and the effective implementation of its projects. The constant social traffic of people, signs, and commodities that trespassed the boundaries between strictly defined urban and rural areas was but a sign of the disconnection between state governance projected on populations and markets and the fragmented reality of the social. Colonial governmentality linked the political rule of the native and the economic exploitation of her labor power. A general economy of power relations that attained micropolitical levels characterized colonial rule and its demarcation of juridical distinctions.[7]

The Indigenato was a juridico-political regime that established socio-legal hierarchies, adjudicated privileges, denied rights, classified subjects according to race and place, and established fixed origins and potential destinations, reducing the unfolding of difference—enhanced by the fragmentation brought about by colonial governmentality—to a dualistic scheme.[8] It produced broad effects that went beyond the juridical definition of the native subject and the obligations that subjecthood entailed in terms of taxation, labor, and compliance with local customary authority, private capitalists, and central colonial administration. Systems of education and labor, identification and circulation, as well as punishment and control, were intricately linked, legally regulating the life of a subjectivity that had recently abandoned the condition of slave and had become a "free laborer" under fascist-capitalist conditions.[9]

The construction of the customary, evolving over several centuries, entailed the elaboration of a series of legal fictions. By means of juridical fiat, these legal documents established boundaries, demarcated spaces, and defined social categories, forming a discursive gridlock superimposed on the rapidly changing terrain of the colony.

As a policy on and a policing of the customary, the regime of the Indigenato was aimed at governing a social world of antagonism and articulation, as well as of production, exchange, consumption, and fiscality. These political and economic practices were entwined, forming two interrelated sets of issues that can be assembled under the rubrics of the "labor" question and the "native" question. The juridical codification of the opposed realms of the indigenous and the nonindigenous traversed both the field of dissemination of power and the field of circulation of value, as an extended political economy. The institutions that ruled both fields—subjects as natives and subjects as workers—were intrinsically linked. Processes related to the control of a labor force—the issue of nascent social classes and social identities formed in relation to markets—were entangled with the disciplining of a native population through politically shaped and legally enforced racial distinctions.

This political and moral economy was founded upon both monetary and ethical values. The civilizing mission of the Portuguese state addressed the "moral obligation" of the native toward labor and the pedagogic mission of the state in educating and providing a work ethic to its subjects— even more so after the shift to Fascism and extreme Catholicism. As in the present moment, the law understood as a program of "development" constituted a blurred space where the juridical and the political were indistinguishable.

The Indigenato system had been preceded by various pieces of legislation that, since 1899, determined gradations of citizenship in relation to various forms of forced labor,[10] establishing the legal category of the native under the authority of customary chiefs. A history of hundreds of years of coexistence, articulation, and later conquest of customary authority led to a period of "effective occupation" inaugurated in 1895 by the defeat and exile of Gungunhana, the main chief in southern Mozambique. These events marked the annexation of the south of the territory, which allowed the colonial regime to articulate with a previous system of local chiefs. In the center and north, the rule of private companies shaped political sovereignty and military occupation at the local level.[11] Private concessionary companies enforced their own labor and taxation policies addressed to local native populations. Multiple jurisdictions overlapped, as the colonial territory recognized by international law (after bilateral treaties and ultimatums) was also subdivided into several areas ruled by private companies. These public and private legal subjects articulated their juridico-political rule with a myriad of local customary chiefdoms. Practices of enforcement of local order—as shown, for instance, in the historical emergence of the ethnic identity of the Chikunda, or liberated slaves who became "mercenary" warriors in central Mozambique[12]— illustrate how the construction of the customary had been engineered by the flux of concessionary, speculative transnational capital as much as by the embryonic colonial state.

Beyond power and production, besides codification and capitalization, violence defined to a large extent the contours of this colonial scene. Forced labor became one of the main commodities produced, most often destined for the mines in the Transvaal. Violence permeated the rule of a feeble colonial state, and its dubious "effective occupation" was entangled with the sovereignty of speculative capitalist concessions over vast, often-unproductive territories. Scattered garrisons and private companies' armies controlled the territory and routinely conducted military incursions to round up laborers. Concessionary plantations exploited the natives, and the taxes levied on the local population were often their main revenue.

The juridical construction of a realm of primitivism—the customary— accompanied the harsh process of "primitive accumulation" that added value to the space of the colony. This legal process encompassed the transition from an era of slavery, to one of forced labor (*xibalo*, the Portuguese version of corvée labor), to the full-fledged codification of the native as the subject of "custom." The status of *indígena*, the object of the Indigenato juridical regime in the 1930s, was first codified through colonial legislation on labor and taxation implemented in the late nineteenth century, which defined the subject of customary law as a worker and, later on, as a fiscal subject.[13]

Beginning in 1890, policy on the colonial administration of the Mozam-bican territory was deeply transformed;[14] the territory went from being a province of the metropole to acquiring higher degrees of political and financial independence. Up until then, Mozambique had sent deputies to the Portuguese assembly, and colonial laws were enforced in the colony. The metropole managed the colony's budgets. This situation was trans-formed by a new generation of colonial administrators[15] who transferred higher levels of authority to governors, encouraging the capacity of the colony to dictate its own legislation and achieve financial independence.

Antonio Enes, the main architect of modern Portuguese colonial policy, thoroughly reorganized the colonial administration in terms of state and citizenship, reforming aspects of local governance and customary author-ity. The three pillars of these policies were pacification, the encouragement of white settlement, and the reform of labor legislation to force the native population into work. New provinces were created and territories merged. There were transfers of sovereignty from the state to private companies. Concessionary corporations were given the task of military pacification, administration, and economic development of their regions. These incur-sions led to an effective occupation of the territory that blended aspects of private capital expansion with the progressive juridical consolidation of state power. The political economy of concessions' entitlements was articulated with the juridico-political sovereignty of the colonial state. The law conjoined public and private forms of sovereignty over the space of locality and its native population.[16]

The administrative changes in the political status of the colony included labor reforms. In 1880, labor legislation was adjusted in accordance with the colonial administration's needs regarding the emerging colonial plan-tation economy. In 1890, legislation concerning *prazos* (plantations leased to Portuguese colonists) dictated that the natives were required to pay part of their tax obligations in labor.[17] After 1894, an African subject who infringed any law could be subjected to correctional work as a penalty. These developments led to the new Labor Code of 1899, which sancti-fied the "moral and legal" obligation of the native to perform work and included a provision for the natives to "improve themselves by work, ac-quiring through work a happier mode of existence." This legislation ended Portuguese liberal policies of assimilation of the colonies, reinforcing the distinction between citizens and native noncitizens, crucial for labor policy and taxation. The colony was thus construed as a large labor camp for the native population, in which the law enforced the obligation to work as a "free" laborer in an emerging capitalistic economy: a primitive-accumulation process pivoting around the juridical distinction between citizens and subjects.

Concessionary companies established their own labor and tax regulations to be enforced within the territories that they controlled, although in accordance with colonial laws.[18] The companies' private armies of *cipais*—native police forces—rounded up laborers for public works and labor on the plantations. Military campaigns became a common practice to control rebellious populations and include them as workers and taxpayers. Large numbers of natives started moving from one region to another to avoid being recruited and taxed.

New policies for the surveillance of natives through the issuing of passes and identification cards were introduced to control the everyday labor and circulation of colonial subjects. A policy of *aldeamentos*—or collective villages—was progressively developed. These regulations, along with labor legislation, provided the basis for new policies of "development," which reached their peak in the 1930s. Infrastructure, roads, transport, railways, forced labor, and, later on, harshly legally enforced free labor contracts initiated this process of development, which had its juridical counterpart in the transformations of labor policies and tax legislation that reshaped the status of subject populations, the political realm of the customary, and the scope of native authority. This politico-economic process of speculation and extraction implemented by concessionary companies lasted until the 1930s, when, under a policy of nationalization aimed at reinforcing state sovereignty, the Portuguese Fascist "New State" regime of 1933 did not renew the concessions' contracts.[19]

The laws related to the labor question constituted a template for the juridical codification of the indigenous.[20] The Labor Code of 1899 first articulated the distinction between citizen and subject: all native subjects had a "moral and legal obligation to work" toward "their subsistence and to better their social condition." Customary authorities were endowed with power to recruit forced labor and to sanction with correctional labor those who transgressed the law. Technically, it was this law that initially established the status of the native and the nonnative. The juridical codification of the dialectically opposed realms of the indigenous and the non-indigenous traversed both the field of proliferation of power and the field of circulation of profits: the establishment of a general, extended political economy through the double frame of the Enlightenment's spirit of the laws and the capitalistic law of value.

The Labor Law established the distinction between the native and the nonnative (*nao indígena* or *civilisado*) in categorical terms reminiscent of the civilizing-mission discourse of colonialism and its investment in the development of a primitive subject. The adscription of this primitive nature to the indigenous native (almost a nonbeing) helped to solve the challenge, for the metropolitan architects of colonial rule, of the passage from the abolition of slavery to the colonial dependence on forced labor that contradicted the very "civilizing" image that the colonial powers attempted to project. According to this legal philosophy, the nonnative enjoyed full citizenship rights and was placed under the jurisdiction of Portuguese civil law, while the native was subject to local native authorities and customary laws, along with the laws of each respective colony.

Other legal institutes that codified the contours of forced labor deepened the opposing dialectics between citizens and subjects. These offices and norms blurred the alleged distinction between the law (juridical norms) and the political (colonial administration). For instance, the Office for Native Affairs and Emigration, created in 1903, restructured the relationship between forced labor and migrant mine labor, giving the colonial state control over private companies. Two further regulations, a new Labor Code in 1914 and a later one implemented in 1928, redefined the category of forced labor, linking it to practices supposedly pertaining to free markets and voluntary workers. The latter code, a direct legal precedent for certain key issues within the Indigenato regime, overruled previous labor legislation. It instituted forced cropping, a compulsory regime of cultivation that aimed at fixing the natives to their villages of origin, where they would work on their own land and pay taxes. The code prohibited compulsory recruitment of native workers by the state for private companies and required that forced labor be compensated.

There was a fluid continuity between the statutes of slavery and the legislation codifying mandatory labor. The Indigenato system was a juridical scheme that organized governance at the local level in its threefold mode of implementing legitimate authority, constructing ethnic differentiation, and mandating an obligation to work. The *indígena*, the native, was the monad that supported the edifice of colonial rule through its Janus-faced status as both subject and worker: this monad was a subject both of a colonial foreign power and of a local customary authority, and its identity was determined by the mandate to perform forced labor.

As this brief account of the grounds of the Indigenato illustrates, the examination of the history of the legal and political demarcation of the customary and of the classification of the territory's populations locates the question of forced labor as a juridical succedaneum to slavery[21] at the center of a historical discussion of rights in an African political context. Current processes referring to civil society and citizenship necessarily must be observed through the prism of the legacy of this horrendous institution of political economy. The slave is the figure that precedes the colonial subject, who is someone with the "moral and legal obligation" to perform forced labor. The ideological construction of the slave as a subject deprived of humanity is the political and economic precedent of juridical architectures of indirect rule such as the Indigenato.

The code of the Indigenato updated a host of previous pieces of legislation addressing labor issues that restricted citizenship rights.[22] In effect, the code expanded former penal laws and criminal codes from the nineteenth century. This legal writing codified a vast socioethnic landscape which presented various groups organized under a diverse array of political structures: empires, para-states, chiefdoms, or, rather, stateless, segmentary structures that eventually would be labeled and classified as tribes by administrative ethnography and colonial policy.

The *indígena* was defined as the native subject of customary law. Citizenship, granted only to colonial settlers, was constructed in opposition to the realm inhabited by rightless natives, only a few of whom would enter into a process of assimilation that would eventually bestow upon them the status of civilized people.[23] Civil law was set against customary law, the elusive archaic norms supposedly pervasive in the rural areas. A gradual colonial policy of granting certain political rights to the natives, set forth by metropolitan liberal circles in the mid-nineteenth century, had been followed by a much more restrictive orientation, well expressed by the architects of Portuguese high colonialism, Royal High Commissioners Antonio Enes (the advocate of a civilizing mission through forced labor) and Joaquim Augusto Mouzinho de Albuquerque.[24]

In 1917 the intermediate category of the *assimilado* was legally established. This was a sort of second-class citizen who had assimilated to metropolitan, colonial culture and who was not obliged by the law to perform forced labor.[25] *Assimilados* from various ethnic backgrounds had identity cards issued by the state that differentiated them from the *indígenas*, most of whom were issued with only temporary passes. Despite the longstanding status of "assimilation" in the colonial juridico-political imagination, it was only in 1961, with the abolition of the Indigenato, that "integration" was codified in full. In the 1960s the keyword would be "acculturation." But by 1950, only a tiny portion of the native population in the colonies had attained the status of "civilized" (only five thousand in Mozambique).

In juridical terms, the colonial regime divided the social into three categories. Politically, nevertheless, colonialism fostered a proliferation of elite
groups within a highly stratified society. Ideologues of the regime defined
several existing elite groups that had to be taken into account in a process
of "integration": settlers, *assimilados*, urban salaried groups, customary
authorities, and ethnic elites such as the Chinese and Indians living in
Mozambique.

The Indigenato classified the "indigenous" into tribes, presupposing
a common language and "culture." Within these tribes, individuals were
subject to the direct authority of customary chiefs.[26] The regime determined residence rights and access to land according to affiliation with
various ethnic groups. Alongside the production of "traditional culture,"
"customary law" was also codified by colonial functionaries and ethnog-
raphers. This construction of a realm of law outside the law, of a space of
"traditional" norms and political subjectivities, was essential for the consolidation of the colonial state apparatus. A series of norms from a given
customary law were collected by administrative ethnography as legitimate
jurisprudence for resolving local disputes within the territory of chieftaincies. A tripod formed by ethnic provenance, territorialization, and ancestry sanctioned the subjection to a certain codified type of customary law.
Meanwhile, civil law regulated the lives of the citizens (settlers and some
*assimilados*) as well as the disputes between citizens (or the state) and the
*indígenas*.

The colonial regime modernized precolonial forms of power, deeply
transforming them or creating them by juridical fiat according to the requirements of control and political economy.[27] The Portuguese regime
harnessed precolonial forms of local power; some lineages and forms of
succession were retained, and others were corrupted and transformed.
Precolonial territories were subdivided under the authorities of several
inheritors of a chief. New lineages were created, overpowering the authority of precolonial politico-religious chiefs who were not acquiescent to
colonial rule.

In a 1954 reform of the Indigenato code, indigenous peoples were defined as "subjects of the Portuguese state," while *assimilados* were defined
as having acquired Portuguese citizenship after fulfilling several requirements, such as speaking Portuguese correctly, having a profession, and
being enlightened (*sic*) with regard to Portuguese civil law.

The abolishment of the Indigenato regime in 1961 was brought about
by a combination of pressures, which were external (international labor
law and Western organizations' concern about forced labor), metropoli-

tan (changing conceptions of the labor force and economic development), and local (mounting activity of various anticolonial organizations). In 1960 new regulations softened the status of forced labor and curtailed the authorities' power to sanction those natives who infringed labor laws and contracts. In 1961, forced cropping was banned and later that year the statute on *indígenas* itself was revoked. In theory, all native subjects in the overseas colonies had become Portuguese citizens. A new code for rural labor, from 1962, liberalized labor contracts, allowing the natives to freely choose their employers and granting them more freedom to circulate and find new locations to settle and work. It also abolished public beatings and other colonial forms of punishment. Natives found themselves with more freedom to change jobs, negotiate meager salaries, and circulate in and out of cities.

The end of the Indigenato regime and the subsequent demise of a system of forced labor did not end governmental control of coercive labor markets. Usually, labor recruitment was conducted by district administrators, plantation officers, and customary authorities under conditions of a harsh regime of force, and the dualism of these categories persisted in various ways. Those formerly defined as *indígenas* became Portuguese citizens but the *regulados* (chieftaincies demarcated by the Portuguese regime) were maintained, as well as the customary laws, which were still enforced in parallel to civil law. Paradoxically, it was with the abolition of the Indigenato that the position of the *regulados* was reinforced, and they became part of the state at the level of local administration. Even though the *indígenas* could then opt for civil law and civil courts, nonetheless, in rural and suburban areas, the majority were still under the rule of customary authorities or urban *regulos* (customary chiefs). Following the abolition of the Indigenato regime, chiefs' local rights of rule did not change substantially. They continued to be in charge of labor recruitment and maintained their commercial duties and ties to local administration and companies.[28]

By the mid-1960s, a few years after the abolition of the Indigenato regime, the majority of the population still had not been granted citizenship rights. At the same time, a stronger intervention at the local level on behalf of the colonial state produced even more variations in the political structures at the level of communities. This was the context at the beginning of FRELIMO's anticolonial guerrilla war in 1964. In the face of this threat, the colonial regime launched counterinsurgency campaigns that enhanced the repressive power of local customary authorities. On the ground, the end of the Indigenato did not imply major transformations in citizenship rights, forced labor, rural local governance, or colonial forms of control, even if colonial regulations were somewhat loosened. Solidified in the late 1960s, the colonial legacy of this juridico-political regime was the enforced dualism of legal categories that attempted to organize through binaries a very complex and multiple social field.

## From African Socialism to Democratic Reform

In terms of legal configurations of state and citizenship, the project of "popular justice" constituted the key juridical concept that formed the spine of the Socialist order. Popular justice was first created and experimented with in the "liberated zones" that FRELIMO established in a territory still controlled by the colonial state. The immanent force of law, a violence that is the foundation of the juridical and its potential enforcement, was condensed during the anticolonial war. The state harnessed the imagination of that violence constitutive of sovereignty, asserting that the nation's legality was founded upon the "people's power," a notion that equated the sovereignty emanating from the newly liberated people and its expression as legal order. Popular justice was founded upon a collective will to power. It introduced a type of legality that included the "law" yet was broader in scope, encompassing the whole order of the social. The people, the law, and the political were located in a contiguous, unmediated relation. The force of law that animated this trilogy was based on the military nature of the party-state that emerged out of the anticolonial struggle and achieved independence in 1975 as a diplomatic-political apparatus. The law as popular justice, incarnated in People's Tribunals that ranged from the Supreme Court to the local courts, was a juridico-political form of the national-popular movement of those wars of maneuvers, nationalist departures, and populist arrivals.

The discourse and praxis of the early independence regime aimed at a dialectical *Aufhebung*, or destruction and lifting of all proliferating difference construed by the colonial regime. Key aspects of this process have returned within the current democratic regime, led by the former party-state, for instance, in the current management of the customary and its effects in terms of rights and entitlements.

The consolidation of the FRELIMO party-state system at independence in 1975 was intricately linked to the policy on former customary chiefs. At its first session after independence, the FRELIMO Council of

Ministers abolished chieftaincy in order to carry out a "total transformation" of rural Mozambican society.[29] In the early political battles after independence, "struggles toward national unity" were set against all forms
of the customary and what was considered by the *doxa* of the party as
the "obscurantism of all tradition." Despite the fact that postcolonial trajectories presented a complex range of political variations according to
regional differences and local history (during the anticolonial war, some
chiefs were hailed by FRELIMO as allies; others were ousted, imprisoned,
or killed), the law was clear in its stance against the customary.

The Socialist project, as a mode of political organization and a mode
of production, marked the stance of the central government toward chieftaincy and its reorganization of locality. The violence of war was the other
main vector that shaped customary authority. Along these two indiscern-
ible axes, the state developed a project of modernization of the rural
areas through collective villagization, aimed at absolutely transforming
the countryside. Shortly after independence, FRELIMO implemented a
general policy of construction of large communal villages in which rural
populations would be settled in groups ranging from 250 to 1,000 families,[30] as part of a state policy of Socialist economic development.[31] While
the villagers would construct their own homes, other buildings, and infrastructures, the government would provide personnel, machinery, consumer goods, and water. The villagization project drew its inspiration from
the political and spatial experience in the liberated zones conquered in the
north since the launching in 1964 of the anticolonial guerrilla war from
Tanzania, where Ujamaa policies of collective villagization and development provided a model for FRELIMO.

Villagization followed a double project of Socialist governance of the
countryside: one project was aimed at addressing the political economy,
while the other engaged with juridico-political issues of governance and
jurisdiction. Villagization would reformulate rural economic production, consolidating "people's power" in the countryside as people elected
representatives to village popular assemblies, as well as popular judges
and other local officers. The most crucial effect of villagization for local
governance was the dismantling of the colonial system of local customary
authorities.

The Socialist programming of collectivization was aimed at redesign-
ing the political economy of the nation-state as a mode of creating a vi-
able Marxist system of governance and shaping the projected New Man.
Notwithstanding FRELIMO's policies, social structures based on local

logics of kinship and hereditary succession never actually disappeared
after independence. For example, the 1979 Land Law, which stipulated
that all land was the property of the state, was designed to strengthen new
local state structures at the expense of the kin-based institutions that had
previously controlled access to land. In practice, however, in most rural
areas land tenure remained based on principles of acquisition and inheritance through kinship structures and customary authorities.[32]

Moreover, as RENAMO mobilized numerous chiefs across the country
against the government, these authorities restructured some expressions
of customary rule and also reinstated traditional practices such as spirit
cults. The civil "war of spirits," as it was defined by anthropologists, further extended the connections between violence, spirit forms of healing,
and customary rule.[33] More than three decades later, the power of chiefs as
juridico-political authorities is still widespread in the rural areas; initiation
rites shape subjectivities, and legal institutions created by the party-state
regime combine aspects of a Socialist ethos with supposedly antithetic customary norms.

Numerous scholars and political leaders—inside and outside Mozambique—have underscored FRELIMO's fierce repression of customary
authority, law, and ritual as one of the main causes of the explosion of the
civil war. Later on, at the peak of its failure, in the context of war and dev-
astation, collectivization would be seen as the other main cause for the rural population's rejection of state policies. Many experts agree that in the
early stages FRELIMO enjoyed widespread legitimacy; its policy against
chiefs had been heralded as a positive measure against the inheritance of
colonial governance, and villagization was considered successful while it
delivered some of its promised economic fruits. Only later, with historical
hindsight, would collectivization, economic socialization, and the rejection of chiefs be seen as the main causes of the support lent to RENAMO
by vast rural populations in the center-north of the country.

The back-and-forth movements in terms of the state, the customary,
citizenship, and community are made evident by the trajectory of legislation on land, from the late colonial regime to Socialism and to the current
liberal democratic reform. It was within the debates on a reform of land
law that the almost taboo question of the customary was discussed again
within the highest political circles of the FRELIMO government. Let us
examine the genealogy of this reform.

The colonial regime applied several juridical norms until the adoption
of the 1961 Regulation of Land Occupation in the Ultramarine Provinces.

In this legal text, land was classified into three groups: urban land, located around the main cities; land around villages with local systems of production; and the rest of the land, considered by the state as "free" and thus available to foreign investors. Land that was shown to be in use by the populations of local chieftaincy structures could not be sold by the state. In reality, colonial laws justified the state's allocation of large areas to Portuguese settlers and foreign investors in plantation companies. Extensive territories that were actually being exploited but that local agricultural systems held in reserve by using different pieces of land in different seasons were annexed by the colonial state or given to investors.

After independence, the 1975 Constitution declared all land to be the property of the state. Land use was secured by anyone who applied for it. On the ground, frequent and sometimes violent conflicts arose throughout the country due to disorganized practices of land allocation by local state structures to investors who promised to put the land into production. In 1979 a Land Law was passed that did not recognize any "customary" rights whatsoever. The focus on the so-called "family sector"—households and small communities—was related to its reorganization into state cooperatives. This law was enforced in the context of collective villagization and the dismantling of the system of "traditional" chieftaincies. The civil war and immediate postwar context created a condition of extended conflict over land resources, particularly after the return of millions of refugees and displaced populations. The transition to a market economy in the early 1990s generated the need to transform the legislation on land and natural resources.

In 1995, one year after the peace agreement, the FRELIMO government presented a new National Policy on Land, sanctioned by the Council of Ministers, which liberalized aspects of its former Socialist policy. This piece of legislation was a legal precedent for the subsequent reform of land law and the recodification of traditional authority. The decree resystematized land tenure, transforming the rights of the private sector and corporations, as well as the "family sector," which was the Socialist term for the rural "customary." But the decree was already a transitional document. In the legal discourse of 1995, the label for this sector was shifting toward "local community." For instance, "local communities" could consult and negotiate with private actors such as companies and become coinvestors, always under the control of the state units. Importantly, the articles referring to the "family sector" stated the official recognition of "customary laws" with regard to "access to land and its tenure." This "includes various systems of rights of transference and inheritance as well as the role of local leaders with regard to conflict resolution and legitimation and legalization." According to the decree, the future law would have to be "flexible enough" to accommodate various "systems of rights" in each region and to "ensure the rights of large producers, who occupy areas that are legally attributed by customary laws and cultural patterns existent in their areas." The legislation on land tenure, the decree argues, should consider these "practical customary systems," which already "functioned in an efficient way in the majority of cases of land occupation by displaced people" who had returned after the war to their territory of origin. The decree stipulated that "the recognition of customary laws can help define the limits of collective groups defined by juridico-cultural concepts (for instance, all the members of a lineage or clan), allow them to obtain formal titles and be considered the same as associations." The postcolonial developmentalist discourse that considers "communities" as private subjects of civil law bears the mark of colonial legacies and its organization of rural locality.

The decree of 1995 was never fully implemented. There was wide political opposition within the government to the recognition of "traditional chiefs" and "customary law." Two years later, a new Land Law was passed following extensive research and national debate.[34] This was the first piece of state legislation that explicitly recognized "traditional authority" and its legitimate capacity to enforce "customary laws" and allocate parcels of land, something that had been happening de facto and was tolerated before the adoption of Decree 15/2000 on the recognition of chiefs. The key politico-economic role of chiefs at the local level in relation to land and conflict had already been recognized in the 1997 Land Law.

## "Legal Pluralism": From People to Community

In the mid-2000s, during the peak of juridical reform of the state, the proposed Law of Organization of the Judiciary System aimed at recognizing roughly 80 percent of the country's customary courts, which were informal instances of various sorts (mosques; Zionist churches; associations of healers, neighbors, and elders' councils; chieftains). In semiurban areas, the former Socialist secretaries, as well as the old People's Tribunals, were still at work, combining oral traditions and written registers, customary law and state codes. These tribunals, renamed "community courts," still based their legitimacy on the previous party-state system, even though since the democratic transition they are no longer considered to be part of the state.

The proposal of this law generated debates about the potential for conflict between a type of customary court and the spirit of official law, which stipulated that the deployment of the judicial system must coincide with the democratic administrative structure of the country. Other aspects of the debate addressed undercurrents in the country's political transformation. Law 10/92 of Judicial Courts, still in force then, established that the courts were "organs of sovereignty that administer justice in the name of the People." This law stipulated new general principles and excluded the community courts from the structure of the judicial system. This juridical document presents a subtle rhetorical overlapping of meanings, in the sense that the "People" invoked is not the one originating in the liberal tradition of "we, the People," more in line with the democratic regime, but, rather, the figure that emerged in the postindependence revolutionary Constitution of 1975 and the subsequent Socialist-oriented legislation of the People's Republic of Mozambique. This figure of the People was replaced during the democratic transition by the more diffuse concept of the "community."

This transition was made patent by the reframing and renaming of the former revolutionary People's Tribunals as community courts. These represent a form of customary court, enforcing a mix of official written law and oral customary law. These ex–People's Tribunals of the Socialist period had their origin in the liberated zones of the revolutionary anticolonial struggle. These courts are currently located in a liminal space, both geographically and in relation to their political legitimacy. The legal debate, within the reform of the state, focused on whether these courts should be dismantled or kept—and if maintained, whether they should be located within the future structure of the judiciary, despite the fact that they present a mix of formal and informal conflict resolution practices, and that the last time that lay-judges were elected by popular assemblies was in 1987, under the Socialist regime, according to the practices of nominations and popular assemblies of the party-state system.

The legislation on the recognition of "informal" justice illustrates how the alleged "community" is an outcome of the letter of the laws, as is amply demonstrated in key examples, such as Decree 15/2000 on the recognition of traditional authorities and the 1997 Land Law. One of the main features of the 1997 law was the category of "local community." During

my interviews with consultants who drafted the text of the law, held in
Maputo in 2003, they presented the concept of the local community as a
new, innovative legal construct. It is extremely difficult, however, to identify actual communities that fit the arbitrary and vague definition that the
law stipulates. The law is one of several adopted in eastern and southern
Africa in the 1990s under the auspices of the World Bank. It constitutes
another legislative instance of the state of structural adjustment: a negotiation between FRELIMO elites and donors, a liberalizing policy that
works toward gradual privatization while maintaining state control over
certain key sectors.

The transnational vector intervenes, mediated by the central state apparatus, in the locality and its "customs." Within a general liberalizing
orientation whose aim is facilitating the purchase of land, the Land Law
stops short of creating a proper market for land. New legal subjects, such
as private parties and corporations, are entitled to acquire land. Yet, as
during the rule of colonial regimes throughout the continent, rural "community" land is to be collectively owned. The reference to "customary"
norms and authority connects the two pieces of legislation on "community," the decree on "traditional authority" and Land Law. Through both,
the central state secures its control over and intervention in the field of
the "customary," be it through the prerogative of "recognizing" legitimate
chiefs or the "consultation with local communities" that local district administrators conduct, as stipulated by the Land Law.[35]

The Land Law defines a "local community" as "a grouping of families
and individuals, living in a circumscribed territorial area at the level of a
locality or below, which has as its objective the safeguarding of common
interests through the protection of areas of habitation, agricultural areas,
whether cultivated or fallow, forests, sites of sociocultural importance,
grazing lands, water sources, and areas of expansion." Yet the accurate
demarcation of a community's boundaries in order to endow "local communities" with property titles for communal land is a very difficult process
with respect to the implementation of the law. The often arbitrary and
uneven implementation has created great difficulties for the mediation of
conflicts between communities and large investors. During my fieldwork,
when pressed at a seminar in the Ministry of Justice, a UN senior legal
expert on a short visit from his agency's headquarters affirmed that "the
communities define themselves and know perfectly well their borders."
Who is entitled to represent a "community" in juridical, political, or economic negotiations is also ambiguously stated in the legislation, generating

conflicts at the local level in the case of economic transactions and occupations by foreign investors. The decree on traditional authorities stipulates that these authorities will be elected as representatives by the "communities," without clarifying the accurate mechanism for that process.

Community spaces overlap with the customary and state administration, while new legislation uncovers leftovers from the colonial past. Current demarcations of community land, which are being undertaken by either state ministerial units or NGOs, are imprecise processes. Sometimes, what is being demarcated are the limits of former colonial chieftaincies. There is also the question about whether the local chiefs, as administrative agents within the community, are part of the state administration. Another point for debate is whether the "community" should be understood as a private juridical subject or as a public administrative unit ruled by customary authority. The position of the legal experts who drafted the law, interviewed during my fieldwork in Maputo, was unambiguous: the community is a private legal subject. During a discussion session on land law reform with high state officers and technicians that I attended, one of the foreign consultants who played a central role in the research and drafting of the law affirmed that a community was juridically equivalent to a private company. Perhaps more important and complex is the fact that the legislation on community grants collective rights, something that could preclude the securing of human rights, which according to international law are inalienable and individual.

The elusive "local community," a creation of the nominalism of the state of structural adjustment, constantly reappears in legislation (such as the Law on Forests) and in jurisprudence on customary authority, and so on. By juridical fiat, these local political spaces are now located at the center of developmental policy and capitalist expansion.

Communities are considered as private juridical individual subjects, in the Land Law and in the "Process of Vision Towards a Reform of the Judiciary," developed in the mid-2000s with funding and technical assistance from Scandinavian countries and conducted by a federal commission on the reform of the justice sector. Yet juridical distinctions between private and public, state and society, foreign and national, and formal and informal become blurred when confronted with actual political conditions on the ground. There exist alternatively moments of conflict and overlapping but also of collaboration among various legal institutions. For example, some cases are submitted from one informal mechanism to the other, while others are sent from one instance of the formal system to another instance within the informal one. The passages and shortcuts blur any attempt at the categorical division. At times, people might appeal at the state level a sentence passed in an informal institution A case of sorcery accusation can be sent by a state district judge to be tried at the legal department of the Association of Traditional Healers of Mozambique (AMETRAMO); or a sentence by a community judge (a legal figure, which in 2003 floated in a juridical limbo) could be appealed at the lower levels of the state system. On occasion, Mozambican and foreign NGOs function also as instruments of conflict resolution, and their members sometimes also send cases to the state courts. Bitter conflicts arise at the local level between different political and juridical structures that compete for the monopoly over conflict resolution practices within a community. Examples include a FRELIMO party structure acting against a RENAMO-backed chief or two competing chiefs with different political support.

The "formal" and "informal" systems of justice, although represented as separate fields, are articulated. In this scheme, two metaphysical orders face one another. The Enlightenment's spirit of the laws[36] encounters other, plural, disseminated spirits of an *Afro-eccentric* juridical regime.[37] These are the spirits active within the customary courts, where a chief incorporates the souls of the ancestors, or the spiritual ethos that permeates conflict resolution at mosques or evangelical churches, as well as the normativity imparted in the local branches of the Brazilian Universal Church of God's Kingdom or in the sorcery accusations sent by the police to be evaluated by spirit mediums at the officially recognized AMETRAMO.

The distinction between informal and formal systems of justice has extensive currency within Mozambican expert discourse. In the letters of intention submitted to the World Bank, the Mozambican state has declared its commitment to consolidating the rule of law in the country. This modernist concept, linked to a liberal democratic conception of the political and the juridical, excludes any kind of legal "pluralism" or recognition of "customary laws" within the orbit of the state apparatus. This is a contradiction posed both to state units and to foreign donor agencies that work toward the construction of a dual system that encompasses both formal and informal justices, with strong interfaces between the sectors.

The distinction entails a fundamental paradox. The informal legal system in Mozambique absorbs roughly 80 percent of the legal disputes, therefore subverting any possible attempt to consider these processes as located outside a centralized state system. Indeed, the state that attempts to instantiate sovereignty, govern a territory and its population, is also encompassing within its limits this inflation, this proliferation of juridical sites and nodes of conflict resolution. If the sphere of so-called community justices can also be considered a part of the state machinery, this would put the concept of the state into question. Through legal reform and politics of recognition, the postcolonial Mozambican state is acknowledging the paradoxical condition of its basis and limits.

These legal texts, apex of the juridical sovereignty of a state, are produced by a mix of contracted foreign and national employees. For example, the Land Law was written by a team of experts from the inter-ministerial National Land Commission and foreign consultants from a UN agency. This legal instrument of rural development is deemed as having been produced through the most democratic process to have taken place in the country's recent political history, as its drafting followed a broad and heated debate at the level of the national "civil society." Moreover, the drafting of the law was preceded by extensive socioanthropological research throughout the country, a feature that was already present in the Portuguese "colonial ethnographic state," which had also commissioned anthropological fieldwork by Portuguese social scientists to support the drafting of the 1961 colonial legislation on land.

These legal developmentalist projects give an overall sense of a state of constant becoming where every juridico-political order is permanently immersed in a rapid transition. Yet, during my fieldwork, law students training to become prosecutors and officers in the judiciary stated the obvious, telling me that "on the surface everything seems to be changing through all these reforms, but those who are inside the system acknowledge that actually not much is happening." During interviews, lawyers at the Supreme Court, working on the Project of Reform of the Judicial Sector based there, complained that nothing got accomplished during the time between the visits of the foreign consultants, in this case, lawyers from an Institute for Human Rights, a state organization that submits projects on legal reform to a European Development Agency and that organizes seminars with the main officers of the judiciary to discuss the process of reform every three months in Maputo's five-star hotels. Prominent Mozambican development experts who took part in discussions on the project for the legal reform of the state argued in private that, with this whole reform process, the government was only "killing time," favoring long and convoluted processes that would delay any decision making but would still look good in the donors' eyes.

At these local places of resonance of global flows, the fate of national sovereignty is defined in this most prosaic everyday life of the "development-industrial complex," lost within the thousands of pages of expert consultants' reports piled up in the ministries' archives. In the dead hours to be killed in the local offices, during the months that pass between exchanges between Europe, Washington, and Maputo, during the time of every draft of every letter of agreement signed by the donors and the Mozambican state units, between the periodic visits of the missions of aid officers, the sedimentation of time also develops the law and its social effects.

## Postcolonial Customary

The connected historical trajectories of state and locality had produced the spaces of the colonial "customary" and the Socialist "family sector." The contemporary political context has recodified the space of the local as "community," blending a post-Socialist ethos, neoliberal socioeconomic categories, and the efforts of some of the local intelligentsia to recognize legal pluralism. The reform of "community justice" is one of the main effects of this programming. The other central effect, key for the post-Socialist scheme of governance, is the recognition of chieftaincy, or "community authority."

In June 2000, the Council of Ministers passed Decree 15/2000, the cornerstone of a novel political and administrative order in regard to locality and the legitimacy of customary authority.[38] This legal document was based on the principle of devolution of entitlements to localities and their democratization, central to the policies of decentralization of the state. During the early stages of the transition, foreign actors who had played a major role in brokering the cease-fire between FRELIMO and RENAMO posited that general elections were necessary to balance opposing militarized forces and render them more accountable, and that this process should include the state at the local level. Local elections would allow "civil society" to emerge out of the centralized Socialist party-state. Donors put pressure on FRELIMO, because they did not expect the ruling party to be willing to share power at the local level, even in provinces where RENAMO had the support of the majority. Both political parties embraced a conception of "customary authorities" that considered them to be located at the lowest levels of the state administration, with the underlying assumption that traditional authority would once more play a role in local governance, this time under the form of a representative democracy.

Shortly after the passing of the new 1990 Constitution, before the war ended, sectors within FRELIMO in alliance with donors had already explored the potential of customary authority. In 1991, the Ministry of State Administration had organized a Ford Foundation–funded ethnographic research project on "traditional authority" that conducted field research, interviewed former chiefs, and held assemblies with local populations. It produced policy reports based on an idealized, ahistoric view of "African authority." This research project eventually evolved into a USAID-funded unit located within the Ministry of State Administration dealing with issues of administrative decentralization and local power, its significance peaking around the time of the general elections of 1999.[39]

In 1994, just before the first general elections, the government passed significant legislation regarding the devolution of various governmental functions to "municipalities," and mandating local elections throughout the national territory. Drafted with input from the ministry-based research project, the new legislation explored potential ways for "traditional authority" to be incorporated into local dynamics of state governance, setting precedents for the much-debated decree on "community authorities" in 2000.

The policies of decentralization of the state transformed the landscape of governance, and the question of the customary was crucial within these programs. The first important juridical step taken toward political decentralization was the Municipal Law of 1997.[40] This document, which mandated democratic elections in thirty-three municipalities but not in any rural districts, reversed the initial attempted policy of democratization and decentralization of 1994. Decree 15/2000 and a law on local state organs further reshaped the political space of locality in the country. It reconfigured the level of state intervention in that space and its articulation with local figures of power, in the name of "administrative decentralization."

It is crucial to note that it was a decree from the executive branch, only later regulated by the Ministry of State Administration, and not a full-fledged law publicly debated and passed by the National Assembly as many donors had requested, that regulated the new policy on customary authority. The decree clearly illustrates the new post-Socialist political condition of negotiations among sectors of the ruling party and between those sectors and donor agencies. It also shows the permanence of dynamics of power linked to the previous regime. It represents the condensation of several years of internal debate within factions of FRELIMO on the very sensitive issue of traditional authority and the historical legacies

(colonialism, allegiance to RENAMO) attached to it. Although it constitutes the key legal instrument stipulating the degree of the state's recognition of community authority, it is fundamentally ambiguous and broad in
its scope. The document represents both a juridical and a historical syn-
thesis, where the relevance of "custom" and its authorities is recognized
and derided at the same time. It brings together under the new label of
"community authority" figures of power from customary systems and others from the Socialist period originally created to replace chieftaincies at
the level of the locality.

The decree refers to "community authorities," which can be elected
by the communities and thus enter into a process of legitimate recognition by the state. These authorities may be "traditional chiefs," defined
as "persons that exercise authority following the traditional rules of their
respective communities." But these community authorities may also be
many other types of local leadership, such as leaders of dynamizing groups
(former party-state cells, an institution that remains unevenly scattered
throughout the country), Socialist "neighborhood secretaries," religious
authorities, or other notable persons.

The category of authority invoked is too broad, and the mechanism for
the election of community authorities by the loosely defined "community"
is never specified. The document mandates that "forms of articulation"
are needed between local state organs and the state. While community
authorities should be representatives of a locality, the legal text presents
them as lower ranks of the state administration. The clearest example of
this governmental engineering of the "customary-as-community" is the
provision that entitles a "state representative" (who is in charge of "formal recognition" and the official inventory of local authorities) to "mediate conflicts emerging within the process of legitimation of community
authorities."

The decree establishes many functions that community authorities
must perform; key among them are taxation, census taking, voter registration, law enforcement, conflict resolution, local development, adjudication of land tenure, and labor recruitment. Within the rubric of rural
development, the decree enumerates authorities' responsibility in terms
of enforcement of the law, policing and punishment, as well as education
and health. The legal document that regulates the decree's implementation stipulates that they must "promote local custom and cultural values"
and participate in investigations on local folklore.

With respect to law and justice, the first two sections of the article on "obligations of the community authorities" in the decree establish two important facts. First, community authorities must communicate to the community the content of state law and the deliberations of state units. Second, the decree reverses a central policy that the postcolonial state had implemented after independence, which had placed party organs against the institution of chieftaincy. The decree mandates that community authorities have the obligation to "articulate with community tribunals in the resolution of conflicts of a civil nature, taking into account local customs (*usos e costumes*) within the limits of the law."

However, the new jurisprudence does not specify what kind of custom is to be enforced or mention the regional variations in customary laws; neither does it comment on whether local authorities, in their unchecked enforcement of "custom," can transform or update it as they see fit. Thus, the application of "tradition" in matters of conflict resolution becomes arbitrary due to the nonexistence of overarching authorities to codify and control the enforcement of custom and punitive sanctions.

The customary appears within national politics as occupying a structural void, which the new "democratic" politics has opened up at the local level.[41] This implies not only the harnessing of a reified, essentialized, precolonial "tradition" for purposes of advancing the rule of law but also the blending of "people who exert chieftaincy in agreement with the traditional rules of their community" with Socialist local authorities, religious leaders, members of community courts, advisers to chiefs, and so on. Another controversial issue, already mentioned above, is that the legislation grants collective rights, whereas, according to international law, human rights are inalienable and individual.

The adoption of this legal instrument was a response by the FRELIMO state to the pressure of donors, as well as to internal administrative and electoral needs. At the same time, this policy maintained a status quo. The juridical text endowed local state administrators with the potential to regulate local power. On paper, mayors would calibrate disputing claims to legitimacy and determine who would be recognized as an "authority" and the extent of their prerogatives. However, locally, the actual implementation of the law was dictated by contingency and administrative ruse. The mayor of Angoche, the main town in the coastal area in Nampula Province, won by RENAMO during the 2003 local elections, told me during interviews on the process of legitimation: "We wanted to recognize several chiefs, but the provincial government did not send us the proper banners and flags."

The Mozambican example of reforming the "customary" to transform it into "communal" reflects the current form and borders of the state in contemporary Africa. The relationship between the juridical and the political, between the legal norm and the state apparatus, is tenuous, as though the law surrounded the edifice of the state, being both its foundation and its expression. Thus, the broad juridical reform implemented in Mozambique is aimed at instantiating the neoliberal notion that what is actually being transformed is the "state."

## Jurisprudence as Historiography

Classical political philosophy has defined sovereignty as being founded on the letter of the law. The pretended juridical nature of the modern appears as an operation in which the spirit of the laws incorporates myriad other spirits and legalities. In Africa, as exemplified by the Mozambican case, the postcolonial state fashions itself through the construction, within positive law, of the customary as its negativity. The state functions as a dialectical machine that attempts to hegemonize multiple localities. Its juridical discourse engenders differential moments, local norms, and ritual forms of sovereignty, only to sublate them within a final historical *Aufhebung*.

Yet the connected histories of the state apparatus and the customary presented above do not show the legal dialectics of two opposed concrete entities. Rather, they disclose a broader political field in which the borders between them become indistinguishable. This field is regulated by norms other than the rule of law of the current democracy, which reifies a network of situations and institutions into a state apparatus as the supposed main locus of the political, famously divided into three branches of power.[42] In this juridical democratic narrative, the spirit of the laws unfolds from its source in the Constitution, as the organizing principle of the state, in order to domesticate its other: the customary law of the nonmodern, "traditional community."

The plurality of norms in the African locality sheds light on a more general context. In reality, there exists an earlier historical contamination: the state as the alleged dialectical incarnation of the Spirit[43] had always been articulated with a plurality of other specters.[44] This alterity—"magic," "sacredness," or various forms of the customary—was already present within the origins of the state as condensation of the spirit of the laws.

Other norms and different ethics, as supposed dialectical others located within encounters of "recognition," are crucial for the state to enact its sovereignty

In reality, the narrative presented above of the attempt by the state to juridically construct the customary shows that both fields are located within the same plane, which leads one to question the historical status of the precolonial. Beyond actual vernacular practices and formations, the precolonial customary was a realm legally shaped by colonial law, administrative ethnography, and the governmental practices of private concessions and military posts that reshaped the entire landscape of local kin-based authority.[45] What is the political meaning of the current democratic politics of recognition?

The event of colonialism, despite its short temporal duration, produced nevertheless a rupture in history, a scission that established a "precolonial" time. The state of structural adjustment aims today at defining the future by reference to this ghostly past time. As the question of the customary plays a key role in the definition and demarcation of the nation-state, legislation and policy projects work by referencing a homogeneous precolonial past and an idealized and reified form of chieftaincy as "African authority."

Through a legal-historicist move, the state sets the past to work in the present as an infinite flat political temporality, reflected in the state's jurisprudence. This flow of events would stretch back to an origin that should determine the outcome of the future political community and that should materialize through its crystallization in the legal construction of the customary. The "precolonial" is an absent presence located at the heart of both the colonial and the postcolonial states' attempts to delimit the realm of the customary. At any given moment, this image loaded with a surplus of political sense reemerges, blurring the boundaries and hence showing the unstable borders of a reified, fictive state apparatus.

The postcolonial nation-state constitutes a regional space of paradoxes and anachronisms. A quotidian alchemy of struggle and negotiation marks the limits of the state's recognition of its alterity within this disjoined territory. In Mozambique the state currently reflects upon the legacies of colonialism, Socialism, and the civil war as the historical conditions of its present, through the relations between the poles of violence and the law, that is, instantiations of war and politics.

These narratives of dialectics between the "modern" and the "archaic" are deployed in a contested symbolic field that shows how jurisprudence can also be understood as constituting an implicit official historical narrative. The legal reform of the state functions as a public theater or amalgam of texts that allows us to revisit the recent past. The law aims at exerting a jurisdiction over time. "History" itself becomes the object of development, as new legislation promoted by foreign aid agencies rewrites the contours of the recent political time—for instance, through the reinscription of the customary within the social.

# CHAPTER THREE

# The State of Things

The history of the law traced in the previous chapter produced a particular type of state, which defined the domain of the customary as its opposite vector. The contemporary moment in Mozambique engages this history in itself as an object of political and juridical reform, giving rise to a form of state that requires a theoretical reframing. This chapter explores dynamics of state sovereignty put in place by the postwar democratic transition and the reappraisal of the customary. At stake is the concept of "customary citizenship," a form of political belonging in which local allegiances and histories intersect with formal, juridical citizenship as ascription to the nation-state.

## Maputo I: The State of Structural Adjustment

Maputo, mid-2000s. The feeling of the end of an era permeates the city and its public spaces, especially in the messages of the main media outlets—a couple of television channels and news shows, a few newspapers and leaflets distributed by fax—whose claims and predictions are echoed in myriad conversations amongst elites and others in the know. The last few years have brought a series of politico-economic transformations to the nation-state. Ten years following the end of the civil war the country continues on a path of national reconciliation, healing of social and communal wounds, economic and political liberalization, and the rebuilding of ruined infrastructure. While national elites still keep their grip on the direction and outcome of these processes, more than 60 percent of the national budget derives from various forms of foreign aid and international loans. Donors and financial institutions oversee the continuity of

the peace process, the juridical reform of the state, and the reconstitution of the economy. In this context of reform of the party-state system
and the deregulation of markets and political associations, "civil society"
is a central concept or slogan that is constantly reiterated in the public
sphere.

Maputo, 2003–4. The city, yesterday ravaged by war and scarcity, and
filled with semi-ruined buildings, is now thriving, overflowing with capital from private foreign investment, national elites' shares of privatized
companies and land, donors' aid, and illegal trafficking of various kinds.
Many new banks are being opened. An official stock market begins functioning, while operations at the city port are conceded to a European company for the next fifteen years. Corporations and investment consultancy
agencies begin to operate from their bases in the posh areas on the coast.
Legal and illegal markets intermingle and feed each other. As the majority of economic activity is located within the so-called informal economy,
it could be argued that this sector is effectively the formal economy of the
nation.

In 2003, the newly developed urban areas that host the elite and middle
classes seem but a satellite of Lisbon, with Brazilian inflections. Portuguese television and radio are ever present and widely followed. These Lusophone spaces mean that on any given day at street cafes and offices the
daily intricacies of Portugal's politics and soccer are being discussed, amid
references to European politics and society. Brazilian novellas, music, and
films are more influential and present than African cultural productions,
with the exception of South Africa, a regional power that is the other central political and economic reference.

An aura of violence permeates the public sphere. Crime is on the rise
and the downtown areas have become increasingly insecure. The legal
monopoly on violence has become privatized, and British and South African private security firms proliferate. The recent political and economic
transformations have also been marred by political crime. State officers
investigating details of large privatizations of banks have died in suspicious accidents. The country's main investigative journalist, who had re-
searched alleged misdeeds and dubious business conducted by relatives of
the president and other supposed front men and collaborators, had been
machine-gunned by unknown men while driving his car in the affluent
downtown area.

Law and justice are objects of everyday conversations. City dwellers in
the middle-class areas publicly, yet discreetly, debate issues of legality and

illegality in the country's current moral economy. According to the word on the street, the country, despite a public commitment to the ideological stances of early postindependence, appears to be on a rapid downward spiral produced by the whirlwind of politico-economic changes. There is still secrecy and censorship, and the circulation of information and alleged rumor is closely monitored; the transition from decades of centralized rule and intense social control is deep but slow.

In the evenings, families and neighbors gather around TV sets to follow the intricacies of the trial of the man accused of executing the journalist, as if it was yet another popular Brazilian soap opera. He has escaped twice from high-security prisons, and eventually the accusations will involve people who are close to the president of the Republic; even his son will be eventually put on trial. People discuss the depositions of witnesses and defendants, the alibis and betrayals of friends and acquaintances; they listen intently, evening after evening, to the sinuous, elaborate perorations of lawyers, prosecutors, and judges that take place amid an august blend of protocol and décor.

A different temporality intersects with the transformations of this present. In conversations in homes, offices, and cafes and on sidewalks, a past epoch often emerges: "In Samora's time . . . ," a person would say, followed by a litany addressing the current moment of dubious arrangements, decayed ethics, impoverishment, and abandonment of independent morals and national sovereignty. The reference to the deceased revolutionary leader is the marker of a previous, seemingly long-gone era of higher moral and living standards, despite its vicissitudes of authoritarian rule and war.

The sense of an end of an epoch, a certain listless nostalgic affect, blankets the social mood, as the people confront changes in the economy, a boom in growth rates, a hyperkinetic displacement of political personnel, and feverish preparations for a new general election in the year to come. As the ruling party's old guard takes charge yet again, everything seems in disarray, suspended, as though all might be transformed as political structures are reconstituted, economic flows redirected, and a new, younger, generation assumes positions in the state apparatus. Yet most people in the urban middle classes seem to think that despite all this, nothing will really change.

As an icon of this state of things, the image of the president of the Republic is reproduced everywhere. It circulates profusely, as though leaving a trail of elusive yet material remains, cementing the unity of a nation immersed in a process of reuniting divided sectors and factions, remembering the dismembered body politic. The president's name appears in public spaces and speeches, in stadiums and in the events they host. The portrait of the president is ubiquitous, affixed in public offices, ministries, courts, the halls of the popular assembly, the palace of government, and even the residential villa that the president has built for himself, as if a mirror game of portraits might reflect the presence of he who walks these spaces and holds the key to the purported transition of power.

The 10,000-meticais banknote carries the same portrait of the president, placed below the coat of arms of the Republic, with its AK-47 rifle juxtaposed with a plow. Alongside the iconography of the bill representing labor, natural resources, and power plants, the leader's visage metaphorically backs the value of money. A political economy is summarized in that small note, telling the story of the succession of power from the time of revolution and the people's republic, with its planned centralized economy, to the current time of privatizations, postwar structural adjustment, foreign aid, capitalization, and investments in the new liberal democratic republic. The president has led the country for the last eighteen years, since the accidental, untimely death of the first revolutionary leader in 1986.

The sensation of decay and overall transformation is twofold. First, it refers to the impossibility of the president's running for another term, since he has lost support from the old guard of the ruling party. Second, the sense of having a terminal condition encompasses the party itself; having ruled the nation since independence, the party now appears at a dead end, after a decades' long rule that spanned Marxism-Leninism, war, and liberal democracy.

The juridical reform of the state transforms history itself into an object of socioeconomic development. Like the nation-state, immersed within historical transformations and political transitions, the capital city and its social meanings are also undergoing a process of reconstruction. The downtown streets still bear the names of revolutionary leaders from Mozambique, Africa, and other regions of the world. Yet investment flows into the urban space, especially the city center, and in posh residential areas, old buildings are refurbished and new buildings, villas, compounds, and entertainment venues emerge. Bars, clubs, and theaters cater to the national elite, who mingle with the large expat community of diplomats and development consultants. Branches of European and South African banks open in central points. New churches also proliferate throughout

the town. A globally powerful Brazilian evangelical church, which broad-
casts its shows late at night on national TV, has built a megachurch on one
of the most elegant avenues near the coast. A particular icon, the AK-47,
is disseminated throughout the urban space, linking past and present.
The rifle appears on the national flag, recalling the revolutionary times
of the People's republic. It can be seen in the hands of young soldiers
from the national army, which, since the democratic transition and under the tutelage of foreign security forces, is composed of FRELIMO and
RENAMO soldiers; the same rifle is carried by the innumerable guards
working for private security organizations, many of them ex-combatants
in the civil war. Also, while famed French architect Eiffel had designed the
train station of colonial Lourenço Marques as well as a cast-iron house
in the downtown area, today in a nearby market, as part of a European
development agency project, local artisans sell to the many tourists small
replicas of the Eiffel Tower made with pieces of AK-47 rifles destroyed
during the disarmament period after the peace accords.

The end of an era was also palpable in an interview I conducted with
a foreign consultant working on state reform, a Scandinavian lawyer who
was in charge of programs at one of the European development agencies
funding the reform of the judiciary and who was advising on new legislation and citizenship rights. Her status within the development community
and her views on the political context and reform of the state are representative of those of a wide array of foreign advisers with whom I spoke. We
spoke for a few hours at her office inside the high modernist fortress that
served as an embassy in the elegant tree-lined suburban area that hosted
many diplomatic organizations. Abundant sunlight coming through the
large windows illuminated the office and large desk, which were in a seemingly organized state of chaos, with many reports and files piled up all over
the place. The law and development expert gave me a candid assessment
of the national context in the current, delicate moment.

She spoke about general, rampant "corruption," as foreign aid money
was, she claimed, channeled toward private accounts. (This reminded
me of my conversation with a young lawyer working at a ministry office,
who had told me how his uncle, employed at a high level in the national
bank, spoke about the accusations of corruption in the language of a
previous ideology: "We are implementing the primitive accumulation of
capital . . .") Yet, she affirmed, the bloc of main foreign donors was not
deterred by this. At the last meeting of the cabinet of ministers with the
board of donors, the prime minister asked for a budget of $600 million

and obtained instead an offer of $720 million. Hence, the government can assert that, although it receives plenty of critiques, it has the full support of the international community, which sees no wrongdoing.

She was quite frank in affirming that the country's postwar peace process and structural adjustment were successes, and this situation gave the government elites plenty of space to negotiate and demand support from donors—for instance, for funding the sumptuary infrastructures being built to host a summit of the African Union. The government was forcefully "demanding" increasingly higher donations to rebuild the city and for other projects from "furious" donors, who had to acquiesce to these demands in order to preserve the functioning of the country without substantially changing its governmental structures.

Our conversation turned to the upcoming national elections and she expressed similar arguments to others I had heard from highly placed foreign development consultants and foreign legal experts, only enhanced by the centrality and responsibility attached to her position. She seemed certain about the doomed near future of the ruling bloc. "FRELIMO already knows that they are going to lose both the local elections next year and the general ones the following year. But we are concerned because they will not abandon power smoothly. Moreover, RENAMO does not have any sound political program or administrative structures in place with properly trained people. The population does not vote. They are fed up with politics. You cannot win elections anymore solely appealing to a rhetoric of struggle for independence. There is a whole new generation now, born and raised in the postcolonial era. There might possibly be many social conflicts after the elections."

In 2000 and 2003 I interviewed tens of state officers and foreign development consultants during many hours passed at the premises of official units, with their endless delays. Those were days spent at offices filled up with stalled documentation, operating at different speeds depending on the alternatively slower or more rushed demands and rhythms belonging to the logic of either state units or donor agencies. At one of those offices, housing a unit located between the judicial and executive branches, my dialogue with a young lawyer signaled in the direction of yet another power, operating behind those two: "The state is XXX [he named a Scandinavian development agency]. . . . I used to be under contract with UNDP [United Nations Development Programme] and now we operate with contracts from this agency, which funds our unit. My colleague employed at the unit working on land reform has a contract with XXX [a multilateral agency based in Europe]. . . . Yet we are national officers. When I worked for UNDP, the fine print in my contract stated very explicitly that 'contracted personnel are not UN functionaries.'"

While different areas of juridical and economic reform of the state are allocated to various state agencies, under the coordination of the World Bank, the dynamics of many projects that take the law as their object of development are as follows. Funds are made available, for instance, by a European development agency operating in the field of reform of the country's constitutional and legal regimes as well as the justice sector. The consultants—researchers based in the country and high-ranking officers periodically traveling from their headquarters to supervise the implementation of projects—function as brokers to secure funding from the main agency, later finding state offices as counterparts where these projects can be based. Multilateral agencies apply for funding provided by an individual European donor, proposing projects targeted at particular sectors or working with individual units within the government. Different groups of experts will work on various kinds of reform legislation, subcontracting various local consultants to draft the legislation, including national officers.

In 2003–4, independent European consultants working on temporary contracts for a multilateral agency based in Geneva approached a state unit that was working on questions of legal pluralism (customary law and "community justice") in order to produce a joint research project on local management of conflicts. The Geneva organization encompassed issues of land tenure and rural development within their portfolio but did not operate on questions of justice per se. The project was focused on the management of conflicts over land at community courts (the former People's Tribunals), including aspects of their capacities and needs (training, infrastructure, funding), which constituted a very sensitive issue within the new democratic regime in Mozambique.

The project was designed by the European independent consultants working for Geneva (they had previously worked for USAID) with minimal input from Mozambican researchers working at the state unit, and then the multilateral agency and the national state unit jointly applied for funds from the Scandinavian agency mentioned above. When the project was presented, the donor agency's office in Maputo pointed out that the vast majority of disputes over land were not adjudicated at the community courts but rather at other customary spaces such as chieftaincies or elders' councils. The team of experts then adjusted the program slightly and resubmitted it to the donor agency.

In Maputo in April and May of 2003 I met with a few senior state

officers who had held low-level positions in the previous colonial administration until 1975, and who continued working at their posts in the judiciary during the new postcolonial dispensation. Similarly, in the current
state of structural adjustment, agents can work for both the state and the
donors at the same time. I was present at meetings in which a prominent
representative from the ruling party in charge of different projects pertaining to the juridical reform of the state—among them the new legislation
on the status of community courts—offered very high ranking officers
in the judiciary to work as consultants on these projects, to draft the new
laws. The contract would be funded by two European agencies that supported the reform of the sector.

A month later I interviewed a Mozambican lawyer who had a degree
in administration and was an adviser to the National Assembly on a
project to reform sectors of the executive branch that was designed and
funded by USAID. She was technically under contract with that American
agency. Different party blocs in the National Assembly had agreed that
she would organize the agenda and the schedule for transforming certain
aspects of the executive. She had a long and varied résumé as a state officer, spanning the beginning of Socialism to the current neoliberal times.
Soon after independence, she had visited areas controlled by RENAMO,
meeting with customary authorities. At the time I interviewed her she was
also in charge of USAID / National Assembly projects in rural areas, especially some conducted in connection with the largest corporate metallurgic
project in the country. An expert in rural development, she affirmed that
based on her experience, she was "against traditional authority," which
she defined as utterly "antidemocratic," while at the same time acknowledging that it necessarily "had to be accommodated somehow within the
new democratic system."

Several experts I interviewed in 2003 (Mozambican lawyers, foreign
development consultants, judges, and state officers) underscored the ways
in which structural adjustment and the privatization of the public sector
were transforming the national juridical structures. The opening of the
economy to foreign investment had brought about a homogenization of
contract forms and a proliferation of new types of regulation more suitable to the Anglo-Saxon legal traditions of investors and companies from
South Africa and Europe. The economic boom related to finance and enclaves of production carried with it the effects of international legal regulations on business that progressively influenced the rest of the judiciary
and legal apparatus.

In mid-2003 I met one of the most important local social scientists, a former organic intellectual of the party-state system, who still supported the government, yet from a very critical perspective. He emphasized the influence of foreign actors on national governance and Mozambique's situation as a political and economic satellite. He traced relations between war, politics, and the economy, explaining how the main lines of the current democratic system had been designed in the context of the peace accords. He claimed that what was needed was the connection between state and society that had existed during the heyday of Socialism but that had been severed by structural adjustment programs. Although he described in detail the complexities of articulations between ethnic cleavages and political identities throughout the country (with the reconstitution of old alliances and the emergence of new local parties, even some phantom organizations evidently promoted by the ruling party), he affirmed that the "international community" carries a lot of authority and weight with respect to major governmental decisions. He affirmed that the RENAMO opposition was not prepared to govern, so the donors turned a blind eye to a lot of bad governmental practices implemented by FRELIMO. He predicted that the ruling party would win the next elections by a very small margin or that they would rig the election as in the past, but that this would not "produce any sort of violent response because the political process and security are controlled by South Africa, and then they would send troops, as they recently did in Lesotho."

Around the time of this interview, I met with a young associate general attorney of the Republic at her office downtown, where she directed the Anti-Corruption State Office. She had been trained in Lisbon and Marseille and had attended several seminars and workshops in the United States. She was naturally wary of me at first, not knowing "who hired me"; later, we talked at length and more openly about the joint economic and juridical reforms of the state.

The first part of the interview was devoted to the centrality of the law in the process of restructuring the economy. She affirmed that juridical reform was under way but said that it had not gotten to the most important part yet, which was to replace the whole system of continental Roman law with Anglo-Saxon common law. She explained that, in an indirect way, the process of economic reform and the opening of the public sector to business produced a transformation of the legal system, from Roman law (the Portuguese system), which she described as slow, complex, and too rigid because of being so formalist and formulaic, to common law, which she defined as faster, simpler, and more expeditious. "Corporations want flexibility in arbitrage, negotiations, and mediations."

The second half of our conversation glossed over the place of a multiplication of justices within the ongoing process of legal and economic reform. She was adamantly opposed to the project of "legal pluralism," which she defined as a program engineered by foreign interests, drawing an analogy between law and language that evoked the project of a nation-state put forward by the revolutionary regime "in Samora's time," with its consecration of Portuguese as the national language and its ban on local language, imposing state unity over tribalisms. "Legal pluralism debilitates the state; at present we have to strengthen the official legal system."

She supported the idea of community courts being the lowest echelon of the judicial system, from which citizens could move on to appeal to district courts, and higher. When asked about the problem of community courts enforcing, as she said, "custom and nonwritten laws," she answered that there was an evident legal void in the current system, yet these courts must be reformed and new judges must be elected—although, she affirmed, somewhat disingenuously, that "current lay-judges study the law, and in the end they make their decisions according to written jurisprudence." These were not merely individual remarks. Some of these views were being widely discussed and reproduced by an advisory industry that conceived of law and justice as infrastructures, as objects of development.

In the years 2000–2005, a decade after the first general elections held in the postwar transition, innumerable workshops and symposia on the juridical reform of the state and the transformation of the judiciary and national legal regimes were held in Maputo. Among the many I attended as an observer and sometimes as a participant in conversations with teams from state units, a large event organized by the Supreme Court and a European development agency working on justice reform stands out for its relevance, its effects, and its cast of participants.

The three-day event held at the end of May 2003 had as its main object the design of a "vision" for the justice sector specific to Mozambique, and it took place at an office of the Supreme Court outside the city and at a luxury hotel downtown. Speakers included foreign consultants subcontracted by the European agency who were visiting the country for a few days, experts from the agency who were based in Maputo, high-ranking officers from the judiciary and legislative powers, and teams of Mozambican lawyers and consultants from different ministries and agencies. The event illustrated some of the dynamics of negotiation, agreement, and op-position in relation to political orientation and funding within the state of structural adjustment. The discussion concerned justice reform in Mozam-bique and presented the law as an object of development. The debates ad-dressed the new "spirit of the laws" being implemented in the country: the dismantling of Socialist institutions of justice, constitutional separation of powers, and financialization of the law.

The president of the Supreme Court introduced the event by saying that the task was to discuss the destiny of "a broader field of legality" that would include both the judiciary and other sectors of the state. He referred to Mozambique's new global context of reference for the state reform, presenting the country's new, modernized legal system as more akin to Brazil's and quite different from Portugal's and the rest of the sys-tems in Lusophone Africa. He was at pains to emphasize the need for the judiciary to be autonomous from the executive branch, fundamentally in terms of financial independence, so that the sector's budget could be man-aged without interference from the Ministry of Justice.

The other main actor at the workshop was a Scandinavian NGO, whose legal consultants were contracted by the main agency funding and advis-ing the reform of this sector. When I spoke with the main consultant in the delegation, he confirmed that they were working on similar projects of reform of the judiciary in Niger, Tanzania, and Guatemala, and they had previously advised on the reorganization of prison and police sectors in postwar Serbia. Yet, despite their global reach, they advocated "unique, singular" projects in each country.

At these sessions, the emphasis was on the joint issues of "indepen-dence" and "transparency," which were decomposed into three main aspects: the need to see it as a field encompassing many spaces and prac-tices; the relevance of centralizing its control within the executive branch; and an individualistic approach geared toward each citizen's access to jus-tice as a good, or a commodified service.

The main consultant from the NGO spoke in English, with simulta-neous translation. During his presentation he constantly pointed to dia-grams and schemes on a board and to PowerPoint images that offered detailed representations of the executive and judiciary sectors as well as the intricate steps and sections of the processual "vision" being discussed. He introduced himself merely as a "coach" of the process of reform of the judiciary. He relished his job as "provocateur," able to stir up the debate and lead it in certain directions. Although it was evident that he and his team of (European and South American) young lawyers constantly traveled around the world to promote and evaluate similar reform projects, he insisted on the fact that the process should yield a program tailored toward such a "unique" country and the "special" audience in attendance. The key concept he proposed was that of "flow," which would enable the inclusion of all subsectors operating within the justice sector: police, prisons, courts, and so on. Although he described the justice sector as a "strange animal encompassing functions belonging to the three constitutional powers," "the process of reform," he affirmed, "must be coordinated by the Ministry of Justice, with other sectors only adding a few points." This would strengthen the "right spirit of independence of the sector."

Then slowly, but very clearly, he developed the concept of justice understood as a service. He expanded on different aspects of this, asking rhetorically who is served by the system of justice, who the consumers are, what the characteristics of the manager/purveyor of justice should be. He referred to the ongoing decentralization process, which would facilitate the development of new management tools to make the system more "accountable to its customers."

Developing his ideas through schemes that he drew on a board, he described different "business areas" within the state apparatus, evoking justice as one such business and aiming at defining the "clients" of the judiciary sector. He affirmed that a certain "ambition" was needed to produce the document that was expected as the final product of the exercise, which should describe "the real world—that is, what kind of society you want to have and the place of the law as a means of measurement."

In agreement with the corporate logics of the moment, when the discussion turned toward the "values" that the judiciary should enforce, the European consultant emphasized "celerity." At the end he reinvoked the main theme of the workshop: "A vision is a dream. Today you might not yet see how to achieve it, but we will define a time horizon, and our technicians will strategize on how to arrive at that point."

The consultant was followed by a Supreme Court Justice. This man, son of a Portuguese settler who had worked in the administration of colonial concessionary companies, had been a young member of the brigades of popular justice a couple of years after independence and had later occupied low-ranking positions in the postcolonial judiciary system. In 2003, he echoed some of the perspectives advanced by the representative of the international donors. He first emphasized "independence," which he then restricted to the "act of judgment," a sign of, he said, "independence of powers from absolutism," which should result in independence of the judiciary from the executive branch. This remark, which was evidently meant for the donors managing the reform, who promoted a discourse of transparency regarding "corruption," was followed by an economic approach toward the law. "Transparency," the judge affirmed, helped "fair justice to arrive to the consumer at a lower political and financial cost."

The main morning session continued with debates on these matters, and toward the end the main politician working on reform at the National Assembly, a FRELIMO MP, spoke, perhaps implicitly rebutting the views of donors and the justice who had spoken earlier. "We have to design a sustainable system for the next twenty-five years, independently from each person's dream. It is not possible to think of a decentralized system of justice in a country where 60 percent of the budget comes from foreign aid. It is therefore necessary to coordinate this reform of the sector within the broader context of a constitutional reform."

The session ended with a second, shorter intervention by the Supreme Court Justice. It represented a mix of the usual post-Socialist nostalgic rhetoric ("in Samora's time") with current pragmatism. It warned against the creation of new mechanisms of control within the executive branch. He began by quoting a speech from 1975 by Samora Machel: "We must create popular power to serve the masses." He then moved on to practical policy issues: "Since Samora's time our mode is to create a structure only when there is a deep need. . . . An evaluation of the number of legal cases in our courts could be an adequate sign."

Toward the end of the day, the consultants led a debate on the "logic of justice" organized around the dissection of two main themes: the "mandate/purpose" and the "machinery" of the judiciary. Although their framing of these themes—heavily focused on the overarching issue of transparency—was informed by a technocratic discourse that seemed to be aimed at miming the self-evidence and cleanness of justice as a service, the discussion increasingly took on animist contours, almost depicting "justice" as a live entity with volition, needs, and desires.

The workshop ended with the main foreign expert announcing that two days later they would meet with the "political heads of the reform process" in the executive and legislative power. The final debates brought up a new theme, mentioned by some key participants, that slowly began to emerge as crucial: the consideration of the "legal pluralism" that already existed in the country, essentialized and reified as a given datum, as if its historical construction could be ignored. The workshop closed with a poignant question posed by one of the FRELIMO MPs that addressed the juridical nuances and loops of post-Socialist transition: "Legal pluralism already exists in this country. Are we going to produce new legislation to address it, or will we continue working mainly through the people's courts?"

## The African State: In Theory

The Weberian conception of the state presents it as a community that successfully claims a monopoly on the legitimate use of physical force within a given territory.[1] The Weberian ideal-typical model of the rational-legal bureaucratic state has become normative in much of the literature on postcolonial states, insofar as the capacity of a unified apparatus to successfully impose jurisdiction over a territory and a citizenry by means of its legitimate monopoly on violence is the measure by which such states are evaluated. This model is ill adapted to understanding the contemporary Mozambican state, where jurisdictional power is fundamentally flawed or contested. For instance, according to the canonical Weberian definition, the state possesses an administrative and legal order, subject to change by legislation. Yet in Mozambique, external powers in the form of transnational development agencies have engineered the liberal democratic regime that emerged from the peace accords coordinated by the international community, producing the legislation that will shape the new democratic regime. Donors design and fund central areas of state reform, including contracting foreign or national private consultants to write the letter of the law, to then be passed by a national assembly. The state's fundamental ground as the sovereign constitution of a juridical order, whose authority is exercised through jurisdictional powers, is denied when the law itself is the object of developmentalist reform and foreign aid. At the same time, official jurisdiction is also strongly challenged by local agencies that formerly belonged to the state apparatus, such as those studied in this ethnography, as well as by other normativities and historical forms of violence.[2]

Rather than a unified sovereign apparatus, the Mozambican state should be conceived of as a segmentary state, composed of various types of agencies that are not fragments stemming from an ideal totality that is lacking (failed, collapsed, or weak state), but rather loosely tied segments of different assemblages. Its citizenry is also segmented into various sectors, with different degrees of entitlements. Studying the state in its positivity, as a space where struggles over sovereignty and modalities of governance unfold, sheds light on effects of statehood concealed by the reification of the political as a centralized institution.

Much of the Africanist literature on the state loosely follows Weberian or Marxist lines. These institutional approaches differ in how they define state legitimation and the extent to which the Western model is understood as a normative telos. At the most abstract end of the spectrum, one finds deployed a conception of the state as an apparatus, structure, or institution that exists in a position of sheer externality to local political forms. In the most normative understandings of the state as a modern rational-legal ideal type, it appears as an idealized telos, drawing on Weber's evolutionary history, in terms of which the postcolonial state is understood as deploying a less "developed" mode of legitimation based on charismatic, traditional, and patrimonial forms that stand in a more or less complex relation to the imported rational-legal formal apparatus. A variation of this view understands the state in terms of a "dual-publics thesis," in which the rational universality of the Weberian state is opposed to the normativities of traditional publics on the ground.[3]

A trend displayed by African thinkers working during the 1970s and 1980s from a structuralist Marxist perspective, proposed analyzing the state as an abstraction of class relations that reflects and upholds global capitalist structures of domination, in which the national state apparatus is merely a mask for class interests of an economic comprador elite and a bureaucratic political class who control it and have access to its resources.[4] During the nationalist and developmentalist period, both Marxist and nationalist historiographic and political analysis of state-citizenship relations focused solely on the problem of indigenous control of an inherited, extraneous state apparatus. State power was understood as a nativist and structural-functionalist quest to refashion the state as an autochthonous entity, obliterating its *longue durée* history and its roots in various social forces beyond the agencies of an apparatus.[5]

A later, much more nuanced version of the nationalist-Marxist approach locates the position of the postcolonial African state vis-à-vis citizenship in the context of the legacies of colonial governance and its inheritance of a colonial "bifurcated" and decentralized form of power, where white colonists and elite natives, who made up the central state, had access to citizenship rights and were ruled by civil law, while the majoritarian rural native population of subjects, located in ethnic enclaves, were ruled by "traditional authority" through customary law.[6] In this approach, postcolonial regimes are understood as having deracialized the central state but as having failed to de-ethnicize local structures of power related to custom, replicating aspects of the colonial distinction between citizenship and subjecthood.

While being grounded in an analysis of the particularity of the African nation-state and the need to find historically situated understandings that do not replicate the Western political norm, this nationalist-Marxist approach also rejects aspects of the nationalist-nativist narrative. At the same time, while retaining roots in Marxist political analysis, it rejects the centrality of political economy as an explanatory framework, moving from the labor question to the native question, decentering the analysis of market and accumulation dynamics in favor of a study of an apparatus of governance. Based on the ethnography of a state, the chapters that follow explore the idea that normative parameters from Western liberal theory need to be expanded in order to understand African political dynamics.

Another crucial contribution offered by these studies on the specificity of state and citizenship in postcolonial Africa is the focus on the centrality of locality and the customary in contemporary governance, as opposed to most current analysis, which focuses on urban political elites and the state's self-presentation as a single apparatus and a unified legal subject. The present book examines the centrality of the rural customary and the locality within the reform of the postcolonial state and citizenship. It deepens this approach by examining ethnographically how the liminal field of the periurban needs to be understood as a central political space, part of a continuum between village and city where parameters of sovereignty and social inclusion are currently defined.

Another research approach is to examine the state apparatus from the perspective of "politics from below," focusing on the continuum between state politics and society. This model is that of the "rhizome" and envisages the state as a "multiplicity," with various points of entry and origin, forms of authority, and social networks, where traditional and modern elites are linked through clientelistic networks of patronage and accumulation. This trend emphasizes the study of the "historicity" of the African state, defining it as an imported agency that had to be "grafted" onto local endogenous structures.[7] This process defies the hegemony of the imported state logics through the exertion of control and pressure, adapting through various eras of transnationalization and governmental modalities—colonial control and extroversion, postindependence development, and neoliberal structural adjustment and reform). Some authors using this model have studied the transformation of the African state from the viewpoint of the "privatization" (or later the "criminalization") of the state,[8] which allegedly takes place through the "discharge" of public functions, which are transferred to private actors (e.g., customs, taxation, security). This approach takes into account a new round of linking the African state to emergent global flows.

In these types of studies, the debate on the African state is generally contextualized within the frame of the relations between state and society. Different perspectives give various names to the "social" component of this equation and enumerate different actors forming it: grassroots movements, trade unions, kinship structures, traditional power. Yet they mostly take for granted, in different degrees and despite attempts to nuance it, the existence of a unified state apparatus and an illusory border separating distinct political fields.[9]

These theories on the specific form of the African state illustrate the fact that the African postcolony exceeds the parameters of classical normative theories of state formation. In the light of such normative definitions, African states are most often evaluated in terms of lack, defined in terms of everything that apparently they are not, as failed states or negations of a universal ideal form. When the state is considered in its own positivity, in terms of what it actually does and produces, a different theoretical framework can emerge, one that sees the African state as a strategic situation that articulates colliding forces (as in Foucault's definition of power). Questions about the dynamics of sovereignty, governance, or law with regard to the crucial question of the local and its demarcation open up new perspectives on who is a sovereign authority that enforces the law, collects taxes, or provides services.

The Weberian definition of the state sees it as an apparatus that imposes legal jurisdiction over a given territory. But who actually governs the space of this postcolonial nation? The Mozambican case study shows the porosity of the supposed boundaries of the state, revealing political relations between an alleged state apparatus and a multiplicity of other actors, both at the level of the central state (transnational agencies, illegal networks, corporations) and at the level of the locality (chiefs, customary structures, religious leaders, former Socialist institutions). The emerging picture reveals a transient entity, a political assemblage of different kinds of agents interacting in a quest for hegemony. Within the dynamics of power in the continuum between "state" and "society," "customary citizenship" is today a key technology of governance as well as an open field for political struggles by different actors.

The state appears as an elusive element that circulates, articulating social relations, among disparate fields: institutions, norms, subjectivities. This condition refutes the idea of a strictly "national" state, with jurisdiction over a single unified territory and enforcing legal violence upon its citizenry. In terms of the current political economy and its influence on international and national law, what emerges is a state form shaped by the current dominant *dispositif* of neoliberal developmentalism: a political assemblage that could be defined as the state of structural adjustment. Let us examine the conditions of emergence of this state.

## Neoliberal Governmentality

Different political and economic analysts agree that the mid-1970s saw the beginning of the implementation of neoliberal policies of state reform and structural adjustment of the economy, especially in the postcolony.[10] In the light of a crisis of a long cycle of capital accumulation and Cold War geopolitical dynamics, marked by the rise in oil prices, the abandonment of the gold standard by the United States, a burgeoning debt crisis throughout the global South, and the explosion of Cold War conflicts and armed struggles, new formations of governance were implemented in regimes of the global South that would later be extended to the United States, the United Kingdom, and Western Europe. The following sections trace the unfolding and contours of neoliberal governmentality and the place of the state and the law within it. The latter part of the chapter illustrates the effect of this on Mozambican governance and its political economy of citizenship rights.

There are two main trends in the study of the state under neoliberalism. One emphasizes economic issues, addressing the interplay of the state and markets and studying how the state apparatus is transformed as capital flows and trade are allegedly deregulated. The other, inspired by Foucault, approaches the state through an interpretation of his problematics of modern power in terms of governmentality and subjectification and focuses on technologies of governance, global flows, and micropolitical effects across a variety of institutional and social settings.

The approach proposed here utilizes the basic findings of these two trends, yet locates them within a distinct perspective. The ethnographic

material collected in Mozambique on the state, the customary, law, politics, and the economy leads to a questioning of the categorical distinctions
between "state" and "markets," "national" and "transnational," or "economy" and "juridico-political" that operate, to varying degrees, in these
approaches. Questioning these distinctions, the perspective presented
here studies the neoliberal condition as a strategic situation of power that
articulates elements from the law, the political, and the economy within an
extended assemblage defined here as the "state of structural adjustment":
a general economy that encompasses various fields, constituting a system
of production and exchange regulated by contingent power formations.

Late capitalism is constituted by a politics of expansion of finance capital at the expense of other forms of capital, increasing debt and a number
of legal regulations that transfer controls and resources to private capitalist enterprise. One of the main characteristics of this formation of power
is its promotion of a new configuration and sense of the juridical, defined
as the "rule of law," which transformed previous definitions of the concept.[11] Neoliberal governance redeploys the law as a juridico-economic assemblage consisting of a multiplicity of laws and norms expressed in both
legislation and technical knowledges, with a host of authorities, sites, and
techniques. Through this assemblage, state institutions (executive or legislative powers) in conjunction with extra-state units (donor development
agencies, transnational financial institutions, nongovernmental organizations) regulate strategic situations of power, capital accumulation and
circulation, and processes of subjectification. The following two sections
explore the two central dimensions of this juridico-economic assemblage.

## Down by Law

Neoliberal governmentality subordinates the political to the functioning
of a market economy, according to a doctrine in which markets should
regulate the state. The art of government is presented thus as the creation of managerial frameworks and parameters designed to maximize
private profit and subsume all social activity and imagination, including
the "public sphere" and "civil society." In particular, studies of neoliberal
governance that examine the way in which "markets" constitute a fiction
that the neoliberal state aims at realizing have been helpful for interrogating the legal fiction of the "state" as a unified apparatus or as a single
juridical person.[12]

The figure of the law is central to neoliberal governmentality, yet its meaning is recast in a new, different light.[13] Whereas within the rule-of-law paradigm of an earlier, nineteenth-century liberalism, the juridical functioned both as the foundation of state sovereignty and as a limit to the power of the state apparatus, in neoliberal governmentality the "Law," as a multiple assemblage of juridical and paralegal fields, is deployed rather as a method of "conducting the subjects' conduct"[14] through a juridico-economic regulatory logic of the "framework" and the rules of a market economy understood as a rational game.

A key paradox of the political project of neoliberalism[15] is that its proliferation of state legislation, which reformulates the relation between state and markets, is presented as a decentralization of the state and deregulation of markets. Moreover, this political model propels an increasing securitization of society according to the principles of the preservation of human capital and promotion of individual freedom.

Studies of neoliberalism have emphasized the centrality of the production of legal and paralegal expert knowledges, geared toward the normalization of various social fields. The assemblage pivots on the articulation between rules and norms, giving rise to a normalizing society in which political demands and identities become juridical matter and in which discourses on law, rights, and justice constitute the hegemonic frame for the field of social contestation. This assemblage thus promotes a reconfiguration of the meaning and content of the law, one that equates rule of law with a system of rights deeply dependent on economic freedom and a logic in terms of which distinct fields of social practice come to be seen as managerial problems amenable to regulation by technical apparatuses and disciplines.

Neoliberalism replaces the abstraction of moral universals and equivalences of the law with the immanent technicality of the social norms produced by particular societies. As central theorists have noted, neoliberal governance is thus marked by an economistic prevalence of norms over rules. While the law excludes and penalizes transgressions, normalization avoids the dichotomy between legality and illegality. Normativity is equated with normality, and norms are immanent in the questions of order or morality that they regulate, purportedly emerging out of a community's evaluation of its own ethical standards. Norms are set and evaluated in reference to positive knowledges—hence their enactment appears to be more technical than political. There is not a single point that marks the final achievement of normalization. Rather, regulation oscillates among a range of mediations by expert discourse and practice. In distinction to juridical models of sovereignty, normalization underwrites the neoliberal discourse of transfer of entitlements and responsibility from the state to society.

However, it is important to note that governmentality as a modality of power's exercise does not supersede the juridico-political, but rather, both law and norm coexist in neoliberal juridico-economic formations. Legislation proliferates at the same time as—or, indeed, as a result of—normalization.[16] Different social fields are still policed by the juridical punishment of illegality and transgression, and the law becomes the principal technique for normalization. This insight is not always clear in the broader literature on governmentality, yet it provides a productive site of engagement for the Mozambican evidence.

The ethnographic material collected on the practices of the Mozambican state shows that instead of the alleged overcoming of law by norm, neoliberal governmentality generates a "normalization" of the law, through which expert discourses permeate legal procedures, and juridical technologies become enmeshed with paralegal technical disciplines in the production of normative regulatory mechanisms. In the neoliberal reform of the state and society under the logic of market exchange, the law moves from transcendence to immanence, and its supposed unity disseminates into myriad sites of normalization and evaluation. Formally, the law retains the discourse of equivalence, judgment, and punishment, but in actuality it operates by measuring quantities and deviations according to a calibration of normalcy and pathology. Far from being considered an abstract principle, the law is deployed as a technocratic domain of particularities, immanent in the social; the law does not concern morality and punishment but rather displays an economistic rationality in calibrating the demand and supply of social transgressions.[17]

## The Laws of the Market

Neoliberal governance aims at reifying the fictional nature of the market through legal technologies that calibrate state functions and personal attitudes with regard to parameters of economic enterprise. This section describes the juridical framework of economic policies geared toward freedom of capital accumulation and flow.

One of the central ideological foundations of neoliberalism is the equation of wealth creation with growth that is solely guaranteed by the logic of market rule. Markets are presented as immanently stable, self-regulating mechanisms whose correct functioning, when undistorted by external intervention, ensures the creation of wealth and its distribution throughout all sectors in society.

There are two main approaches to the state within neoliberal doctrine. One assigns the state apparatus merely the role of providing a "framework" for markets, while the other endorses intervention in public policy issues and the promotion of "civil society" under the logic of markets. The latter approach endorses the active prevention of social conflict via economic logics while nevertheless rejecting the redistribution of income, private property, and wealth through taxation or welfare intervention.

The various analyses of neoliberal governmentality see the state as centrally engaged in enforcing private property rights through the juridical enactment of policies such as the deregulation of markets and the dismantling of trade tariffs and barriers for private business. Neoliberal governance implies the increasing financialization of capital, a logic that expands into society at large, with speculation and virtualization influencing the field of the political and social development. Social relations are mediated by a contractual logic, in which the social is instantiated through freely negotiated contracts between individual legal subjects.

Another basic tenet concerns the liberalization of business, insofar as private enterprise is seen as the main creator of wealth and generator of social progress. Thus, all legal barriers to capital flows such as tariffs, taxation, and controls must be removed, and taxes must be substantially reduced, in order to pursue an increase in capitalist economic production that should lead to a general improvement of social variables. Therefore, neoliberal governance legally enforces the privatization of economic assets and social sectors and deregulation of property rights, through which economic areas previously regulated by the state are deregulated and placed under private management. While government is allegedly minimized in order to unleash the efficient productivity of private agents, the figure of the citizen is replaced by that of the consumer. State-granted rights are presented as commodities for consumption, according to a rhetoric of "access" to justice, education, health, or basic infrastructure.

The neoliberal logic couples economic competition with deregulation, which purportedly provides the best means of increasing efficient productivity. Free markets and trade are considered to be the best mechanisms for alleviation of poverty. Hence, some of the poorest nation-states in the world adopt "strategies for poverty alleviation" recommended by international institutions, where different aspects of state reform are aimed at the liberalization of the economy.

The neoliberalization of the state is presented by policy makers as a process of discharge of functions, transfer of resources, and privatization and deregulation of socioeconomic sectors. Similarly, most analyses of neoliberalism describe the changing characteristics of the state in the contemporary moment, yet they do not question the given nature of the state itself, presupposing a juridical core that underlies various subsequent versions of this apparatus (the welfare state, the socialist state, the neoliberal state, and so on). This state could supposedly undergo deep transformations, adding and dismantling functions and services, without having its true nature or juridical sovereignty affected. As shown in the remainder of this chapter, the ethnography of African postcolonial conditions leads the theorization of the state in different directions.

The grounded analysis of neoliberal governmentality and capital in postcolonial Mozambique reveals articulations of fields and flows that belie the normative distinctions between state and market or civil society, public and private spheres, or national and global/transnational. Localized, concrete dynamics of governance belies the picture of a unified apparatus (the state), which under advice and pressure from agents external to the nation-state (donors) adjusts and reshapes a given field located outside itself (the economy, markets).

Rather, what appear are flows of power, capital, and information that reshape political and economic governance. Examples can be found in the broad programs of juridical reform of the state, where social development projects channel transnational funds and expert knowledge, reinventing the scope of the allegedly differentiated field of the economy and placing sectors such as justice, education, or customary authority that were formerly outside its reach within "markets" operating under new logics of consumerism, financial efficiency, and fiscality.

The ethnographic data on these formations of governance reveal fragmentary, interconnected national and transnational agencies, linked by the circulation of capital from investment in enclave economies, funding for reform of state units, aid and development programs, as well as illegal flows. Within this condition, fields of the political (good governance, transition), the juridical (rule of law), and the economic (free market, deregulated business) are interconnected under a single logic of legal reform of a state that is not being reduced, or retreating, as it is claimed. This reform has as its main aim the imposition of an economistic logic of governance and the social that can be defined as a state of structural adjustment.

So-called "structural adjustment" has constituted a key aspect of neo-liberal governance since the 1970s. The Bretton Woods institutions (International Monetary Fund, World Bank) recommend reforms of the state apparatus and the economy that imply cuts in public expenditures and stringent fiscal policies. Structural adjustment programs consist of loans given to nation-states in order to fund state and economic reforms. The credit lines are to be deployed in decentralization, deregulation, privatization of the public sector, and reallocation of public resources and expenditures, as well as the freeing of markets and trade. Usually the process of granting loans includes conditions from the transnational creditor agencies that put pressure on national governments to carry out the recommended reforms.

Neoliberal conditions of governance in the postcolony are thus fundamentally structured by a logic of debt, as nation-state sovereignty is curtailed by increasing national public debt. Meanwhile, transnational institutions and national elites negotiate the conditions attached to the funding of national budgets for administration, development, and security, which leads to policies of decentralization, privatization of the public sector, liberalization of trade and labor markets, and unrestricted influx of foreign capital.

The next sections provide an analysis of the distinctive way in which neoliberal structural adjustment, or juridical reform of the state, markets, and civil societies, unfolds in postcolonial Mozambique. They survey the context in which the reappraisal of locality and indigeneity plays a key role within the decentralization of governance in the continent, showing that an analysis of alleged distinctions between state and customary is crucial for understanding how legal reforms on citizenship transform the socioeconomic management of local populations.

## The State of Structural Adjustment

In postwar Mozambique, the juridico-economic assemblage of neoliberalism can be defined as a state of structural adjustment, which represents the political status of a society at a given moment, as in the original notion of the concept of "state."[18] This moment is composed of various overlapping temporalities that together prolong a politico-economic model based on emergency measures that were initially presented only as temporary. The state of structural adjustment can thus best be conceived as a dynamic field of opposing forces: a strategic condition of power organized around logics of debt, accumulation, privatization, and entangled processes of inclusion and exclusion. This politico-economic machinery of governance fuses national state units and transnational agencies, making public and private interests indistinct. Analysis thus needs to be situated in relation to the crucial role that the law plays, through the juridical reform of the state and the regulation of the social in terms of market logics. In the case of Mozambique, as well as many other African states, the legal recognition of customary law is crucial to the formation of new dynamics of citizenship.

The dynamics of the state of structural adjustment goes beyond the "privatization of the state" in postcolonial Africa.[19] Beyond the strictly economic aspects of neoliberalism, it references a general economy of governance in which markets, flows of finance capital, investment, and enclave extractive economies, as well as aid money, loans, and debt, play a crucial role in state governance. The state of structural adjustment is marked by the denationalization of key public state sectors, such as the crucial process of the privatization of fiscality, whereby tax collection, customs, and even security and surveillance issues related to them are transferred into the hands of foreign corporations. The privatization of areas of a given state apparatus is but one aspect of a larger political condition that involves a continuum of micro- and macroeconomic dynamics. Its political features cannot be reduced to the alterations of the markets, as shown, for instance, by the way the juridical demarcation of the customary is also a technology of rule inserted within a general economy, with deep political effects at both central and local levels.

At the central level, the state of structural adjustment implies an accelerated temporality, enhanced by the speed of flows of financialization and indebtedness. It also means the shortening of the horizons of development, as socioeconomic planning envisions briefer temporal frames. At the level of the local state, locality is saturated by the multiple temporalities of competing authorities and overlapping legal regimes. At the locality, the allegedly past-oriented sanctions of custom encounter and shape the supposedly futuristic orientation of official law that aims at subsuming all local forms.

Within this state, foreign donor agencies fund entire areas and units of state governance. For instance, donors mandate ("recommend") a juridical reform of the state aimed at privatization, decentralization, and deregulation of structures of governance and the public sector of the economy in order to produce both a democratization of governmental structures and a liberalization of the economy. This juridical reform is led by an array of foreign agencies under the logistical, organizational, and ideological aegis of the World Bank. These agencies support the research and drafting of legislation, governmental policy, and official documentation, through funds allocated to ministries and judiciary units and logistical support. They also organize and fund specific projects (e.g., on municipal governance, training of judges and functionaries, "empowerment of civil society").

Let us examine aspects of how the law becomes an object of development programming within this context. The design of new legislation illustrates the confluence of different agents within flows of governance that do not conform to normative categorizations of the state as a unified apparatus. Foreign actors participate in the drafting of new laws that reform the national economy or state governance. This mandate emerges within rounds of negotiation on budgets and loans between officers representing the nation-state and consultants from transnational agencies, generating recommendations and conditions attached to the disbursement of loans or the funding of basic state functions and key development projects. Within a confluence of diverse interests, foreign consultants working together with high-ranking state officers subcontracted by donor agencies draft projects of constitutional reform and national legislation to be passed by the legislative body.

Relations between foreign agencies, consultants, and national actors are highly fluid, demonstrating the difficulty of maintaining clear distinctions between the foreign and the national. In the process of research, discussion, and drafting of law projects and policy programs, national state officers occupying positions in government act as paid consultants to foreign donor agencies, within the framework of specific projects and budgets. National intellectuals and technocrats who consulted for the development of projects (e.g., land legislation, privatizations, or judiciary reform), or advocated in favor of particular policies vis-à-vis government agencies, are later employed in a state unit funded by a foreign agency to implement programs in related areas. Often, national functionaries who participated in consultations go on to work at international finance institutions, monitoring their home country or engaging in negotiations with former colleagues. Formal national governmental units might include a combination of national state employees and national or foreign consultants, who might act independently or be employed by a foreign development agency. Sometimes a national state officer might resign from his or her post at a state unit, only to be hired back later in the same position by a foreign organization, performing similar duties yet now formally a consultant paid a higher salary by the donor agency. The status of intellectual ownership of research funded by donor agencies, conducted by national experts alone or in collaboration with foreign consultants, is ambiguous. The bureaucratic sector of the "state apparatus" encompasses several overlapping layers, where civil servants perform various public and private roles at the same time, profiting from their posts and functions and channeling funds to political bosses who control the flow of personnel and resources from legal and illegal funds, national budgets, and foreign aid.

Within the current joint private-public governance, different regions of the national territory are informally allocated to various foreign governmental agencies. These agencies implicitly divide the performance of different tasks of governance or the funding of local states among themselves. A whole province or sector (education, health, reform of the judiciary) can be informally allocated to a country or development agency. Governmental functions such as primary health care, education, and infrastructural projects are undertaken by units belonging to donor agencies or by foreign or national nongovernmental organizations linked to an international umbrella organization. These NGOs are supported through foreign funding given directly by states or by agencies funded by states.

While foreign development agencies grant soft loans or gifts of aid money to fund the juridical reform of the state or the functioning of certain key governmental areas, sometimes pressure on negotiations is applied so that key, hugely profitable economic sectors are, following a concessionary logic, allocated to public or private corporations from the country of the agency advising and supporting state reforms. Across Africa, the transfer of assets from the public economic sector to private hands has been ongoing since the end of the Cold War and the era of the developmentalist state. Transfer includes the privatization of state companies, communications, security, the concession and alienation of state-owned land, and the exploitation of energy and natural resources. Moreover, in some cases, private companies manage the national treasury and pay the interest on national debt. In others, charitable foundations funded with state money or with foreign aid channeled through state agencies undertake infrastructure or welfare projects. On occasion, grassroots social networks led by religious or traditional leaders channel development funds and implement projects. In some cases, such as Mozambique, constitutionally recognized customary authorities receive loans and technical assistance for projects in collaboration with transnational financial institutions, under the legal and logistical umbrella of the federal state but also bypassing its formal jurisdiction and national sovereignty. Also, a host of private intermediate actors linked both to corporate economic interests in security or natural resources and to high-ranking political officers exert pressure on policy makers or legislators or negotiate on behalf of these closely interconnected sets of interests, very much in the manner of Western "lobbying."

This state of affairs is directly fueled by structural adjustment programs, whether under the rubric of funding from finance institutions, the conditionality attached to loans for the transformation of public bureaucracy, or as a result of new dynamics opened up by the privatization and decentralization processes. Yet the state of structural adjustment is shaped by more complex processes than just the privatization of economic assets. The postcolonial state has been formed by the alternation between private and public sovereignty, between autocracy and democracy—from the precolonial moment, to the early colonial concessionary and mercantilist structures, to the full implementation of a colonial state, then through the uneven trajectory of the postindependence state. This *longue durée* perspective reveals the similarities between current dynamics and those of early, precarious colonial formations and concession companies. The fragmentation of the national territory occurred under logics of temporality, speculation, and indebtedness that are comparable to those of current structural adjustment programs and the "retreat" of state practices articulated with the work of NGOs.

The conjoined private and public nature of early colonial enterprises is not merely replicated at present in a supposedly "neocolonial" era. Emergent processes shaped by neoliberal ideology that locate the rule of law at the center of an economic governmentality mix an alienation of public resources with processes of entitlement devolved to entelechies of individuals and "communities." Let us examine the Mozambican case more closely, especially as it presents particular features vis-à-vis this general model of governance. In this case, the forms of a latter-day protectorate mingle with the recasting of the power of local elites.

The postconflict context constituted the framework for the new liberal democratic regime, where the two main camps in the war became the main protagonists. International actors, such as religious orders and transnational organizations, followed by financial institutions, brokered a peace accord between FRELIMO and RENAMO. At the end of the Cold War, the Socialist bloc, and the apartheid regime, the peace process and democratic transition created a positive politico-economic situation for national political actors and foreign institutions overseeing the process. While the process of peacekeeping and security unfolded, in the beginning enforced on the ground by African, UN, and transnational armed forces, the post-conflict situation facilitated the enforcement of conditionality on behalf of the donors who provided most of the budget and logistics for the country's reconstruction. The serious threat of a return to armed conflict in the first decade of transition functioned as a powerful disciplining force for the engineering of political and economic changes, agreements between enemy camps, and even between factions of the ruling elite, as illustrated in the decentralization of the state, new land legislation, local reforms, and recognition of the customary.

While Weber recognized that the modern state originated in violence, many contemporary studies fail to fully consider the foundational role of colonial and postcolonial violence in the structuring of African states. Yet the violence that both grounds the legal order and enables law to function as a mode of legitimation is a key vector for studying the contours of the state in the African postcolonial context. In the first place, the postcolonial state inherited forms of violence and bylaws that have their origin in the arbitrariness and violence of colonial governance. Second, the framework of the Mozambican democratic regime stems from the effects and consequences of a devastating civil war, and the democratic, liberal order emerged under the looming threat of a return to conflict. The legitimacy of liberal official law has been overdetermined by the massive violence of the past, and today, the violence at the basis of the law appears self-evident and unmediated. Moreover, a political imaginary based on the possible return to a state of civil war reveals the weakness of the state's claim to a monopoly on violence against the territory. While the literature on collapsed and failed states takes into account the place of war and conflict in shaping contemporary African politics, it approaches it within a negative dialectics that opposes violence to social order. A case like Mozambique illustrates the other side of violence, its positivity within the logic of a political system. War, along with dismantling a state, destroying its material infrastructures, and decimating its population, is also the foundation of a democratic politics. The legacies of violence from civil wars and the muddled political logics they generate can be better understood by analyzing the political pragmatics of disorder and the reproduction of crisis as a mode of governance than by interpreting them as the failure and collapse of an allegedly weak state's sovereignty.

Under the tutelage of international financial and security agencies, the juridical reform that propelled Mozambique's transition from Marxism-Leninism and civil war to liberal democracy produced a confluence between post-Socialist dynamics and neoliberal programming, showing the particularity of the Mozambican case within the overall context of structural adjustment states. Even though the consecration of private property rights is a key aspect of transition from Socialist regimes, the confluence of national elites and transnational actors produces transformations in political structures and channeling of resources that go beyond the "privatization" of the state apparatus.

In 2004–5, 60 percent of the Mozambican national budget was based on foreign aid money, in the form of loans or gifts. Hence, governance was deeply embedded within practices of conditionality, and yet this did not imply an absolute weakening of the power of the post-Socialist elites, who found new ways of thriving politically and economically in the new adjusted economy. Post-Socialist dynamics blended with neoliberal policy. Consider the case of the foreign donors' promotion and funding of "civil society" as a fundamental aspect of transition to liberal rule of law, when in practice many of the nascent institutions that fell under this rubric in the mid-2000s had their origin in the structures of the party-state system. Donors' programming and funding, social forums, legal-academic debates, and media coverage considered the FRELIMO youth and women's branches, the national peasant organization (a major source of political support under the previous Socialist regime), and even the FRELIMO-led Association of Traditional Healers of Mozambique all as part of civil society. Other public debates pondered the inclusion of newly recognized urban customary authority as civil society entities. Other civil society organizations, including those that led important campaigns on reform of the land law or legislation on women, family, and gender issues, were formed by state officers or by their relatives and close affiliates.

Mozambique privatized a majority of its economic public sector and many former state agencies and functions, yet of crucial political significance is the fact that national elites still control privatized areas and functions in agreement and collaboration with transnational political and economic elites. High-ranking state officers or individuals connected to elites are in positions enabling them to grant and renew contracts, oversee their enactment, or cancel them. Parallel markets that blend legal and illegal activities and capital flows proliferate, mixed with governmental structures and open business markets. Urban security is privatized, managed by companies owned by high-ranking military officers or ministers or by foreign companies with ties to elites. Initially, the demobilization of the FRELIMO and RENAMO armies provided personnel to private armies and police platoons.

Land around Maputo and other main urban centers, as well as in coastal areas, was privatized and transferred to governmental elites or was organized under joint ventures with foreign investors for economic exploitation or tourism. The process of transfer of urban land in the mid-2000s was private and opaque, given that there was a juridical void in terms of new land legislation promoting privatization, still in the process of being discussed and designed. Legally, all land continued to belong to the state; hence, only "rights of use" could be granted, although for terms up to many decades.

Within a general privatization of key state functions since the late 1990s, custom services and tax estimation and collection were transferred to foreign security agencies, and private companies patrol maritime borders. Private corporations enforced security and regulations through private armies hired from security companies, while Asian and South African companies exploited maritime resources. Foreign affairs agencies and diplomatic representation underwent a process of privatizations and outsourcing as well, with businessmen in other countries acting as honorary consuls, charging fees and conducting business on behalf of the Mozambican state.

Private companies from the United Kingdom and South Africa took over telecommunications and also provided computing systems and communication infrastructure for government and development programs. European state companies obtained the concession on water circulation in main urban centers. Timber and cotton concessions have been given to private investors, some of them close to the ruling elites. The dynamics of labor and production in some of these concessions in the north is strongly reminiscent of older colonial modalities of enclave extraction and population control.

The precariousness of state agencies led to the privatization of development and infrastructure projects, which were handled by national and foreign NGOs. Donor aid and development projects were often channeled through organizations led by government officers or through people closely related to them. National private companies with ties to government elites obtained funds from donor agencies to conduct development and infrastructure projects.

Thus, since the late 1990s, the transition to a market economy in Mozambique was more complex than the mere retreat of the state, apparently materialized in the end of state subsidies, the sale of public assets, and structural adjustment policies of decentralization and deregulation. New forms of legislation were not aimed at merely reinforcing and freeing markets or engineering the state's relinquishing of all control or articulation between state and markets. National and foreign capital entered a political process of articulation and cooperation in joint investments. Thus, with respect to the state's role in the national economy, the general socioeconomic context revealed continuities between the Socialist system and the new logics of market rule. For instance, in Nampula Province the 1990s witnessed a resurgence of a colonial-style concessionary cotton industry. Indeed, since the late 1990s, Mozambican state officers have emphasized the benefits of articulating the private sector with public state enterprise. At the same time, there is a strong impetus for state-private partnership in donors' policies for "good governance."

Certain analysts argue that neoliberal political and economic reforms in Mozambique have reshaped the state's influence on the economy without entailing a withdrawal of the state. As evidence of this, they cite the sale of state assets involving official institutions, the fact that state officers regulate the activity of the private sector, facilitating the work of corporations and joint ventures, and cases where government officers and party members became owners or managers of privatized companies. Yet these examples don't necessarily provide clear evidence for the continuity of the state's influence, even under modified circumstances.

Rather, the Mozambican case, with its interrelation of public and private actors, suggests that the crucial point for analyzing the role of the "state" in the neoliberal moment is the ideological orientation of the public sector materialized in concrete economic policy. The most relevant question is not whether the state participates as a partner in economic ventures but rather the key fact that within neoliberal logics it is not an ideology of general interest that orients the public sector. In this new environment, the logic of the market has colonized state practice, presenting the fiction of the unified single state apparatus acting as an individual subject of rights among others.

Within its broad program of privatizations, praised by the World Bank and other multilateral organizations as one of the most successful in Africa, the state still maintains control, or a majoritarian percentage, in many enterprises. But the orientation of the public sector in a regulated economy is very different from its orientation in a neoliberal economy. In the former, economic assets are owned and managed by the state, their activity geared toward a general public interest, not profit and capitalist accumulation. In this economy, the surplus can be allocated by the state to nonprofitable sectors and welfare. Under neoliberal state logics, public investment is determined according to the rules of market investment and profit. These economic dynamics also show that the state of structural adjustment represents an amalgam of previous Socialist structures and policies with a new neoliberal politico-economic logic.

As a legal-economic assemblage, the state of structural adjustment also entails an attempt to reconstitute state sovereignty and its juridical foundations through the juridical framework of articulation with private capital. Here the spirit of the laws makes an economic appearance under the fiction of the distribution of assets and goods. The fact that the state participates in the economy does not imply the reproduction of a state apparatus or the continuity of the state. Rather, the ideological ruse of the state as yet one more individual subject of interest conceals a fundamental conversion of the nature of the state itself. Let us examine the social effect of these juridical and economic transformations.

In a context of weak governance structures, where peace and security were unstable and economic extraction was located in a few profitable enclave areas, donors enforced conditionality only insofar as it related to the granting of contracts for privatization of certain assets and an overall reform of salient aspects of law and governmentality. Otherwise, control over funds and projects was loose, and bureaucratic delays and detours were long and common. Hence, a new version of the postcolonial gatekeeping state took shape as the former Socialist economic sector was privatized and new political economic formations channeled transnational capital through a continuum of national and foreign elites. The difference with previous gatekeeping formations consists in the structural continuity between agents and sites of political and economic power, which break down the normative distinction between national and foreign, within a public/private state of structural adjustment.

Superficially, aspects of Mozambican post-Socialist dynamics might appear to be a manifestation of what has been called an African "shadow" state.[20] Relying on international recognition of political sovereignty, this state, based on autocratic patrimonial relations, is able to weaken official state agencies and manipulate access to formal and informal markets. The shadow state (informal, commercially oriented networks) functions beside, yet intersects with, official bureaucratic agencies. This analytic approach may help dismantle liberal juridical assumptions by showing the interplay of legality and illegality at the core of state agencies, yet it still assumes the existence of a bounded, unified state apparatus based on jurisdiction, with which "shadow" networks interact.

More importantly, by focusing on the actions of political actors within the nation-state boundaries, it fails to examine how these structures of governance are based on global flows of capital and information that present the image of a fluid transnational structure of governance not limited by national boundaries. Attention to the actual nature of capital flows, illegal activities, or prebendalism shows the continuity between public and private, as well as foreign and national, actors. It also highlights the fragmentation within governmental sectors and agencies, as well as a deterritorialization of economic enclaves and extraction and export that reinforces the image of a continuum of political networks, which exceed the unity of a state apparatus.

This political condition of a continuum of sovereignties generates the figure of a state that is not an apparatus but rather a relation. It evokes the original meaning of the state as a condition, a strategic situation of power.[21] Within this form of governmentality, dichotomies between state and customary, private and public, and formal and informal are unsettled. As the second part of this book illustrates, in vast rural and periurban territories the alleged categorical distinction between state and society is disrupted by connections between official formations of power and local chieftaincies, religious institutions, vernacular ritual forms and memories. This fluid state of things or political condition produces a variegated field of citizenships, a realm where political technologies of governance encounter different claims of entitlement and belonging.

While most of the above-mentioned processes took place in urban milieus, the state of structural adjustment also fundamentally affected rural areas, ranging from privatization of state-owned land and concessions of large portions of rural territory to the recognition of customary authority and traditional justices, as well as the re-creation of local community. These various processes were interconnected and represented another aspect of the continuum of forces that is the state of structural adjustment, where neoliberal planning and donor support for decentralization blur the scope and boundaries of the state apparatus at the local level. In Mozambique, locality is saturated with para-state sovereignties such as former Socialist party units, NGOs, and religious authorities, all of which perform local state functions, and "community authority" is recognized by the state as legitimate local government.

At the level of the locality, the confluence of rule by traditional chieftains, the preponderance of kinship norms and ritual, a plurality of mechanisms of justice embedded within older political and religious institutions, and the unfolding of autochthonous imaginations of land, territory, and power consolidates the juridico-economic category of "customary citizenship" as a central process within the overall neoliberal reform of the nation-state.

## The Dilemma of African Citizenship

The dilemma of citizenship in Africa centers on the question of how to produce juridical reforms of the state that might grant universal democratic citizenship in the context of the historical resilience and political relevance of the customary. The fate of the nation-state in a globalized age is still determined at the level of locality.

The democratic transitions and structural adjustment programs of the 1990s and early 2000s transformed the nature of the state and politics in Africa. In the wake of these processes, the dilemma of citizenship unfolded around the opposition between dynamics of political rights and customary politics, rules and entitlements. Schematically, this opposition can also be mapped onto the dichotomies of urban/rural and individual/communal Both ruling elites and the governed populace appeal to both democratic inclusion and neonativist claims based on soil and tradition. Questions of rights and custom mingle in a delicate political choreography, and past dynamics of state politics and clientelistic networks persist in new forms as elites and masses strategically adapt to new global dynamics of power accumulation expressed in international law and transnational capital, as well as to the openings produced by the retreat or restructuration of state sovereignty.

In the last couple of decades, debates in academic and policy milieus have centered on institutional approaches to strengthening "civil society," largely envisioned according to Western conceptions of law, rights, and institutions. Often, these debates touch upon the undesirability or strict impossibility of translating normative Western liberal conceptions of democratic citizenship into African postcolonial contexts. For one thing, in their modes of constitution and forms, public spheres and processes of inclusion are radically different in Africa and Euro-America. Certain African sociopolitical movements acting on the ground espouse a conception of citizenship that can be considered broader than that based on the hegemonic liberal conception of the rights of the individual, which sometimes masks inequality under the guise of special rights and a politics of recognition.

In much of Africa today, whether through governmental ruse or population's demand, the issue of democratic rights is entangled with questions of indigeneity, ethnicity, and various "traditions" that aim at enforcing differentiated types and levels of citizenship. Legacies of colonial rule complicate these matters on two counts: through the colonial construction and reshaping of the customary and through the program of duplicitous governance that assigned the majority of the population to the status of subjects without access to civil society and civic rights. This double bind is one of the basic structuring principles of governance that the postindependence regimes had to reform. Processes of resistance to colonialism, which gave way to postcolonial politics and state formation, were largely shaped in response to the structure of colonial power itself.

The articulated histories of state and customary presented in the previous chapter illustrate how, since the Indigenato regime, Portuguese colonial governmentality enacted a version of indirect rule that defined citizenship in restricted terms. Civil society formations and the realm of civility and rights were shaped by the feeble colonial state. Rights of association and the public use of reason were granted only to white colonists and a small minority of "assimilated" natives. The vast majority of the autochthonous population was confined to ethnic enclaves and was ruled by "customary tribal authorities" that fused various forms of power. These distinctions largely took place within an enforced administrative division between the urban and the rural realms. Yet, the elite group of *assimilados* constituted a key element; as a liminal category between foreign citizens and native subjects, they formed the ruling postcolonial multiethnic elites who still hold political and economic power at present.

The FRELIMO regime made this colonial legacy the target of its radical Socialist reform. As in most newly independent African states, the regime faced the political tasks of having to reform national citizenship through three interconnected axes: reshaping the differentiated structure of state sovereignty, transforming the nature and strength of customary power, and bridging the urban-rural political and administrative divide. This political task is still being taken on by the post-Socialist version of the FRELIMO regime at present, yet within a very different transnational context, one that has produced the reappraisal of custom, the return of chieftaincy, and the recalibration of previous Socialist institutions of local governance. As in much of the continent, the last few decades of democratization and the expansion of citizenship in Mozambique have been centered on reform at the local level.

The policy of granting democratic entitlements is still played out in terms of the differential access of populations to civic inclusion, justice, and freedom along an urban-rural divide and inclusion of rural communities in the national polity through submission to tradition and customary authority. In economic terms, the citizenship divide also persists today as legacies from colonial and early postcolonial times in terms of access to socioeconomic resources and labor, as well as state restrictions on indigenous movements, which today concern internal migrants seeking work. In this regard, the key question of access to land also defines a broad conception of postcolonial citizenship, manifested throughout the continent as claims of autochthony and indigenous rights to land and expulsion of "foreigners" by self-proclaimed "sons of the soil."

The debate on citizenship in Africa centers on the question of whether democratic rights alone should define citizenship or whether allegiance and subjection to custom should supplement belonging in a national polity, therefore expanding the scope of a liberal conception of the citizen. This situation also represents a key predicament for a continent where the opposition between national citizenship and local ethnic "identity" has been played out in highly violent terms.

The dialectic between rights and custom is also reflected in the division between individual rights of liberal citizenship and communal rights of tradition-based claims based on autochthony, indigenous identity, ethnic affiliation, and regionalism. These demands for communal or collective rights found in different regions of Africa are complicated at present by the ubiquity of the question of "community" as a key tool of neoliberal legislation and socioeconomic programming.

This general context has particular variations. As shown by the legal reform of custom, land, and chieftaincy developed in Mozambique in the 2000s, the post-Socialist condition, retaining aspects of the communal ethos and aspiration of the Socialist program, overlaps and articulates in complex ways with the neoliberal categorization of "community." The entangled state of structural adjustment materializes on the ground among the blending of remainders of Socialist communalism and the emergence of neoliberal communitarianism through chieftaincy's sovereignty, local institutions of justice, or ritualized politico-religious performances.

Postcolonial regimes charged with the task of reforming the framework of citizenship nevertheless maintained, in various ways, the structural double bind of citizenship and subjection/subjectification. At present, the discussion about citizenship in Africa can thus be framed by the opposition of the figure of the individual rights-bearing citizen and a broader set of political entitlements, horizons of social justice, claims to ethnic identity, and customary belonging. The latter include ways in which citizenship, beyond the juridical, is enacted in quotidian issues of relatedness and ritual, corporeality and subjectivity.

In the light of the main legacies of colonial and early postcolonial regimes, still impinging on African politics in the current global neoliberal moment, new forms of national inclusion and localized belonging are emerging, which eschew the dichotomous divides between central and local state, citizenship and subjection, civic rights and custom, civility and tradition. In the last few decades the joint dynamics of democratic transition, juridical reform, neoliberal economic opening, and structural adjustment produce a novel form of inclusive exclusion that is also an arena for political action and demand: a blend of citizenship rights and customary entitlements.

## Maputo II: Law and Custom

In Mozambique around 2000–2004, the issue of "legal pluralism," or the coexistence of multiple juridical regimes within a nation-state, was ever present in general discussions about the reform of the state and the economy. The debate on a plurality of justices was related to the exit from the party-state system and what was perceived by some factions within the government as its rigid legal and political structures. Debates and planning meetings on local government, the judiciary, and land reform or development were all permeated by themes related to various perspectives on the status of the "customary" vis-à-vis a national, unified system of justice. From World Bank documents, to consultants' reports, to "ethnographic" campaigns conducted by state judiciary or legislative units, the key issue of the customary was central to broad juridical aspects of the overall reform of governance and the economy. Even factional politics within the ruling party and the jockeying for positions of influence within the new process of juridical reform of the state also dovetailed with the debates on legal pluralism and its place within community courts.

During those years, most debates on the transformation of the nation's juridical regimes involved references to the realm of the customary. Through discussions on land tenure, recognition of local rights, the new role of chiefs within local government, and the fate of the former Socialist juridical institutions, the space of "traditional" practice that had been banned since independence acquired a renewed force and became a crucial element in planning the legal reform of the state. This debate was as much a sign of ongoing political changes influenced by negotiations with foreign agencies as it was a sign of a slow but steady change of guard, as a new generation of politicians oriented toward governance management increasingly occupied higher positions within the state apparatus.

During the first half of the 2000s the discussions held by politicians and expert consultants placed the realm of the customary at the intersection of private and public spheres, between the rationale of state governance and the logic of private markets. The customary was thus once again, as during late colonial times, at the center of a legal and economic governmental program of resource extraction and management of populations through their placement in spaces of differential inclusion.

Land was the main economic resource available, and as such it was the centerpiece of the program of deregulation and opening of the economy, which was aimed at removing it from state property and control and opening a market for titles of use, as mandated in the recently passed Land Law. The growing debates on land reform held by politicians, investors, lawyers, and consultants took into account different aspects of customary tenure, titling, and the key role of chiefs as custodians of land property.

These debates took place in a paradoxical, somewhat anachronistic milieu. Young Mozambican lawyers who were central actors in the reform of the justice sector and were advocates of legal pluralism" told me in interviews and private conversations that they had grown up at the height of the Socialist regime in a context where, throughout their training in high school and college, they had been taught that the customary had been effaced from the nation-state. When some of them returned from graduate work in law in Portugal at the beginning of the democratic transition and joined teams of jurists in conducting field research on local forms of conflict resolution around the country, they were astounded. They told me that the idea that in the early 1990s they could interview "chiefs" sounded to them almost like science fiction, having grown up under the certainty that those "puppets of colonialism" were but vanished relics of a long-gone past.

In Maputo in September 2003, I interviewed a high-ranking FRELIMO officer, a representative and director of two commissions, one on state reform and the other on traditional authority, at the National Assembly. He had been governor of Nampula Province in the 1980s during the civil war and later had been appointed minister of state administration (1995–2000). An example of the second-generation of FRELIMO leadership, he was a leading voice in the process of decentralization of the state and enhancement of local municipalities. Referring to the current democratic transition, he spoke about the past two years of "electoral war" in the country. He had managed a northern province at the heart of the civil war and, people covertly whispered, had allegedly supported the magico-military pro-FRELIMO guerrilla groups of the Naparama.[22] His current discourse on the customary was based on personal experience. Not only had he begun collaboration with local chiefs on issues of development and governance at the height of the civil war, but he also told me that he had conducted historico-ethnographic research on chiefs in the area.

He offered a type of modernist, juridical myth on the actual meaning of postindependence state policy on the matter. He explained how during colonial times there were de jure chiefs (legitimate rulers) and de facto chiefs (appointed by the colonial regime), two echelons of power between which there were constant secret consultations. The "legitimate" *regulos* mostly supported FRELIMO during the anticolonial guerrilla war, for which they were persecuted and killed. Understandably, FRELIMO saw chiefs only as de facto authorities, imposed by colonialism, and repressed them en masse. By the mid-1980s, a group of second-tier state officers expressed the need for an articulation between the local state and former chiefs, something he started implementing in Nampula, in relation to development and infrastructure. "The less 'developed' an area is, the more the legitimacy of a chief's authority is diminished," he affirmed. In his view, history had brought about social transformation, and the time was ripe for policy changes. He affirmed that progress was sweeping the nation, from roads to industry to a new role for customary chiefs.

The officer used the term "community leaders," rejecting the term "authority" because, he said, no other authority could be allowed to overlap or compete with that of the state without creating the risk of conflict. As the head of the ministry, he accomplished a deep reform that dismantled important aspects of the centralized state administration. "Decentralization was the vogue; it was being carried out all over the world by then." In his view, the policy reform concerning local chiefs implemented through the legal reform of the early 2000s had been successful. The chiefs were well suited to collaborate with local development. He made no mention of the nuances of the partisan clientelism involved in the current "recognition" of chiefs, the local struggles over chieftaincy offices, the ambiguous status of contenders from different lineages, or the disputes and competition between returned chiefs and still-existing Socialist authorities (village secretaries and community judges).

In Maputo in 2003, information about chiefs was being constantly collected and analyzed in a tiny office replete with computers and filing cabinets in the Secretariat of Local Government, an agency within the Ministry of State Administration. This unit illustrates very meaningful trajectories within the state of structural adjustment: it had emerged out of an ethnographic project on legal research and local consultations funded and organized by USAID shortly after the end of the war. The program, which aimed at stirring a public debate on the issue of the customary and the potential future recognition of traditional authorities, was initially housed at that ministry as a nongovernmental project, evolving later into an official state unit, with funding from different donors.

At the office, at any given time, six to eight employees could be seen working busily, classifying data. In the run-up to elections, the pace at the small unit was hectic. Via telephone, email, and fax, information on the behavior and practices of "traditional authorities" was constantly collected from different regions in the national territory: a chief's political allegiance, collaboration with local government, the electoral tendencies in his district, and so on. The unit's computers were constantly fed with this information, submitted by nodes of local administration scattered across the national territory. The administrative and quasi-ethnographic endeavor of the local state aimed at making visible the often obscure dynamics of the newly recognized traditional powers. The state apparatus's local ramifications and the condensed authority of its centralized units exercised constant surveillance vis-à-vis this newly uncovered political actor. These practices of control were flawed by a trajectory of suspicion and repression, a history of a continuation of war through political means. In this process, a juridical textual medley emerges, constituted by the innumerable pieces of information on traditional authority—names, numbers, movements, tendencies—mixing fragments on law and custom, collected by administrators in rural districts, by secretaries of dynamizing groups in

villages and neighborhoods, by community judges, or by various other local party cadres. This juridical amalgam of texts was aimed at making de-
cipherable the blurred contours of local power, there at the nodes where
state and customary encountered each other on a daily basis, in a dialectical movement of suspicion and seduction, of co-optation and deception.

In the mid-2000s, while chiefs were making a comeback under the new
policies of development and juridical reform involving recognition and
reconciliation, former Socialist institutions of popular justice at the local
level were being dismantled. I participated at several meetings at various state units where aspects of the reform of justice were discussed and
in which various lawyers and consultants raised their voices asking about
the true current status of the ex–People's Tribunals: "Are there still any
courts left?" one of the Mozambican lawyers would ask, in disbelief. "Yes,
a few are still active in XXX [a small district in a northern province]" was
the confident response, which ignored the reality of the hundreds of such
courts still active in rural and periurban areas, far from the capital and the
industry of law as object of development and accessible only to those interested, avant-gardist lawyers or state officers willing to undertake week-
long visits to the provinces, investigating as consultants for donor agencies
or for the purpose of drafting new legislation. For instance, in mid-July
2003, I was present at meetings held at Ministry of Justice units, where discussions regarding the status of the former People's Tribunals were held.
The sessions were attended by a FRELIMO MP (who was at the time
one of the top representatives leading the National Assembly's Commission on Legal Reform of the State), a team of high-ranking officers from
the Supreme Court, a small group of Mozambican lawyers from various
branches in the Ministry of Justice, a senior consultant, a high-profile expert from a multilateral organization based in Europe, and two European
consultants (a sociologist and a lawyer) working for the agency and based
in Maputo.

Within the general reform of the judiciary, the current and future status
of community courts was uncertain. In a move that diverged from decades
of Socialist ban on custom, these local courts were positioned by the recent
democratic turn of events within the realm of "community justice" and
hence of "customary law." Their exact future meaning and scope would
depend on an ongoing and heated debate taking place within government
units and foreign agencies on whether the country should have a dual system of justice, with customary/community courts, or whether these should
be included in a unified system, under new regulations.

The donors had established a precise schedule for the research and drafting of the laws, which had to be ready a year later, to be discussed and approved by the Assembly before the uncertain outcome of the general elections of October 2004. In terms of the dynamics of funding and advising the juridical reform of the Socialist system of justice, the multilateral agency was not offering financial support but rather expert advice, as well as brokering an agreement between different units of the Mozambican state—executive, judiciary, legislative—and the Scandinavian agency providing funds for this aspect of state reform. A singular characteristic of the process was that the representatives of the legislative branch were proposing to hire senior members of the judiciary as consultants to draft the legislation on community courts, subcontracted by the Scandinavian agency providing the funds. The Commission on Legal Reform of the State at the National Assembly would make US$100,000 available two months after the meetings, to be allocated toward the drafting of new legislation on community courts. The same agency was supporting the organization of seminars and workshops to discuss the future direction of juridical reform and the role of customary law within it.

The first day of the Seminar on the Vision for the Judiciary mentioned earlier in this chapter involved meetings of thematic working groups that would present their conclusions and proposals during the second day. The participants met at the premises of a state unit located outside Maputo, a legal research center, where tidy offices and meeting rooms proliferated, surrounded by a park of manicured lawns, patches of wild grass, and colorful flowers. In the distance, clouds were getting darker, bearing down on the treetops and the electrical towers. Within the premises, near the main offices, a plaque marked the cornerstone of the future "Museum of Popular Justice" announced at the opening session of the workshop, along with the launch of a CD collecting scanned magazines, newspapers, and other documents related to law and justice from the immediate postindependence period.

At the workshop sessions, the working group on community courts was composed of three experts from a new center for legal research and training of judges, one officer from the Ministry of Justice, and one other lawyer. The representative from the Ministry of Justice asked about the status of the community courts, given that they were not included in the Constitution. He asked rhetorically whether they were actual courts, and of what kind, given the fact that at the moment they were placed under the jurisdiction and control of the Ministry of Justice. Then, this expert made reference to the cultural heterogeneity existing between northern and southern regions, emphasizing the need for the central state to strongly regulate "legal pluralism," giving the example of the potential for shariʿah law in the Islamicized north of the country. He elaborated further on which state organs should oversee the proliferation of informal justices, stating that at the local level in the provinces, the managers of the Notary Register supervise the work of community courts, as representatives of the Ministry of Justice. Local mayors supervise the demarcation of jurisdiction between community courts and chiefs. The key issue, he finally said, was the training of new community judges on questions related to the rule of law and new official norms, as well as transparency, because of alleged rampant corruption prevalent in these courts.

One representative from the legal center housed at the Supreme Court also focused on the question of judges: the last popular assemblies that elected judges having taken place in the mid-1980s, it had to be determined who would be elected as new judges, and through which, new, democratic mechanisms.

During the second day of discussion, the main Scandinavian consultant leading the workshop introduced the two main axes ordering the discussion, which brought echoes of past colonial social ordering: the "presence" of justice and its distribution throughout the country and the status of customary law, either as part of the formal system of justice or as liminal space within a dual system. At the workshop, the president of the Supreme Court stated that pluralism is embedded in the bedrock of African history and has produced multiethnic nations, something that cannot be transformed through mere administrative measures. Legal pluralism cannot even be discussed. Existing institutions of justice need to be adapted to this reality.

This perspective opened a debate on the future of the former People's Tribunals. Various speakers from the Scandinavian research center and different state units launched into a discussion on what kind of law would be implemented at these courts. This was a conversation about how different forms of customary law would be articulated with the newly reformed official state law being implemented in the country. It was also a conversation marked by a liberal sense of law, that is, an understanding of all social entities—persons, communities, corporations, the state itself— as individual legal subjects.

Even though the debate on these courts was centered on community justices and collective "new citizenships," the conclusions, steered by the

Scandinavian consultant ("The manager in me comes out," he said at one point toward the end), ignored any discussion of community or collective rights and referred back, time and again, to personal, singular rights: "how to bring justice to the individual person," the "man on the street," consumer of justice-as-service, represented by a small silhouette of a person in the slide show presented by the foreign managers of the process.

Interestingly, the discussion, which echoed other important conversations being held at high levels of the reform process, expanded on the potential of a unified versus a dual judiciary system in which the question of customary law played a central role. After several experts from ministries presented views on articulation of official law and custom, the president of the Supreme Court supported the articulation of the official system and other normativities, with the formal tribunals as instances of appeal vis-à-vis customary or former People's Tribunals. The main foreign consultant affirmed: "You come from a legal culture in which the People's Courts were located within the juridical system, and perhaps that was not such a good idea. But at present these courts can function as an interface between formal and informal systems of justice. You are placed in a unique position to accomplish this." The debate opened onto new, complex terrains when one of the main MPs working at the National Assembly Commission on Legal Reform proposed to debate the future (recovered) role of chiefs as local juridical authorities.

The Scandinavian agency that organized the seminar was one of the main donor units funding and advising the reform of the judiciary system. In their Project Document for 2002–5 for the Program of Support to the Justice Sector in Mozambique ("Pro-Justice"), the main emphasis is placed on the centrality of access to justice for the donor's and state's overall project of "poverty alleviation" in the country. The report is relevant for its depiction of the judiciary and the compromised role of custom ("community" or "informal" justice) within it, as well as for the presentation of mechanisms to organize the work of donors.

The report describes the dire context of justice in the country, stating that the agency supports and funds the system of official courts, the training of new judges, and the prison system, as well the work of NGOs that perform paralegal services and advisory work. The report describes the judiciary, and all its different levels of tribunals, specifically mentioning that the community courts used to be part of the official judiciary system but have been excluded since the constitutional reform of 1990, at the start of the democratic transition.

A section entitled "Conflict Resolution at the Community" quotes an analytic paper based on ethnographic research jointly conducted by a Portuguese university and a university based in Maputo.[23] It states that "85% of conflicts in Mozambique are solved outside of formal courts." The report repeats the *doxa* prevalent in developmentalist circles in Maputo, wrongly establishing that "the community courts have lost influence during the last decade due to their inherent political allegiance toward FRELIMO and not having adapted to the current political and constitutional context."

The report describes the Scandinavian agency as the main actor in the field of support to the judiciary and justice reform. The agency states that in the coming years it aims to coordinate the work on the justice sector given the fragility of the judiciary and the Ministry of Justice and the disconnection between them. The agency also serves as technical coordinator of the actions of all the donor agencies working on the justice sector, including agencies from European countries, USAID, and the UNDP. In a similar way to what happens in other fields, the World Bank was overseeing and articulating the work of different agencies in the field of justice and legal reform in 2002–5.

A report produced in 2003 by the Legal Vice Presidency of the World Bank, ("Mozambique: Legal and Judicial Sector Assessment") establishes some of the main parameters that have guided the overseeing and steering of reform projects in the field of justice. At the beginning the document offers the main thrust of these projects, stating that the "Government of Mozambique has highlighted the rule of law as a key factor in its development agenda with the World Bank." This particular orientation (and the way "rule of law" has been conceptualized within the discourse of the development industry in the last few decades) paves the way to a diagnostic on how "Mozambique's legal and judicial institutions have not kept pace with the accelerated economic growth of the country in the 1990's. The state of the sector is perceived by many to be a deterrent to investment and a hindrance to growth."

The World Bank's discourse and recommendations in this report articulate most clearly the idea of transforming the way of functioning and orientation of the judiciary and of key legislation, in order to foster economic development understood as bolstering private investment and recreating free markets. In this regard, "corruption" in the justice sector and the orientation of certain legislation—on labor or land—are perceived by the bank's leadership as obstacles to socioeconomic development. The bank's main task is "not legislative reform but rather reform improving access to justice." This discourse related to citizenship and people's access to entitlements permeates the report on justice, understood as a service and as a parameter within a certain orientation of the economy.

As in every recent document providing diagnostics or advice on the juridical reform of the state, this World Bank report also acknowledges the centrality of a newfound recognition of locality, tradition, ritual, and belief (also in relation to respect in terms of gender and kinship). The report elliptically recognizes the crucial role to be played by customary law, referenced here as a "disposition to alternative modes of dispute resolution" and the "participation of nonstate actors in the administration of justice." The consequences of this context for questions of rights and access to services are not fully explored. Its analysis would mean the acknowledgment of the existence of differential degrees of national belonging and entitlements, or the complex reality of something akin to "customary citizenship."

## Customary Citizenship

"Customary citizenship,"[24] as a localized form of national belonging, is a historical product of juridical technologies of governance. The process exceeds the mere return of sharp colonial distinctions between citizenship and subjecthood, blending in new ways traces from different political regimes, articulating elements of official law, custom, and kinship. From the viewpoint of the locality, membership in a national polity is imagined and enacted through participation in structures of kinship and local relatedness, and acquiescence to official law is filtered through "traditional" norms and the subjection to the authority of customary chieftaincy. The state is viewed as legitimate only insofar as it articulates properly with local forms of ritualized power, amplifying their claims and demands.

Two opposite vectors get entangled around the question of customary citizenship. On the one hand, it is a local perspective on national belonging from the point of view of variegated "communities" and their modes of imagining the scope of the state. It is a localized claim on a more encompassing sense of state citizenship, beyond mere "identity formation." On the other hand, it is a centralized governmental policy of simultaneous inclusion and exclusion, a program of both recognition and denial.

Customary citizenship is thus a contested field, a place of state control and identification as much as a space of local demands for inclusion and an expanded sense of belonging in a national democratic polity. State, locality, and community are not homogeneous blocs. Processes of customary citizenship are fields of forces where many different actors, national and foreign, as well as local state officers, chiefs, religious authorities, and rural and periurban citizens, struggle to impose different senses on local and national rights, hence attempting to reshape the scope of the nation-state.

The condition of customary citizenship can be observed in many African countries under the various guises of autochthony, conflict over claims on land and resources, and various forms of "return" and reinforcement of customary law and traditional chieftaincy. The Mozambican post-Socialist and postconflict context adds specific aspects and amplifies certain features of this condition, specifically around the reversal of Marxist policy prohibiting chiefly authority, customary beliefs, and land rights, while maintaining institutional elements from the Socialist period. In the contemporary Mozambican context of neoliberal state reform and "transition," the vast majority of the population do not enjoy the full rights of modern citizenship but are, rather, subjects under the jurisdictions of multiple sovereignties, all deeply entangled with the legacies of the colonial and Socialist regimes, as well as the civil war.

Both connections and discontinuities exist between the central and the local level of the state, observable through the axis of legal reform. The modernist state apparatus reproduces customary citizenship through vast rural and periurban areas. At the level of the local, the renaming of the "customary" by the category of "community" constitutes a link between the planes of the state and citizenship, as well as a key tool of neoliberal governmentality, with broad politico-economic effects.

Customary citizenship is not merely a derivative aspect of the democratic transition. Rather, it is one of the main defining features of the political in contemporary Mozambique. Through the reproduction and recognition of the customary, the state projects to the international community of donors the image of a "true" African democratic transitional reform. This legislation includes a large majority of the population into the nation-state by excluding them from full rights to local governance, access to labor markets, justice, education, or infrastructure. At the same time, the granting, by design or by default, of restricted citizenship generates crucial effects for the economy of an impoverished nation-state.

In order to study articulations of state formation and dynamics of citizenship in the neoliberal moment, it is important to examine key concrete instances of customary citizenship as a process of inclusive exclusion, such as in the reform of recognition of traditional authority. This example will illustrate the complex nuances and ambiguities in the blending of custom and rights, which seem to present democratic features, yet maintain authoritarian legacies of precolonial and colonial customary laws and rule and their ambivalent trajectory in postcolonial times.

Decree 15/2000 on traditional authority is a patent example of the state of structural adjustment as a temporal condition of power. The decree aims at creating a genuine "democratic tradition" at the local level, retrieving the customary from its internal exile, placing traditional authority in a space still redolent with other local figures of the former party-state. In this instance of the current juridical discourse of development, the customary is depicted as possessing a prehistorical, yet "democratic," nature.

The donor-sponsored ethnographic project's final report that informed the decree discusses the intrinsic "democratic" content of "customary" authority, claiming that traditionally the election of chiefs was "perceived by the community as being democratic."[25] The councils of elders were portrayed as analogous to "electoral colleges" that chose chiefs from a pool of related "cousins," appointing them on the basis of their "belonging to certain royal lineages, their good sense, and good heart." With apparent disregard for the glaring contradiction, the report defined the perennial nature of this office, which ceases only with the chief's death or, in extremely rare cases, with the ceremonial ousting of a chief by the elders. The summary of the project constitutes an ideological narrative on how a "community," which is presented as homeostatic and internally leveled, has maintained in a "clandestine" (*sic*) way a "dynamic, lively, modern" form of local authority. The subtitle of one of the last sections of the text invites a "discussion on the reappraisal of the deepest sociocultural values in African communities." This project constituted a culturalist exercise of essentialization that coincided with the foreign donors' agenda of strengthening "community" and an emergent "civil society."[26]

Despite claims of advancing participatory democracy at the "community" level, the decree actually creates the space for new figures of sheer power: "true chiefs" in the parlance of technocracy and development, who are to be "identified" by the government and "recognized." During the transitional period, factors like perceptions of corruption, endemic poverty, migration, and socioeconomic flux also engendered criminality, anomy, and a profound sense of social disorder. Political authorities and law enforcement agencies do not seem able to meet the demands for local security and order. In this postwar context of insecurity, misery, and

risk, we can see the development of a social discourse expressing a long-
ing for previous epochs, be they colonial or Socialist times, untainted by
patrimonial practices or the corrosion of social values. In this context,
customary authority is conceived by the rural population as referring to
this previous, distant time, associated with a stronger sense of authority
and order. This expectation of "order and discipline" sustains in part the
current legitimacy officially bestowed upon customary authorities. This
process conveys a deep paradox and echoes some of the most conflicting
legacies from colonialism.

The decree of 2000 also refers to national unity, setting the stage for
the co-optation of potential local leaders as nothing more than micro-,
local nodes of the state apparatus. If the chief was an "auxiliary assistant"
of the colonial state apparatus in a time that preceded the nation-state,
at present customary authorities, related once again to the state apparatus as local appendages, must contribute to the "consolidation of national
unity." For instance, they must display the national flag and emblems of
the republic at their residences, wear official uniforms, and secure the participation of the population in national celebration days.

Other paradoxes link this juridical exercise with colonial modalities
of power. Throughout the process of recognition of local chiefs (e.g.,
around two thousand were recognized between 2001 and 2004), both colonial and postcolonial registers of customary authority were indiscrimi-
nately used to determine the legitimacy of chiefs and adjudicate conflicts
among them. For instance, colonial registers were used during the donor-
sponsored ethnographic campaigns conducted by the Ministry of State
Administration during the process that served as background for a new
policy on recognition of community authority. Of course, a myriad of colonial legal institutes and administrative documents had explicitly established the transformation of the customary by the subsequent phases of
the colonial regime. Furthermore, the new "ethnographic" project established by the state and donors in the 1990s to determine the legitimacy of
chiefs did not differentiate between ancient precolonial local hierarchies
and those created ex nihilo and incorporated into the governance of locality by the colonial state. Similarly, colonial cadastral and land registers are
used to demarcate "communal land" or today's space of the customary.[27]
Community spaces and territories of chieftaincies often are understood as
coinciding.

Yet there is often disjuncture between the letter of the decree and local
norms: while traditional authorities must articulate with local state organs

as mandated by the law, often their limits intersect, and land claimed by a single chieftaincy trespasses several state administrative units (*postos*). Furthermore, throughout the country, the implementation of the decree fostered innumerable disputes about succession and the right to occupy a position as an authority legitimized by community and recognized by the state. Chieftaincy being intricately enmeshed in partisan politics, the RENAMO opposition denounced many cases of chiefs being alienated, repressed, or imprisoned for their allegiance to RENAMO. The juridico-political ideology behind the discourse on community depicts it as a homeostatic, internally leveled, and undifferentiated social structure. Internal factionalism and struggles among preponderant lineages seeking hegemony within the community added to the ongoing dynamics of partisan politics and constitute a refutation of this representation. Alongside broad claims and appeals to "tradition," the legitimacy of customary authorities is painstakingly constructed and constantly negotiated through concrete power dynamics. Some local leaders without much consensus in their communities were recognized by the FRELIMO state, whereas some leaders with a visible degree of local legitimacy did not receive official recognition. Electoral politics and party allegiances play, today as in the past, a central role in the process of acknowledgment or repression of local authority by the state. In the peculiar condition of this nation-state, where the state apparatus and its history, ideology, and ritual symbolism are intrinsically linked to FRELIMO, the call to national unity rather reveals an ongoing state of politics as war by other means, in which the new neonationalism demanded of community authorities may be seen as a deliberate policy aimed at RENAMO and its potential allies among the customary chiefs.

## The Fetish of the Customary

The discourse of legal reform produces a fetishization of the customary, which is materialized through political and religious ceremonies of recognition in rural and periurban areas. In this process of self-legitimization, the state makes visible and harnesses a history and an imaginary of natural law and sacred violence linked to war that it tried for decades to obliterate. Rather than a dichotomy, what the juridical reform demonstrates is how the fetish[28] of the state apparatus attempts to fetishize in its turn the customary. Both fields gradually blend together until they

become subsequent moments within the temporality of an extended political condition.

The reform presents customary authority and law as genuinely "traditional" and bearing a legitimacy that resides almost outside historical
time. The realm of the customary is thus constructed by the Afro-modern
sphere of reformers—urban politicians, consultants, intellectuals—as a
space of primitivism associated with nature. The "urban" political and intellectual elites depict customary authority in legal projects and reports as
a sort of charismatic power where what is underlined is its interaction with
the souls of the ancestors and spirits of nature. It is a premodern authority
enacting customary laws, which are represented as a type of norm that has
its foundation in its mimesis of natural forms and forces. Custom is associated with nature and kinship, hence to biology and blood, in a chain of
meaning that is connected to a spiritual charismatic authority, "justice by
reconciliation," and an ahistoric, static time. In opposition to this natural
law of sorts, positive law, the "formal" juridical system, involves nones-
sentialist "cultural" representation. Yet the urban and rural spheres are
contiguous in space as well as in terms of the political economy. The interconnections are so profuse that the distinction exists only at an abstract,
administrative level. The traffic of continuities between both spheres
belies the state's construction of differentiated spaces and temporalities
separated by a tangible border.

The central state's quest to control the locality is constrained by complex relations, which have structured this political field through agonistic,
often violent relations of visibility and concealment. Since early colonial
times, local populations protected and concealed the actual individuals
who embodied authority. The splitting of loci of political power enabled
local sovereignties to maintain their own modes of succession and deployment, alongside the formal "traditional" chieftaincy appointed by the
colonial regime. Sometimes, fake or weak "chiefs" were presented as legitimate authority to the colonial power in order to maintain the true lineages in command. Similar practices occurred under the early postcolonial
regime in areas where chiefs had been duly dismissed and yet managed to
retain their ascendance through relatives who held positions in the newly
established Socialist institutions at the local level.[29]

The state of structural adjustment reproduces, through positive law, a
dichotomy where the urban–modern sphere appears as the realm of culture and the rural as the realm of nature. Juridical and economic reforms
work in parallel. The Afro-modern urban sphere engenders, through a

process of primitive accumulation, the realm of primitivism and "custom." This traditional locality appears as a tabooed space. The modernist elites distance themselves from that realm, implicitly drawing its political—and economic—legitimacy from its existence. The juridical representation of difference structures the postcolonial political field. Through the construction of the realm of custom as a tabooed space the urban Afro-modern sphere shapes itself and legitimizes its quest for hegemony.

The paradox of the local project of legal pluralism is that in its alleged quest for a progressive politics, it seems to validate a conservative political view, which sustains dichotomies of the modern and the archaic. These reformist trends represent a populist legal philosophy, which attempts to reinforce the self-legitimization process undertaken by the urban sphere by making it more "democratic," including both the Enlightenment's spirit of the laws and the spirits of customary law.

This postconflict project of social contract illustrates how the modernist spirit of the laws infers a universal norm and subsumes the plurality of differences under only one positive norm: the rule of law of modern liberal democracy. Law, deployed as historiography, becomes the object of socioeconomic development, claiming to process the historical remainder of the customary and subsuming it back into the dialectical system of the state's jurisdiction.

## Jurisdiction: Within the Limits of the Law

Decree 15/2000 legislates upon "custom . . . within the limits of the law," a turn of phrase denoting the time and space of state jurisdiction under the current post-Socialist/neoliberal dispensation.[30] The principle of jurisdiction illustrates the intrinsic paradox of classical conceptions of sovereignty. It demonstrates that the law grounds its claim of being the source of sovereignty on its attempt to delimit in space a dispersal of multiplicities. Sovereignty has been presented since early classical political theory as abstract, universal, and indivisible, hence neither bounded nor restricted. Yet, paradoxically, it must always enact itself through the minor register of jurisdiction and of the singular case. Jurisdiction thus reveals the impossibility of the law's self-grounding.

Sovereignty's claim to have its source in an ultimate power over life and death is still predicated upon the discourse of jurisdiction, which marks the border between an established sovereign order and its outside. It constitutes a place where the sovereignty of the law confronts its own limitations, where power's juridical utopia becomes spatial dystopia.

The two dominant senses of jurisdiction in Western political history are generic (in terms of subject matter or theme) and spatial (in terms of territory or bounded space).[31] In the Mozambican postcolonial juridico-political context inherited from the colonial West, through the interlude of colonialism and Socialism, the practice of jurisdiction conflates these two separate senses. The broad frame based on Roman law is blended with remnants of Socialist normativity and the increasing influence of Anglo-Saxon common law on areas of private business and public sector reform. In this postcolonial landscape, legal jurisdiction in the new rule-of-law context refers to both authority over legal subject matters and ju-ridical sovereignty over specific districts based on demarcations of land.

While the first definition involves layers of meanings, the second one refers to scales of territory. In the postcolony, the first definition concerns the proliferation of legal, political, and even religious authorities (official or customary or a liminal category between those two, as is the case with the community courts). The second definition refers to the postcolonial dissemination of spaces, the complexity involved in the demarcation of legal districts, and the right to allocate land property as a central aspect of the local political dynamics of enforcement of the law. The genealogy that moves from medieval lord, as primus inter pares, to modern secular state is complicated in a postcolonial setting, where the jurisdiction of official law has great difficulty imposing itself over the various vectors of local power. The "community of tenants" of medieval times is transposed today onto the legal figure of jurisdiction over a local "community," a crucial locus for the enactment of democratic governance.

While the Enlightenment's spirit of the laws aimed at subsuming the remainders of other local logics under a single unified system, the actual logic of colonial governance deployed a duplicitous mode of rule, demar-cating the divergent jurisdictions of the state and the rural customary. At present, a local community brings together the two vectors of territory and population, or, of land and citizens/subjects. In the Mozambican postcol-ony today, the question of citizenship is played out in terms of belonging in a locality, as the problem of who is entitled to pass judgment and who is entitled to be judged (exposure to the law, access to a justice system), a question that still revolves around the rural/urban divide.

The definition of the two juridico-political categories, or rural and urban, illustrates both the absolute potential and the negativity of the

political in the Mozambican context. Locality can mean a space of emancipation, or it can mean the return of age-old policies of violent control
and domination. Territory has been rendered yet another casualty of violence and war, and not only through the charred material landscape that
emerges out of decades of conflagration. Legal reform at the level of the
locality entails a fundamental redemarcation of land, both privatizing territory owned by the state by allowing individual investors to take control of it and determining what constitutes "communal"—"customarily
owned"—land to be returned to the ownership of "communities," once
again led by a customary authority. In this process, different historical
vectors merge and part. Histories of colonially defined customary chiefdoms become entangled around the same concrete conceptual and territorial spaces occupied by postcolonial Socialist histories of "villagization,"
"family sector," or neoliberal democratic community.

The jurisdiction that establishes the boundaries of a locality also de-
marcates the limits of the law itself. The territory's internal borders are
trespassed by floating populations migrating for work or ritual obligation,
located somehow in between citizenship and subjecthood, in between law
and custom: as customary citizenry. The traffic of population, the displacement of objects, the residual presences of historical difference blur the
space that the voice of the law attempts in vain to delineate.

The equation between locality and local population, between territory
and community, is not a perfect sum, as alleged by the discourse of the
state. Something exceeds the operation of connecting a group of people,
linked by some alleged primordial bond, to a piece of land or a district.
What escapes is an ineffable element, a remainder of the history of a given
territory, a lapse of time, a margin of space, a surplus population. This
impossibility of closure of locality or community shows that jurisdiction
is not a mandate but a relation. Colonial or postcolonial legal authority
could not establish the limits of the local. Rather, the local in all its multiple disseminations interrupts the law. Postcolonial history shows that jurisdiction is a dispersion, a deferral in space and time.

The object of jurisdiction is supposed to be a territory and the objects
and relations encompassed within them. Yet this territory does not preex-
ist the deployment of this juridical fiction. It is, rather, constituted through
an extension of spatiality and an expansion of time. The imposition of jurisdiction over territory thus also implies a political history of jurisdiction
over time. The postcolony is not a positive territorialization but a spacing,
the replicating practice of time becoming space in the locality.

Jurisdiction means the spatialization of the temporal insofar as the present, the contemporary political moment, needs to be inscribed in the letter of the law as a trace, before it immediately disappears in the passage of time. In Mozambique, this spatialization of time is enacted through the legal operations that reconstitute the past (recognition of chiefs, reinstantiations of "custom," rewriting of various meanings of war within the text of the political), such that it may act as the foundation of the present and legitimize it, as in the reinscription of the historical customary, which shapes the current governance of the local.[32]

The spacing of time, a political history taking place within a territory, is the precondition for establishing a continuity between temporal moments and their institutional materialization. With respect to Mozambique and its history as a concessionary territory, colony, People's Republic, or liberal democratic state, what justifies the premise that the nation-state is continuous, identical to itself, while undergoing a succession of different political regimes? One of the main arguments in favor of such continuity is based on the way in which jurisdiction is also deployed upon time, as the state traces juridical relations between different historical epochs.

Yet territory is not simultaneous with itself. The postcolonial nation is crowded with diverse historical narratives, multiple local textures disseminating out of the single official space of locality administratively demarcated by the state. Jurisdiction is also a temporalization that connects the different spatial localities, materializing history. Let us see how recent history frames the question of jurisdiction in contemporary Mozambique as a local political struggle between various vectors of law and custom.

# PART II

# CHAPTER FOUR

# A Minor State

This chapter analyzes forms of local governance existing during the first decade of the twenty-first century in northern Mozambique. In the context of juridical reform of the post-Socialist state under neoliberal conditions, socioeconomic fractures and political discontinuities could be observed between the south and the center-north of the country and also between actual political and juridical processes in the northern localities and the imaginaries of reform projected from the capital by the national and foreign intelligentsia.

This chapter analyzes at the local level aporias of the state of structural adjustment that arise along cultural cleavages, economic corridors, and political histories. In the locality, aspects of Socialist governance continue within the new democratic regime, even in embattled areas that had been supportive of the opposition during both the civil war and the first local elections.

The following sections describe the current functioning of these former local Socialist institutions, or "minor states," in which the borders separating political and juridical fields are blurred. These units constitute paradoxical spaces of overlapping temporalities and juridico-political regimes generated by the unevenness of the political transition. The chapter describes the political and legal circuits that channel local conflicts in a periurban neighborhood as a point of entry to illustrate a contradictory entanglement of normativities that, far from the "legal pluralism" discussed in the capital's development centers of reform, is strongly shaped by local political disputes over jurisdiction linked to electoral struggles. Life stories of local state officers, their perspectives on recent political history or current events, and the social context of their daily work in a periurban neighborhood provide insight into the functions of the "minor" sections of local states. While the national recognition of the "customary" plays a key role in the juridical reform that generates the state of structural adjustment, this chapter studies its intended and unintended effects in the locality. The minor state is an example of an institution enacting "customary citizenship" at the local level.

One early evening in mid-May 2004, the provincial capital city of Nampula Province was in the midst of mild chaos. Everything was in disarray as night quickly fell. It was quite dark, as a power shortage had affected most of the city for hours. The noise from stranded cars and people shouting as they ran back to their homes contributed to the unrest.

The province was in turmoil. In a few days, the FRELIMO Central Committee would hold a summit in the provincial capital, during which they would delineate the main action plans that the government intended to implement and also launch the national campaign for the general elections. The usual slow pace of the city would be transformed by two events. Before the summit a meeting of one thousand militants and cadres would take place, as preparation for the campaign, and a large rally would introduce the presidential candidate to the provincial population.

An atmosphere of tension had been revived as friction between the government party and RENAMO had emerged once again throughout the province. That night the power cut was attributed by many across town to sabotage by the "party of the partridge," a name that evokes the shrewd movements of the former guerrillas across the rural countryside. The lack of electricity was considered a potential act of boycott similar to those RENAMO had conducted during the civil war in the 1980s. Speaking with both elders and younger people among the local population, it became evident that many interpreted the upcoming general election campaign as a tense combat. Beyond the effects of an alleged process of national "reconciliation," politics was widely perceived locally as a continuation of the armed conflict.[1]

Throughout colonial and postcolonial history, Nampula Province has been relevant for both economic and political reasons. In 1974, the province was the foremost producer of the two most important Mozambican export commodities: cotton and cashew nuts. African smallholders accounted for a large amount of production during colonial times until the expansion of settler agriculture production in the mid-1960s. By 1964, their contribution was larger than the equivalent in other provinces, a position that was regained after the exit of Portuguese settlers in 1975 and the demise of Socialist state-sponsored collective farm production. Today Nampula is also significant in political and electoral terms. It is the most populated province and home to approximately one-fifth of the voting population, whose long-standing antigovernment stance was already expressed in 2003, during the first local elections, when RENAMO won three of the five cities that held a vote in the province. The issue of the customary and the anti-FRELIMO stance of a large portion of the population, historically sustained by local chiefs, constituted an important vector in the political history of the area until the mid-2000s. The civil war (1977–92) in the rural areas worsened an incipient divide between party-state structures and the rural population.[2] As the guerrillas of RENAMO spread throughout the rural areas of the country, they targeted civilian populations and cut infrastructural and administrative links between the FRELIMO state and a large number of communities, thus removing these populations from governmental influence and control.[3] RENAMO launched a guerrilla war of sabotage, assassination, and general destabilization, discovering later the strategic value of establishing links, where possible, with former customary chiefs who, having been marginalized by the FRELIMO state, were often disposed to collaborate with them. In many areas under its control, RENAMO used local structures of power as intermediaries in its own administrative hierarchy.

The issue of the customary was once again a central political question in the early 2000s, when the reinstatement of custom and the recognition of chiefs constituted key aspects of the juridical reform to decentralize the Socialist state. When I arrived in Nampula Province in 2004, a very large banner covered the entire front of the building that lodges the Provincial Assembly and was displayed for months. It said: "Long Live Local Power." Contrary to what was stated by key political slogans from the past, such as "Destroying tribalism in order to construct the nation,"[4] imprinted on flags in Maputo by the Socialist regime at its nationalistic heyday, the mottoes in the mid-2000s emphasized the advantages of decentralization. "Local power," another euphemism for "community authorities" within the developmentalist circles in Maputo, was a technocratic and political buzzword that alluded to a regional policy of loosening the grip on local political structures through administrative decentralization. The apparent legal deconstruction of the Socialist state apparatus and the "return" of customary authority shaped in new ways the work of local political structures.

## Minor State I[5]

Khakhossani[6] is a densely crowded neighborhood of approximately 14,000 people located in a strip of land surrounding Nampula City, the

provincial capital. A ride in one of the minibuses from the city downtown
takes about thirty minutes. The bus follows the damaged dirt road, which
runs from the city to the *bairros*, or semiurban neighborhoods, passing a
large street market of many shacks. It stops at a busy crossroads, in front
of a carpenter's shop. It takes five more minutes to walk the meandering,
narrow dirt street that, passing a few houses, huts, and informal street
shops, goes deeper into the neighborhood, toward the house that lodges
the minor state and the court.

History takes place. The house is around fifty or sixty years old, nearly
derelict. Once owned by a Portuguese settler, it was later appropriated by
the new independent state after his flight. The walls must have last been
painted, all in bright white, in 1975. Today, the structure appears on the
verge of collapse, especially the roof, and the walls are in dire need of a
coat of paint; large, sickly mildew stains sprawl across them, inside and
out. But this dilapidated house is not just any building. It lodges a minor
state apparatus, each space within it enclosing a separate institution of
executive or judicial powers: the Bureau of the Neighborhood Secretary,
the community court, and the party cell. These structures are immersed in
local micropolitical struggles over contested senses of history, as different
allegiances mean the espousal of different readings of past trajectories of
the state and the customary.[7]

The experiential passage of time shapes the contours of local space,
as shown by the struggles of various juridico-political actors who aim at
imposing on the locality different versions of the jurisdiction of the force
of law. The house lodging the minor state and the effects it produces on
neighborhood dwellers are overdetermined by a recent history of various coalescing legal and economic transformations.[8] The ruined building,
embodying an imagination of a centralized power, is also a reminder of
the fact that alongside the constructions of versions of political history,
the state apparatus is predicated on spatial metaphors of architecture and
hierarchy and depicted as an institution situated "above" society.[9] This
particular house is located on the margin of a peripheral urban neighborhood, on a borderline between rural and urban areas, somehow simultaneously placed inside and outside the scope of official law. Hence, it is
both site and metaphor of the minor state and its decayed yet resilient—
indeed, exceptional—order.[10]

This key locus of a minor politics is the product of a regional history.
In the final stages of the civil war and during the early transition toward
democracy, around the early nineties, a political unit called the dynamizing group (DG) symbolized the party-state system at the level of locality.

Its precedents go back to the politico-military cells set up by the guerrilla war machine during the liberation struggle of the 1960s, both in the open war of the rural battlefields and in the utter secrecy of urban insurgency. Replacing customary chiefs as nodes of local governance, the DG blended the forms of a local state unit and a FRELIMO party cell. It entailed a limited reform of the previous political space of locality because, as did chiefs, it encompassed all forms of power—executive, legislative, and judicial, as well as a local police force—in one single merged form. The DG constituted the embryo of today's minor state. Current local politics stems from the dynamics of war. Immediately following independence, FRELIMO officers held several administrative and political positions at once, as do neighborhood authorities today.

Following independence, conducting their administrative and judicial endeavors through popular public gatherings, local Socialist authorities attempted to, as they claimed, "simplify" the intricacies of colonial law and governance, allegedly making them accessible to the local population's needs. Later, the newly formed People's Tribunals would nominally oppose custom and all traditional ritual, in a move that mirrored the attempt to replace chiefs with party cells. Socialist legality and practices of popular justice conducted in those units also led to a renewal of dynamics from previous institutions, such as an age-old customary court that since precolonial times had served as a space for conflict resolution through the management of spiritual forces. Nevertheless, as in other regions of Africa, the dynamics of reconciliation reputedly active in customary chiefly courts had been transformed by colonial codification.[11]

There are plenty of continuities between the Socialist DGs and current local structures of power, both having originated in the former party-state system. At present, the two main authorities at work in the neighborhood, the neighborhood secretary and the community court, are but holdovers from the authorities in the DGs. The position of secretary was transferred from the DG to the locality, and everyday conflicts, which had originally been solved by the DG's secretary of social welfare, are now dealt with by the community court. Also, two of the judges at the Khakhossani court had worked earlier at that office. The recent political past impinges on the possibilities of the present.

History takes place; its effects are imprinted on the space of the neighborhood, over the dense woods, the distant hills, and the rocky paths—for instance, through marks of violence visible on buildings, on roads, or in nature, as signs of a civil war that in the 1980s reached the outskirts of the city. A history of the enactment of the law in this area is also engraved on the walls of the house that lodges the minor state. The courtroom encloses many layers of historicity[12] and of the political struggles over the enforcement of jurisdiction.

Jurisdiction allegedly deploys a voice that fills a restricted space. It is a metaphor of the sovereignty of an original legal authority and its rhetorical power. It is also a metonymy for the condensation of a network of local relations into a single unified apparatus of state power: out of many multiple murmurs a single voice. The house is located at the center of a battle over jurisdiction. Different local political agents, from chiefs, to religious leaders, to RENAMO officers, as well as the ex-Socialist authorities, aim at channeling and solving local conflicts in order to gain political legitimacy in the neighborhood. It is a current political struggle predicated upon a previous history.

The house bears the marks of the passage of time, its entangled temporalities reinforce an effect of historical depth that for the people in this neighborhood is related to a sense of legitimate justice, even though the court has ceased to belong in the state apparatus. This house has undergone three different political regimes. During each of them it held, for the population of the area, a symbolic charge related to different political systems and regimes of law. During the later stages of the Portuguese regime, it was simply the residence of a foreign settler or, as neighbors say, a mere "landowner," a sign of the system of extraction of which colonial law was at the same time the foundation and the outcome. Taken over by the FRELIMO regime, the house became the site of the party cell (the DG, the main local state unit). In 2004, three decades after independence and emerging out of the post–civil war agreements, the newly installed post-Socialist regime and its neoliberal stance have reconstructed the house, almost by default, not as the People's Tribunal of yesteryear but, rather, as the site of a community court.

The label "community" reflects both a retreat of the state[13] (which means the abandonment of Socialist rhetoric) and also the problematic recognition of the legitimacy of the realm of the customary as juridico-political counterpart of the state apparatus. For the local people who attend the court's sessions twice a week, the courthouse represents a sign from a historical past, which continues to provide the experience of the present with political meaning.

Neighbors explain their seeking recourse at the community court in terms of seeing it as a site of history. In their view, the court still represents a legitimate apparatus of control and provision that has been for decades all they know of the state. They reference recent regional history of the nation-state—its achievements, its struggles—in order to explain the legitimacy of the community court's procedures. In the eyes of these people the "structures" (governmental authorities) still bear the legitimacy of the FRELIMO party-state. Hence, a small edifice in ruins in the impoverished outskirts of the city is a site where the possibility of justice emerges, among leftovers from the political and judicial transformations that the country has undergone in the last decades.

The present-day community courts are the heirs of the project of popular justice launched in the mid-1980s, when at the height of the Marxist regime and facing unrest produced by war, scarcity, and pervasive crime, the state affirmed that legality and order were to be guaranteed by the sovereignty of the people. More than two decades later, in 2004, a different foundation gave legitimacy to a state attempting to control a social order threatened by recurring fears and conflicts. In the north, the role played by state units that had been implemented after independence to ensure the channeling of a Socialist order from the top of the party-state to villages and neighborhoods was changing. Mayors and other local officers were involved in the play of bipartisan politics at the level of a democratically reformed locality. Yet what was happening with the officers of the former DG, which now through new legislation the state was placing alongside chiefs, as relics of a not-so-distant past? What space did popular judges and secretaries occupy in the midst of rapid and uncertain political transformation?

During my fieldwork on rights and custom in early 2004 in Nampula City, in a context marked by apprehension and deep suspicion toward strangers and by mechanisms of tight control still enforced by the state, a certain degree of trust acquired over time and with patient effort led me from a research group on "citizenship" at a local university to that minor state constituted by the current version of the DG. Through young members of those groups I met a community judge at the small white house where he worked as a guard during the week. The judge would later usher me into the peripheral area in which he lived, where he worked twice a week as a judge, as well as introduce me to the other local authorities, such as community judges and neighborhood secretaries. The life stories and work of these officers show key aspects of local politics, of the transitions and transformations of the nation-state as experienced in the locality, and of the particular nuances of distinctions and articulations between the juridical and the political fields, custom and law, in a post-Socialist transition shaped by neoliberal dynamics.

## Minor State II: Secretary

One clear and breezy morning, a few weeks after our first encounter and following several conversations on relations between recent history and the present, I accompanied the judge to his neighborhood outside the city, where he led me to the old house that was the apex of the local conjunction between the political and the law. A man, dressed in a white shirt and wearing old dusty black pants, was sweeping the floor very carefully at the back of the house as he did at the beginning of every working day. He was the president of the Community Council, a local institution created in each neighborhood in 2002, and whose functions are mostly those of a local police force. During the course of my research, I spoke many times with him about his work and also about the history of the neighborhood and that particular house. "What did he do?" I asked the man once, referring to the previous owner of the house. "He was a landowner (*propietario*)," he answered, lifting his eyes for a second to reward me with a huge smile. And he explained further: "He was the owner of this house and those parcels of land, over there." The indeterminate space he was pointing out with his homemade broom was below, downhill, toward the huts and mud houses and palm trees of the neighborhood of Khakhossani. Without stopping his sweeping, he told me, "After independence, the government took over the house for the people, and it became the base of the dynamizing group." In a sentence, he compressed years of narrative of a national-popular project that took over the space of a territory, reclaiming it for a population that would exert sovereignty through the party-state and its local cells.

The entrance to the house led into a large central hall, from which one could access its four rooms. The largest office belonged to the secretary of what in the recent past used to be the DG. Now, the man was referred to as the neighborhood secretary: a political appellation that has given way to a merely spatial one. The house had no electricity, and not much daylight seeped in through the cracked panes, especially in the central area. To the right of the entrance and a few steps along a narrow, dark corridor was located what used to be the kitchen of the settler's house, from whose windows and back door one could see the hills surrounding the neighborhood, some small houses, the palm trees, the sky. Every other day, before the court's sessions began, a group of tall, strong young men, wearing bright T-shirts and holding batons, would sit on the empty, cracked sink for a while, before leaving to accomplish their duties as the newly formed community police.

Across the central hall there was another, smaller room; inside it is dark. A computer-printed sign on the door read "FRELIMO party cell, Khakhossani neighborhood." There, in the dim light, a young man was at work: three times a week the deputy secretary received neighbors and wrote down their requirements and complaints. The minor state stood as an icon that signaled toward a previous political regime that still remained and yet also had been fading away at varying speeds within the nation. Indeed, the minor state illustrates this political afterlife in a present that reproduces features—in terms of sovereignty or the effects of the war— that were first iterated under Socialism. This historical past was folded within the house's ruined walls. In 2004, the house hurriedly abandoned by a fleeing Portuguese settler still hosted authorities from the immediate postrevolutionary moment.

Enter the neighborhood secretary, Mr. Santos. He cut an outstanding figure: he was tall and thin, and his angular face was marked by two intense, deep-set eyes and a small pointed beard. It was a fierce visage, marked by a very serious expression. During the weekdays, when he was on duty, he wore the tailored, dark-green ensemble affected by many local state officers, somewhat reminiscent of a Chinese Mao outfit. A big hat in hand was an ever-present supplement to his semiofficial uniform.

Within the house that formed the base of this minor state, the secretary's office faced the room in which the court conducted its sessions. It was a wide, almost bare space, with a window that let in a lot of sunlight. There was one shelf holding randomly arranged folders and papers, as well as a large cupboard. The secretary worked at a large, old wooden table covered with piles of folders, papers, and notebooks. A large pamphlet with instructions related to the upcoming elections, old issues of the *National Gazette*, copies of laws, newspapers, and innumerable handwritten notes with requests from the local populace provided a sense of an official, bureaucratic space: the precarious site of the state. Opposite the secretary's seat hung the usual large, black-and-white official portrait of the president of the Republic. Behind the table, hanging on the barely painted wall, were two posters of FRELIMO's electoral propaganda. One featured Eduardo Mondlane and Samora Machel, mingling these revolutionary leaders with presidential figures—Joaquim Chissano (president until February 2005) and Armando Guebuza (then a presidential candidate, now the president). The other was an older one from a previous campaign. It was out-of-date, though maybe not for the locals' sense of the political.

The work of a cluster of secretaries—of a bloc, or neighborhood—involved dispensing "welfare" at a microlevel and in the context of extreme scarcity. The secretary went everywhere with a diary bearing the inscription "1995": as if the political took place both in the present and in the past at once. In that outdated notebook he inscribed, in a minute, patient calligraphy, requests, demands, aspirations, and dreams or nightmares, fixing in a bureaucratic language the quotidian, at times slow, at times anxiously accelerated, rhythms of the population. He worked every day at his office, where he constantly received people who addressed him with the utmost deference and seriousness, bringing to him requests and demands related to health, infrastructure, or minor conflicts. Every day, he walked around the neighborhood—by himself or with an aide, the deputy secretary or another man—and sometimes traveled outside his district, to work on some issue with another secretary or a with a small delegation dispatched from "above," as he said, referring to the City Council (local legislative branch). His métier was the solving of conflicts: healing wounds opened by quarrels, disease, or mere desperation.

His activities illustrate the dynamics of ex-Socialist political structures in the city. The secretary transferred the population's demands to the Administrative Post—the official bureau on which his position and the whole of the minor state depended. He solved by himself some conflicts and complaints, acting as a juridical authority of sorts, meeting with the neighbors and their families. Other problems he transferred to the community court, with the Police Station being his last resort if the threat to order reached the limits of insecurity, crime, and violence. He explained his work in terms of "transferring the preoccupations of the population to the state's institutions" and "channeling down the government's orientations." In exchange for this work the secretary did not earn a salary, a state of affairs he bitterly contrasted to "the situation in some nearby districts, where secretaries and their deputies also hold some kind of position within the state" (the "formal state apparatus"), "for instance, at the Municipal Council, or the Military Command."

I first met the secretary, apart from some casual greetings outside the courtroom, on a day when the five community judges went to a house located at the outskirts of the neighborhood to pursue inquiries related to a divorce case. This was an out-of-the-ordinary occasion—seldom did judges leave the courthouse to hold a session at some neighbor's locale—

and one in which the secretary was invited to come along and participate in the discussions. By then, I had already been conducting research at the court for some time, so I was also invited to attend. For twenty-five minutes we walked in a line, crisscrossing the neighborhood along dirty, meandering paths, past the crowds of mud houses—the five judges, the secretary, and myself. We passed shops and small movie theaters set up in precarious brick houses where DVDs of Indian or Hollywood martial arts and romance films were shown and encountered street hawkers and boys herding goats to market, hitting them with sticks.

The purpose of the visit was to encourage a married couple to reflect further on their separation: either to reconcile or to take the necessary steps toward dividing their lives and belongings. At the same time, the judges needed to see the place for themselves in order to evaluate the worth of the house, the piece of land upon which it was built, and the couple's few belongings, all of which were the subject of dispute.

This event showed the political interactions between officers and institutions within the minor state. The secretary was invited to participate in the session as yet another figure with authority over the resolution of conflicts. While technically, this position would make him as a "judge," actually his participation in the case located him in an ambiguous position between two poles, juridical and political. This situation replicates the context of the early Socialist period, during which the position of secretary of a village or a neighborhood carried with it judicial functions.

On another occasion, I attended a session at the community court at which the secretary was also present. He had been summoned once again to pass judgment on a case as an ad hoc, temporary judge. His participation had to do with the fact that a powerful local figure of authority, a sheikh, was the one accused of attempting to retain land that was not his. On this occasion, as in other cases, the plaintiffs, being close neighbors, had attempted to first solve the quarrel a few days earlier at the secretary's home.

A few days later, he entered the courtroom sporting his green Mao suit (almost a uniform among local secretaries) moments after the hearing of the case had begun, gave a brief smile to the people present at the session, received the respectful acknowledgment of the other judges, and sat, like yet one more magistrate, on an old, rickety wooden chair placed in a corner. During the following hour he remained sitting with an expression of utmost seriousness, legs crossed and his proverbial hat resting on his lap, as the sheikh (white shirt, turquoise jacket, red hat) sat quietly and also observed, with a half smile on his face, how his opponent argued his case with much gesticulation. The judges told the man to stop his gestures ("speak like a man; you are at the court").

At the end of the discussion, the secretary asked questions. When he was interrupted by the family of the plaintiff, the president-judge rebutted them ("Be quiet, the comrade secretary is speaking, and we need to know where the case was born, whether there is a matter [to be judged] or not"). The secretary gave advice that helped, in an obvious fashion, the position of the religious (and political) authority. Thanks to the secretary's help, his close neighbor, the sheikh, would prevail, probably due to his local influence, in a conflict where he had no evident advantage if judged only by the evidence and testimonies submitted to the court.

During our first interviews at his office, Mr. Santos dutifully described the responsibilities of his office. When I asked him about the length of his tenure, he looked straight into my eyes, raised his eyebrows, and assured me that he had been "here," serving the motherland, right since independence. "Since 1975?" I asked him, pressing him, searching for a confirmation of several things at once. His affirmative reply seemed to link many loose ends that emerged during my research on local politics. But later on, I would learn that he had been deceiving me. "Mr. Secretary, would you say that in the last few years, after the change of regime, with democracy, elections, the end of the war, many things have changed within the government and for the population?" He shook his head gently and looked at the floor: "No, not much, not really. Nothing has changed."

Mr. Santos was forty-two years old in 1975. In the mid-2000s, he performed his work as though nothing had, indeed, become something else. The micropolitics of the neighborhood, the conflict with RENAMO, the functioning of the minor state unfolded, according to the secretary, as during the early Socialist period. Apparently, notwithstanding the short, if very intense battle fought between RENAMO guerrillas and a small platoon from the government's forces right outside the white house that now housed the minor state, nothing had been transformed since the civil war that neighbors saw and felt closely enough in the 1980s. The secretary affirmed that he continued his work as though nothing had changed; war had followed politics, which in turn had followed war.

A couple of months after our first conversations, I was at a run-down "barrack" in a local street market, not too far from the minor state's house, sharing drinks and conversation with the secretary and the judges from the community court. During a break in our discussions, when Mr. Santos went out briefly, I brought up his work and his life story, in order to have the judges explain the post of the secretary itself, its history, its potential and limitations.

Then, all of a sudden, the man who was clearly the main political force in the minor state, the president-judge of the community court, revealed how he pulled the strings behind the local scene, explaining that, through a series of fortuitous events, he had over time attained more power within the minor state and links to the formal state. This authority allowed him to surround himself with acolytes, allies, and friends within the community court. It also served to support candidacies for the position of secretary, who were appointed by bureaucrats in the city structures of the formal state. That afternoon, during our chat at the bar, the president-judge of the community court suggested that the secretary owed his post to him: "But he never acknowledges it."

The judges explained that Mr. Santos was the fourth person to have held the position of secretary in the area. Later, they traced the trajectory of each man who had occupied this position, his personal qualities, and why he had vacated the office, be it death or a transfer to some other post or zone. When I questioned them about the fact that Mr. Santos had assured me that he had occupied the post since independence, they nodded and, looking at me awry, hesitantly hinted at the possibility that he had meant that he had been occupying various other positions within the local state.

This fact was also explained by the way in which the officers of the minor state considered their work at the neighborhood's political structures as a form of representing, without any mediation, popular sovereignty as enacted since independence. At the level of the minor state, the articulation between party and state, proper to the Socialist regime, seems not to have been completely effaced.

These minor state officers have been here since independence, a moment in which a new temporality, indeed a new way of being, had begun and which, according to the secretary, has not ended yet, without changing a bit along the way. The whole of the territory had been liberated and claimed for the people and for the site of this sovereignty: the state. "To be here since independence" meant neither deception nor exaggeration. For, since independence and the implementation of the party-state system, the whole of the territory had been identified with the state itself—that is, with the ultimate locus of popular sovereignty, whose site within the neighborhood was this old white house in ruins.

In a conflictive area such as Nampula Province, where RENAMO enjoyed a high degree of support and there exists a pervasive antagonism to the labor and symbolism of the state apparatus, the local officer was confronted on an everyday basis with a sociopolitical environment that went from calculated indifference to outraged hostility. This context was fueled as well by the constant oppositional work of RENAMO, which included the blocking of the local state's endeavors, rumor and gossip, and the scattered use of violence. The secretary, almost a caricature of an outdated type of politics, found himself in the midst of a marginal struggle within the current democratic regime and attempted to make some sense of it: "This new democratic thing is very complicated. The elections, for instance. . . . Do you have democracy in your country, with elections and all? Oh, I thought it was something that was developing only here in Mozambique. Well, it is a very harsh thing; mostly because the other parties, instead of supporting the government and helping it to carry on with its duty, just block all its work. They create confusion. We encounter this all the time here in our district. The enemy turns the population against us constantly. They make our work extremely difficult. And the population complains a lot."

As though still being played out against the deathly background of the war, the game of democratic politics constituted for the local state agents a dialectics of friend and foe.[14] The secretary complained: "The enemy is constantly spreading rumors. This morning I attended a meeting, which I had been organizing during the whole past week. A brigade from the government came to *sensitize* the population in regard to issues of the Chupasangue and the disappearances of people. Rumors circulate blaming these facts on the government, and the population feels restless."[15] Halfway through my fieldwork in the city, a story dating from the 1970s had reemerged, about a supernatural vampire-like figure, the Chupasangue, who sucked people's blood and abducted them. The secretary had to conduct his daily endeavors within this impassioned context of fear and violence. He explained that his work involved mostly what could be called micropractices of clientelistic welfare, but it could also expand into invisible realms where spirits reigned and another kind of law was enforced.

Despite the implementation of a liberal political regime based on democratic representation, these authorities held their positions in reference to the legitimacy of the previous Socialist regime, supported by the fact that FRELIMO had remained in power by means of general elections. These authorities merely *remained* within the democratic regime, coexisting with the norms and institutions of the new rule of law, claiming a type of legitimacy that stemmed from the direct democracy of the People's

Republic. The paradoxes involved in the overlapping of political logics in the minor state, although seemingly a political oddity, reflected broader schemes of governance at the level of the central state, where remnants of modes of government that originated within the previous political regime were also entwined with "democratic" forms and norms.

These local authorities alluded to another sort of representation and a substantially different type of election. Secretaries in rural villages or urban neighborhoods had been appointed directly by local FRELIMO structures, whereas "people's judges" were elected in collective assemblies where the population endorsed candidates presented by FRELIMO as "good comrades" and thus suitable to perform just and sound legal procedures. The last election of local lay-judges took place in 1987, the year when the FRELIMO regime gradually began to officially withdraw from Marxism-Leninism. Therefore, according to the present political norms, these local authorities have not been democratically elected. Thus, the minor state existed within a disjuncture vis-à-vis the current political regime in regard to procedures for legitimate appointment to office; it did not result from the legal decree on "community authorities" or the political debates on the future of "community tribunals."

In regard to the status of their political sovereignty as part and parcel of the state apparatus, their elected status was ambiguous. For instance, the eventuality of having to appoint new local authorities if FRELIMO were to lose a general or even a local election had not been regulated. This local situation resembled the dynamics of the central state, where in Maputo in 2003, within the context of approaching general elections, various high-ranking officers and foreign consultants pointed out to me in interviews how urban elites (national politicians, foreign consultants) discussed the eventuality of a RENAMO victory and an ensuing replacement of high-ranking state officers as something that would definitely "challenge the status of the Mozambican democracy" and the "actual existence of a proper state apparatus."

Thus, in 2003, a RENAMO mayor in one of the main cities in Nampula Province ordered the suspension of the secretaries of the city's twenty-two neighborhoods, whom he accused of "acting as political activists for the ruling party." The city, whose municipality was one of five won by RENAMO in the local elections of 2003, replaced the secretaries with RENAMO members appointed by the mayor. The Nampula provincial government of FRELIMO dispatched a delegation to the city to investigate what they saw as an irregular situation in which the mayor's decision violated Decree 15/2000 on community authority.

The mayor's sovereignty collided with that of the provincial government over the loose, abstract legal discourse of the decree, which establishes the norms of coordination between local state organs and community authorities and does not regulate properly the status of the latter or their correct mode of articulation with "traditional leaders" (customary chiefs). One of the potential effects of the mayor's decision could have been that those neighborhoods had two secretaries each. Justifying his decision, the mayor said that "we want to work with people who represent the interests of civil society, not of political parties." The mayor signaled a conundrum of the democratic transition, such as the alleged recent separation between state and civil society, which would be the realm of the private, put in question by the status of ex-Socialist secretaries placed somewhere between both fields. Moreover, the RENAMO mayor's declaration implicitly placed political parties (meaning FRELIMO) on the side of the state apparatus, alluding to historico-political continuities with the previous party-state system.

To counter this discourse, the official national press, linked to the central state's interests, argued that "the people the mayor appointed are militants of his own party." The FRELIMO secretary in the city described the mayor's decision as an illegal "provocation" and filed a juridical demand with the provincial government. This argument reveals a paralegal space that blends the force of law of the democratic legitimacy of a local election with the extrajuridical force that was the foundation for a decision taken on the limits of the juridical.

This argument on the status of former officers of the previous party-state regime, located at the border between the juridical and the political, took place as FRELIMO geared up to restage the dynamics of armed struggle in the context of impending democratic elections. The Nampula provincial governor held a meeting with the local secretaries, assuring them that the government was taking the necessary measures to reinstate order in the municipality. The force of law and the political as a continuation of war seem to have met at a dead end.

## Minor State III: A Community Judge

Community Judge Simao Nipante was a short, slim, very quiet man, with an expression that blended puzzlement, suspicion, and kindness in his small eyes. In 2004, Judge Nipante worked six days a week as a guard at a house belonging to the Ministry of Public Works, as the community judges did not receive any state salaries whatsoever for their work at the courts. "Once, in 1983, Marcelino was quoted in the newspaper saying that soon popular judges would begin to get paid. But it has been twenty years since then, and I do not think that this is finally going to happen." The judge referred to Marcelino dos Santos, one of three members of the FRELIMO revolutionary troika that led Mozambique during the anticolonial struggle and after independence. Judge Nipante would often reminisce of times past at my request, explaining to me the functioning of the court in a sort of historical context. He talked about these events somewhat reluctantly at first, though showing benevolence toward me and to my friend who introduced me to him, whose mother was from the same town as Nipante and worked with him at the house and, after so many years, considered him a relative of sorts.

Nipante was born in Mesagane,[16] in the hinterland of Nampula, in 1936. I would learn later, following community links and circuits of reciprocity, that most of the judges in the community court, including its president, came from that town and had known one another for a long time. Nipante had come to Nampula City when he was in his twenties and had lived at first in a neighborhood outside the city. During our conversations, at dusk, he would point in the direction of the mountains on the dark horizon, enclosed by purple clouds. Somewhere below those clouds existed the semiurban neighborhood in which he had lived during colonial times, for, as a black man, as a native or "indigenous," he was banned from living within the limits of the city in which he worked during the day.

He told me once, in passing, that he had occupied local positions of power in postindependence times, "when all the white men left." In the late seventies, he held posts in the local DG, mainly as secretary of social action (welfare). At that time, the DG was a political structure that also adjudicated justice. In these posts, Nipante used to mediate local conflicts. Thus, in 1982 he was nominated by the local FRELIMO structures to occupy a position as popular judge. After having been elected by a neighborhood assembly, he had continued working at this post until the present day (2004, when I interviewed him).

The judge's career illustrates the nature of the minor state, its current predicament and potential, showing how local juridical institutions evolved from political structures that originated in legal formations organized during the anticolonial guerrilla struggle. From rural Mesagane to the provincial capital of Nampula, the almost seven decades of life of the community judge showed glimpses of the political history of the state, from colonialism to socialism, to the disjoined present in which he lives and works.

One evening, as I was speaking with Nipante on the patio at the back of the government-owned house where he works as a night watchman, he provided me with a succinct scheme of the ongoing condition of micropolitics and overlapping forms of justice in his neighborhood. Throughout the periphery of this northern provincial capital, there were customary authorities who held various degrees of power over their areas of control. The power of these authorities grew the farther they were from the city, achieving its peak in the isolated rural areas where state structures were almost nonexistent. According to the judge, the majority of traditional chiefs in the province currently supported RENAMO. Nevertheless, in a few districts, the neighborhood secretary worked with such customary chiefs, managing to coordinate certain political activities such as holding elections, building infrastructure, or carrying out information campaigns about health and other social issues. According to the judge, "not *all* the *regulos* [customary chiefs] belong to RENAMO. And even some of these work very well alongside the government, only making very clear their differentiation from it at the moment of the vote." The judge was aware of the crucial political effects of the recognition of the legitimate authority of customary chiefs by the provincial government, which had "given them badges and uniforms as it was during the colonial regime." Despite the importance of this fact in terms of both recent history and the current political situation, he nuanced the contours of the process: "The government has not recognized *regulos* in the peripheral neighborhoods of the city but only in the rural areas where there are no governmental structures such as *grupo dinamizador*, secretary, or tribunal, and the power of the *regulos* is strong."

Although this situation resembled somewhat, from the judge's perspective, the much abhorred colonial period, to which he referred with a quiet, detached, and yet obvious contempt, he acknowledged that in many areas the population had begun perceiving what could be understood as a slippage from the customary to the state. The chiefs, wearing the uniforms and badges and holding the pennants of yesteryear, were in some ways seen as belonging to the state apparatus. And if people identified the chief, or a judge, as belonging to the state, they behaved accordingly. He expressed a pragmatic view of current politics, not too dissimilar from the one articulated by high-ranking ministry officers in the capital. Thinking aloud in the semidarkness of the evening, drawing some abstract patterns with his foot in the dirt of the patio on which we were sitting, he wondered why, in this turbulent period, the people still managed to identify the community court with the state, when the tribunal's small building showed on the outside no evident sign referring to a political organization.

Other kinds of authorities, related to the customary, also participated in the struggle to guide people's everyday lives or to become the ones who restore order, thus providing that order with a particular orientation. In Khakhossani, Judge Nipante said, there were both a customary chief (*regulo*) and a *cabo* (lower level of customary authority, linked to land property), who in their daily endeavors supported RENAMO. The judge, when he mentioned this, sounded as though he deeply resented this situation in his own sphere of influence.

In the area, politics was played out through the attempts to impose a legal regime, a struggle to possess jurisdiction over the solving of legal cases. According to the judge, people submitted their conflicts first to the neighborhood secretary or to the various block secretaries, who would in turn send most of them to the community court. In reality, the interface between the political and the juridical proved to be more complex than this, as the competition over the provision of justice took place alongside a disrupted and very conflictive political terrain of antagonisms.

The process constituted a circuit connecting political allegiances with the search for justice: a person who supported RENAMO or plainly opposed the government/state/FRELIMO would submit her conflicts and quarrels to other para-state forms of sovereignty: chiefs, RENAMO party officers, religious authorities. These juridico-political figures all implemented various legal regimes—influenced by customary law, Shari'a, or others—that diverged from those espoused by the authorities of the minor state. Only those people who supported FRELIMO appeared before institutions that bore the symbols of the state (and, hence, of the governing party, which was considered almost its synonym). The legal regime enforced by these governmental authorities, despite its articulation with an elusive sense of "local tradition" (kinship rules, religion, magic beliefs and ceremonies, custom), was constructed around fragments of a past Socialist ethos. The residues of this elusive ideology were aimed at constructing a sense of shared political community under the guidance of a centralized structure. The kind of law enforced by the institutions of the minor state was a loose, almost improvised set of norms that, juxtaposed with aspects of the customary, aimed at providing the cement for such a polity.

Working at a juncture between the political and the law, the minor state (secretaries, community court judges) attempted to exert a potential power, control and surveillance, while at the same time delivering justice. Within the space of the neighborhood, nevertheless, its alleged sovereignty was contested, opposed, and at times simply dispensed with. This peripheral area, Khakhossani, is situated not far from the heart of the city, where the base of the provincial government and the vicarious representation of the central state were located. The area nevertheless constituted an intermediate space between the locus of the government's power and a territory where the population has consistently been opposed to it throughout the last decades.

The minor state worked in a conflictive terrain with regard to governmental practices in the field of justice. It was an embattled space where different kinds of political authorities aimed at imposing their sovereignty over legal matters. Often the population conflated the community court with the whole of the minor state. More importantly, the issue of the law can shed light on crucial aspects of the political in this area: the deliverance of justice seemed to be understood as the circulation of some substantial mode of sociality that restores order. In any given district, these juridico-political authorities might include FRELIMO and RENAMO, party units, secretaries, community courts, religious authorities, and a large hierarchical cohort of customary authorities (*regulo, cabo, mwene,* etc.).

## Minor State IV: Judges

Five judges worked in 2004 at the community court in the neighborhood of Khakhossani. Several of them, like the president-judge and Simao Nipante, were originally from the same hinterland district. Recounting the story of his life Nipante referred time and again to the town in which he was born. By then, I had already gathered that this area held the key to several aspects of the functioning of the minor state.

Mesagane is a district in the province's hinterland, and hence, unsurprisingly, the first allusions to it that I heard in the courtroom drew the usual contrast between the characters of Makhuwa people, who are from the coastal areas, and of those from the interior of the region. The hearing of certain cases had included sarcastic and deprecatory comments on the nature of coastal folk. Later, I encountered other evocations of a rural district that, as it turned out, had been the cradle of several officers of the Khakhossani minor state. Obviously, the president-judge's hometown had to do with the source of the local state's legitimacy.

Hernando was also born in Mesagane. He was a man in his early forties, with bright vivacious eyes and a fine moustache. The president-judge labeled him "our prosecutor." Several days a week, he sat behind a small table in the main, dark, central room of the house, receiving cases and complaints, meticulously registering names and facts, setting appointments for the cases to be heard, and collecting the 20,000-meticais (equivalent to almost one US dollar) fee for each case.

Hernando had lived and studied abroad, and he timidly boasted about this when we chatted during a long walk through the neighborhood that I took with all the judges. Like thousands of other Mozambicans of his age, Hernando was sent at age sixteen to study in the former East Germany. He claimed to have visited several countries, including in his account all the places where his flight stopped for an hour on its way to Berlin. In a small East German city he studied for his bachelor's degree in engineering. He spoke some English and was apparently fluent in German.

After he returned to Mozambique, he attempted to work for the police. But his long experience abroad paradoxically (was it envy or, perhaps, a genuine concern for him?) blocked his recruitment. "They said I was overqualified so they would not know what to do with me; for I had seen the actual 'cowboys' [criminals] fighting in real life—things they had only watched on TV." Today, thanks to his skills, Hernando is a clerk at a local factory, where he translates messages and contracts addressed to foreign companies. The president-judge called him "my nephew," referencing a younger aide born in the same area as himself.

Paulo was the judge who was closest to the president-judge. "My assistant, my right hand," the president-judge called him once when we were downing beers at the local marketplace. He meant a relationship of friendship and professional trust. Paulo was the writer, in charge of producing case records. He carefully noted down in longhand all the details of each argument and each complaint that emerged during the sessions—each case's precedents, unfoldings, declarations, and sentences—and kept hundreds of filed cases. Piles of files, folders, and notebooks cluttered the small table on which he worked every Tuesday and Friday. He performed his duty with sober, affected manners. A rather tall man, sometimes he raised himself above the desk to admonish the plaintiffs with a controlled violence, never losing his sardonic smile.

Deputy President Paulo was the only judge who was not from Mesagane; he was from Zambezia Province. And, unlike the other judges, he was not Muslim. One of the last times I had the chance to speak with him was when I ran into him one Sunday afternoon, amid a large crowd leaving in procession from the cathedral.

The other two community judges were Adelfo and Ignacio. The former was a sheik whose mosque was located a few kilometers from Khakhossani on the road that ran by the street market. There, he held religious meetings, weddings, and, on rare occasions, sessions of conflict resolution according to Islamic law, which was a practice more common in the coastal areas of the province than in the surroundings of the capital. A chubby character who wore T-shirts in very bright colors, Adelfo always rode a bicycle, invariably being the last one to arrive to the court's sessions. He was very soft-spoken and was rarely heard during sessions, though his colleagues eagerly waited for his isolated questions and thoughts, which were based on a deeply entrenched, cheerful common sense.

Ignacio was a short, strong, one-eyed man. Despite being quite poor—like the rest of the men on the tribunal—I will always remember him wearing the old but elegant blue jacket with only one button (along with dark trousers and red socks) that he had on the day we organized a session to take photographs. He worked at the military school in the city, a job he probably got through his connection with the president of the court, who had worked there for thirty years. He was the last judge to be incorporated into the tribunal, but by 2004 he was one of its pillars. During the cases, he listened quietly, for an entire hour sometimes, occasionally falling asleep during the declarations and interrogations, his head on his left hand, probably exhausted because of too much work and early risings, perhaps simply bored by the routine dynamics of the cases. Yet he spoke quite brilliantly in almost every case, usually in Makhuwa, developing very intricate arguments and conclusions that drew upon the slightest minutiae of the plaintiffs' declarations, painstakingly examining representations of desire and intonations of reason. He elaborated complex lucubrations that skillfully mixed various moral views, abstract reasoning, and judgments with the most prosaic, concrete facts of violence, emotion, or despair presented by the neighbors.

Although neighborhood residents who still supported or just feared FRELIMO had respect for these officers and submitted themselves and their conflicts to their authority, their official status was ambiguous, as figures located in interfaces between past and present political regimes, as well as between different fields of the local sociality: politics, religion, kinship. This liminal condition at times undermined, at times reinforced, their legitimacy and the work of the minor state.

On occasion, one judge would be included among the group involved in a trial, as a relative of one of the persons involved in the conflict. At those times relatedness and the law became closely entwined, the judge himself being the kin-based witness and jury member. Those situations made evident the entanglements between the state and the sphere of the domestic. For instance, the president of the Community Council acted as part of the family in a case in which his nephew was involved. The divorce of the couple mentioned earlier was dealt with in an intimate atmosphere in which the president of the court addressed another functionary as "nephew," and this person, in turn, referred to the woman involved in the case as his "niece." In another case, a judge gave his opinion on a divorce case speaking from his post behind the court's table, only to leap across the room an instant later to sit among his own relatives, at the back of the courtroom, behind his niece. This switching of positions and roles prompted aggrieved complaints from the family of the woman's husband.

One morning, before the session at the Khakhossani court began, Judge Nipante reminded the rest of the judges that he had to leave and therefore he would not be able to participate in the work of the day, as the divorce case of his own niece was going to be heard at another court, in Nakasiki neighborhood, a few kilometers away. As he was being granted permission to take a leave of absence for the day, I asked to be allowed to accompany him on his trip. The judges conferred for a few minutes and agreed to let me attend the sessions at another court. First of all, Paulo, the deputy president, had to produce an "official" certificate in longhand that explained to the other judges who I was, that I was affiliated with a local university and attended the court's sessions on a regular basis.

The judges began warning me that the other court might work differently or deficiently, that the judges there did not respect all the proper rites that I had grown accustomed to in this court. They seemed to fear the impressions I might formulate about the justice system if I became acquainted with the workings of other tribunals. With all these caveats, I walked with Judge Nipante for an hour, to another neighborhood, to a court that still had a sign outside bearing the old denomination "Tribunal Popular de Base de Nakasiki." At that court, to which I would return several times, I also observed the enmeshment of official formal law, a pedagogic morality, and kinship rules—a space of resonance for the exposition of most domestic and intimate matters, a place where state law harnessed "traditional" subjectivity, to be reversed in its turn, co-opted by custom.

Different social fields intersected and overlapped, as signs of a fraught recent political history. One evening, after a long conversation with Judge Nipante, in which for the first time we mentioned issues related to sorcery, spirits, and invisible realms, he told me, as I was about to leave the house, and not looking at me but at a distant point, "If you're interested in those issues, then you should talk to the president-judge of the court."

## Minor State V: The President-Judge

He stepped into the house through the back door, the one that opened onto the hill, the neighborhood, the huts down the road, and the purple mountains in the far distance. We had been awaiting his arrival for a while. He was rarely delayed, people told me, unless he was busy at home, still seeing persons in relation to his other occupation. When he finally arrived, he was agitated, nervous. A drunkard had been harassing him, attempting to pick a fight, a few blocks away from the courthouse. "We need a police force here at the tribunal, like the one we used to have years ago. How are we to be sure that the law is followed? How are we to find suspects and bring them to the court? We even need protection for ourselves; people resent us and every once in a while we come under attack."

He slowly calmed down and got ready to begin the day's work. He walked around the house, greeting the secretary with formulaic half jokes, looking at the cases that the young "prosecutor" has been filing for today's session. He glanced at the several people gathered outside the house to wait for him. Acting like the true master of this ruined house, he seemed to look after everybody.

He was a strong man, in his early sixties. On this day he wore the same brown pants and yellow shirt with arabesques that he sometimes sported for several days in a row. His impressive figure exuded an aura of authority, which he reinforced through the theatrical nature of his movements, his emotive yet imposing tone of voice, the looks—at times fierce, at times playful—that he gave to the plaintiffs and defendants.

When he recounted the story of the tribunal at my request, the president-judge began by evoking the violence that underlies the application of the law, for instance, at places like this court. He alluded to those forces that guarantee its enactment: "Where you sit now, at every session, there used to always be two men from the People's Militia [Socialist police–foot soldiers]. Then, *in Samora's time*, people respected us more. Now, you see how people behave at the court, in an absolutely disrespectful manner. In those years, there was fear and people respected the state."

Yet, these days, walking around the area along with the judge, being present at random conversations he held with various neighbors, going out to have more private conversation with him over a drink, accompanying him to some official appointment in the city, and talking with various people at their homes, discussing the court sessions, one got the sense that he was accorded a steady level of respect. Amid the political battlefield that was the neighborhood, the competition for hegemony between local political and religious authorities and the various overlapping legal regimes, the president-judge of the court stood out as a figure of power. He was well known in the area and most people acquiesced to his words.

For people who supported FRELIMO in the area, the authority of the president-judge was undeniable. One neighbor, who had a precarious carpenter's shop on the edges of the district, insinuated that his legitimacy arose from his long-standing career in the minor state, that people recognized his work and effort since he occupied low-ranking posts in the FRELIMO system. Yet other people, who lived closer to the court, suggested in passing that his recognition and ascendance originated in a rather different field, his other profession. This endeavor, which the Socialist cadre called his "private occupation," as opposed to his "state job," was a craft related to invisible deeds and causes and inquiries into the future.

It might be said that there were intricate overlaps between his two professions. Uncovering someone's complex designs and determining the accuracy of some piece of evidence or the justness of an action and the reaction to it informed both his labor at the tribunal (as custodian of the state's law, of a certain ethos of the Socialist project) and the work he performed daily at the small hut located outside his house, which he called "my laboratory of tradition." For the president-judge of Khakhossani's community court was also, reputedly, the main diviner and healer in this area.

After the mysterious remarks of Judge Nipante, I also heard comments about this situation from people I interviewed about how their conflicts were solved at the court. Conversations with members of two families about the few discussions of sorcery accusations held at the court led to some ambiguous references to the judge's fierce authority being based on invisible powers.

A few months after the beginning of my research, when time had accomplished its patient labor, and confidence and some shared emotion had created the proper space, I was, indeed, going to be ushered into his hut, despite his reservations ("You are the first white person that I have received here . . . and I wonder what it is that you are seeking . . . and if you are going to betray me"). On a gray, chilly afternoon, we sat outside his house (made of square mud bricks and with a straw roof) while two of his sons constantly went in and out through the small, low door (it was so low that one had to completely bend over to get in). The hut was located a few steps away from the house, by a tall tree and near some barbed wire that marked the end of his small piece of land. A short distance away his wife and her cousin were kneeling, whispering, drinking some kind of infusion.

Inside the circular hut, a random collection of objects was the setting for the deployment of magic: a straw mat on the floor, the mud pans for the oracles, and, hanging from the walls and roof, many plastic bags holding all kinds of colorful substances and plant material. An enormous collection of small objects were scattered over the floor, everywhere, creating a galaxy of sorts, keeping some secret, disorganized order. It was very dark inside the hut, and the door had to be left slightly ajar to allow in some sunlight. A stool squatted in the corner, for the many visitors—patients—to sit upon and await the prognosis. Lying on the mat, with his legs outstretched, the judge-diviner performed his craft. Here, he seemed transformed from the man who worked at the court twice a week. His facial expression suddenly changed, illuminated by a strange smile. His main activity consisted of divination by means of an oracle, for which he prepared himself for a few minutes by chewing and inhaling some local tobacco, achieving such a degree of concentration that he almost entered into a trance. Other endeavors included crafting talismans (folded letters written in Arabic that include numbers, symbols, and charts) and preparing healing substances with plants and herbs to cure either minor health problems or deep ailments of the soul. But the main activities he accomplished were his predictions of future events, the investigation of secret actions, and the inquiry into dark sorrows.

There were very few continuities between his two fields of activity: divination and justice. Instead of both spaces being interconnected, channeling conflicts and cases from one to the other, actually a deep fracture existed between the world of invisible justice and the world of legible law: "that is my day job, the labor I perform at the state; this is my private work." Although he inhabited both spaces, he kept his labor as an adjudicator of conflicts and his labor as a diviner, a magic healer who reads oracles, absolutely separate.

At the court, where cases related to the alleged action of invisible forces are presented regularly, the judge avoided an overlapping of functions. There was no intersection between the spiritual practices of divining

the future or curing bodies and souls and those related to juridical interrogations, to different insights and predictions into healing the wounds
opened up by conflict.

Other features of that clear distinction between the contiguous spaces
of law and magic emerged during a conversation I held with the judge on
another occasion when I visited him at his house. We came out of the hut,
after discussing oracles, divination, and substances, and both of us were
sitting on mats on the ground, engaged in a long conversation, drinking
large cups of fermented rice beer. As the afternoon slowly died away and
a cool breeze blew from the west, he recalled aspects of his biography
that illustrated the fragmentary logic of articulated layers of life—such
as politics, law, and violence—as experienced recently in this region. At
some point during our exchange, he went into his house and came back
carrying a blue folder containing several types of documents, each of them
narrating a different aspect of his life. The first piece of documentation
he handed to me was a precise marker of that strange dynamics by means
of which the fields of magic and legality were kept separate, in a delicate
sense of adjacency. To assure me that his endeavors as a diviner and healer
were utterly serious, he showed me, smiling with pride, an ID card that
officially certified that he—the president-judge of the local community
court—was also a fully recognized member of AMETRAMO (Association of Traditional Healers of Mozambique). This national union of sorts,
which gathers healers and diviners under the banner of "tradition," was
created in 1991, under the aegis of a FRELIMO regime that was beginning
to accept the need to reappraise customary beliefs and practices. Pointing
out his membership in this association, which is placed under the influence
of the ruling party, the judge was emphasizing the legality and accuracy
of his invisible craft. He stressed the legal status of his activity as certified
by the para-state institution that oversees his profession, an organization
supervised by units of the state apparatus.[17]

Though we met regularly at the court and sometimes went out for
drinks and conversations with other judges, whenever I visited him at his
house, my dialogue with the judge in his hut and "laboratory" concerned
only issues of magicality. To discuss issues strictly linked to the law and
the state, we restricted ourselves to conversations within the court. Another conversation held at his house, prompted by his musings over his
magical craft and his affiliation with AMETRAMO, alluded to issues pertaining to the complex relation between the state and the customary. We
talked about how the government used to oppose AMETRAMO in its
beginning, as it was considered to be part of all the obscurantist decadent

practices that had to be erased. He mentioned how, currently, local medicine men help to carry out health programs related to AIDS and other
diseases, working with NGOs and state units alike. I informed him about
a new policy being developed in the capital by the Ministry of Health
in an attempt to incorporate traditional medicine into state programs.[18]
This took us on a detour into the current reappraisal of the customary
undertaken by the post-Socialist state. He began to second-guess me and
evade answering me, as though again suspicious of my interest. In a region
like northern Mozambique, to talk about these seemingly utterly ordinary
facts conjures up a whole recent history of oppression and war. Later, the
judge's remarks would yield vivid images of this deathly history in which
the customary (chiefs, ritual norms) played a central role in a civil war
that involved ceremonies held by diviners to communicate with invisible
forces, the performance of rites of war, the circulation of magical substances, and the invocation of invisible weapons among soldiers. And yet
despite those continuities between magic and the political in the history
of the region, the judge insisted that his work at the community tribunal
was conducted according to the law, independent from any influence of
spirits.

Continuing my conversations with the judge, the references to questions of law and the customary led to the issue of yet another identity card.
One time, to illustrate who he was and where he came from, he handed
me a very small notebook of sorts, which contained a photograph and
a few pages with formulaic sentences, names, and signatures, along with
numbers and official seals, folded between two brownish covers. It was an
identity card from 1955 issued to a certain Mucimbo.[19] The fierce face of
this man appeared on the wrinkled, yellowed pages of the old ID, wearing
the mandatory hat that was part of the uniform provided to chiefs by the
state. The judge proudly showed me that document, through which the
man was recognized by the colonial state as a *regedor*, the official title for
the higher rank in the hierarchy of customary chiefs in charge of local government functions. This man was the judge's maternal uncle, a key figure
of authority not only in the restricted space of matrilineal kinship relations but also in the more general sense of local political power orders.[20]
When the judge was in his late teens, he was the chief's closest nephew and
also his aide with regard to various political functions.

The contiguity between state and customary in the region was also
shown by the fact that the judge constantly emphasized a division between
his two different endeavors by boasting about the state's endorsement of
his activities in the realm of the invisible.

From colonial and early postcolonial times to the post-Socialist context, the dynamic relation between the state and the customary involved a complex game of alternate articulation and distancing, within a historical context marked by continuities between war and the political. In Nampula, high moments of this dynamics were, for instance, the appointment of many customary chiefs as agents of local government immediately after the anticolonial struggle and, a decade later, the support given by so many chiefs to RENAMO during the civil war, in opposition to FRELIMO's ban on the customary.

Life experiences such as the president-judge's suggest a more nuanced actuality of the customary, beyond the mere fact of its codification by colonial history. Instead of historical processes being the explanatory source of the negative dialectics of customary and state, that dyad seems to be the actual foundation of events at the regional level: a veiled engine of historicity that stems from that very agonistic relationship. History unfolds through a political combat of enmity and attraction, of desire and mutual seduction, between the state apparatus and the customary.

Individual lives embody this historicity. The president-judge's life conjoins several political epochs and shows the unfolding of a local history of domination and articulation between the law and custom. Justice is precisely a crucial realm from which to observe the political transformations of the last decades. Not only have successive legal reforms rewritten a historical narrative of the nation-state, but they have also constituted strong interventions in that historicity; they have been true performative discourses that shaped the imagination of political events.

These events were mirrored in the split subjectivity of the president-judge, a case of "customary citizenship" in itself. He narrated the history of the neighborhood court, describing it in his peculiar, metaphoric language as a pictogram of the intricate connection between historicity and juridical regimes. According to the way he described his court as being located at the edge of the law, it embodied the potential of the present and the unfulfilled promises of the postindependence moment.

The dynamics of the courts showed that in the context of a state immersed in deep crisis, in institutions that were residues from already-superseded regimes, justice was sustained only by the sheer quotidian effort of a group of former local officers. In the view of the ex-Socialist judges, despite what could be seen as errors, petty ambitions, or shortcomings, thirty years after the launch of national independence and after a civil war, they considered themselves to be still attempting to circulate and share an element that carried with it the promise of justice.

# CHAPTER FIVE

# Poetic Justice

This chapter explores ways in which the minor state constantly reconstructs its legitimacy through the performative work of the court that blends custom and official law through an entanglement of orality and writing. It describes the ethics and aesthetics of an everyday enactment of "customary citizenship" in the locality, which illuminates central aspects of a nation-state immersed in deep political transformations.

The sections describe the place of the community court within multiple jurisdictions of conflict resolution. It presents the voice involved in jurisdiction, examining how the law, as the official discourse of the nation-state, is refashioned through its implementation in the locality. It describes a ritualized aesthetic put in place to constantly reconstruct the legitimacy of the state in the locality. The analysis of the work of community courts sheds light on national and regional political processes, such as lacunae, anachronisms, and paradoxes of the post-Socialist transition.

The various sections record the speech of the community judges and plaintiffs, narrating a history of the state and its legal foundations from the perspective of the place that "tradition" occupies within the court. The theatrical rituals and rhetoric involved in the quotidian enactment of justice at the court constantly aim at reconstructing state legitimacy. Through them an elusive element of justice circulates, shaped by repetition and deferral, different from the linear temporality of the force of law.

## Dislocated Law

"That is the limit of the law . . . ," the president-judge of the community court said to me one afternoon, after the day's work had ended and we were standing outside the house, discussing trial sessions. With ample sweeps of his arms he was indicating some fences that lay a few meters beyond the old building housing the court. He explained further: "The law ends here. It is applied only within the territory of the city. Further out there, in the countryside, they do all sorts of other things. . . . They enforce the law of the ancestors. . . . They do 'tradition,' 'custom'; they have *regulos*. . . . They do not search for the one who knows the law but privilege the one who knows culture. . . . There are community courts but they do not implement the law; rather, *they still even do FRELIMO*."

Two meanings of these limits, as strict territorial boundaries or actual limitations of the law's reach, blended in local political struggles. As the judge's remarks illustrated, the extent to which a form of law associated with a state-sanctioned juridical regime was actually enforced was determined by reference to the orbit of urban political institutions.

The neighborhood was for the local state officer the exclusive site for the implementation of the law, with the house of the minor state standing as the point in space that condensed these juridico-political relations. Beyond the city's periphery, in the rural areas, a plurality of other norms held sway, remainders from various histories, with only a loose relationship to any practice associated with the state apparatus.

The spatial frontiers also signaled the limits of legality. The urban/rural divide that was a crucial juridico-political technology of high colonial governance still delimited, thirty years after independence, the process of granting full citizenship by the state. The letter of the law was contested by the quotidian flow of population that traveled back and forth through the region, constantly crisscrossing, as in the colonial past, the various spaces that the law codified. Yet, the subject's position with respect to the juridical distinction between urban and rural areas determined the exercise of various rights associated with the fact of belonging to a nation-state.

During conversations I held with neighbors who attended the court's sessions and in brief interviews conducted at their residences, they would also share a view in which the loose limits of the neighborhood, signaled by random markers, like a building, a road, or a stream, coincided with the limits of the law. Many of them were originally from the not-too-distant rural hinterland or still had family living in the villages, and they referred to the ways in which *milandos* (conflicts) were dealt with or solved there in relation to the authority of custom, elders, and chiefs. They related the term for "conflict" to the various local terms for and senses of "justice," leaving the concept of "law" to refer to official sanction, the state, and FRELIMO structures, akin to the situation in the urban and periurban areas, where a frail imaginary of the state still attempted to impose legitimate authority

amid its quotidian struggle against a host of other local actors that had
RENAMO as its main, if loose, reference.

The struggle over legal jurisdiction in the neighborhood represented
a condensed version of the dichotomous conflict shaping the imagination
of the central state. The neighborhood was a liminal space, a frontier land
between law and other norms, where an emergent "customary citizenship" was molded by the articulation of a politics linked to the central
state and a micropolitics deployed at the level of the body and subjectivity.
As shown by the experience of people attending the court's sessions, this
conjunction took place not in terms of state-defined scale but under the
modality of a minor politics, one in which law and life (body, relatedness,
sexuality, emotion) coalesced in a dimension of subjectification, where a
legal regime is instilled onto the matter of the body, its flesh, its desire.
Let us examine how the possibility of justice circulates through this body
politic.

## Circuits of Justice

A divergence emerges in a corner of the neighborhood. It might be a violent falling out between friends, a mild disagreement between neighbors,
a case of debt or theft, or a sorcery accusation. Or conflict arises within the
austere limits of a household, as the contingent explosion of a process that
has been building up for a long time.

The quarrel may concern a falling out between a disagreeing couple.
Divorce cases involving resentment and debt are most common. In these
cases the court aims at attaining a reconciliation or an orderly separation
and makes sure children are registered with official institutions. A case of
divorce often involves domestic violence. The bare space of a hut, scattered family relations, or a few belongings are also usual objects of dispute. Abuse of alcohol, disease, misery, or the emptiness of a monotonous
life without hope are often the background in which the bitter argument
emerges.

The case is always the localized origin of jurisdiction, whereas locality
constitutes the origin of the postcolonial nation. The universal authority
of the law has to be tested through the encounter with the singularity of
a case, in the same way as the sovereignty of the state has to be enforced
on the locality in order to gain legitimacy. The crucial test for jurisdiction
takes place by means of the passage through the narratives constituting a
legal case. The relation between the law and a case infuses contingency

into codification and instills chance into the teleological history of territorialization inherent in jurisdiction. The universal spirit of the laws must
"fall"[1] into the experience of the singular[2] concrete materiality of local
jurisdiction.

In the African postcolony a case is located within a maze of legal authorities, as jurisdiction cannot organize its place of evaluation. In a periurban neighborhood in northern Mozambique, for instance, a case can be
allocated to one of several competing sovereignties. National history influences the sense of everyday life in the locality. Depending on whether the
plaintiffs or their families side with FRELIMO or RENAMO, or on which
side the civil war located them, they will lean more toward "custom" or
toward official "law." Their quarrel will then be directed toward different
types of legal or political authority. According to political allegiances or
religious dispositions, the disagreement is taken to political units or state
courts, chiefs, sheikhs, or a group of elderly neighbors.

Other examples of cases show the malleability of conflict resolution,
which might include other authorities or units. In one instance, a man, an
ex-combatant from the liberation struggle, had not attended the court
sessions, even though the court had summoned him three times. His
nephews were involved in the fraudulent selling of a piece of land. The
community court submitted this case to the police station and then to the
official city tribunal. In another case, a local sheikh came to the court to
participate in a dispute that involved his relatives and a piece of land in
the periphery of town. Only the two main judges were present at the court,
so the president-judge, given the relevance of the case and the people involved, asked the neighborhood secretary to join in the discussion.

The first locus for dealing with a quarrel, in an attempt to reconcile
the different parties, is constituted by extended kinship structures, which
might include neighbors. Within this first space of customary law, the elders encase the dispute within the norms sanctioned by tradition, which
in this periurban area is influenced by modalities of state normativity (colonial and postcolonial). This is observable in the recent weakening of
the once firm scheduling of ceremonies and in structures of matrilineal
inheritance and cohabitation, debilitated under the influence of state intervention and cultural modernization.

In this periurban environment the networks of state power are pervasive, and families appeal to them in cases where the conflict exceeds the
boundaries of kinship structures and the moral economy. Most commonly,
the block secretary is called up as a representative of the lowest levels of
the state apparatus to attend a dispute in a domestic space. Invested with

the authority of some kind of state power, the secretary can attempt to solve the conflict in conjunction with the families, or he can refer it to other loci of juridical rule, such as the police station or the community court.

Good sense, local history (including incidents regarding personal relations as well as kinship ties), and stylizations of customary law that originate in the areas from which the families come constitute the frame for conflict resolution and reconciliation. The intervention of a state authority such as the block secretary illustrates local governmental practice in the maintenance of social order at the microlevel within the neighborhood. This takes place through the invocation of a grammar of kinship rules imbued with vague ethico-political remainders of a Socialist commonality, as an imaginary of the state aiming to ensure support for the ruling party in the locality.

Through other sites of the minor state, such as block or neighborhood secretaries, neighbors become acquainted with the existence and the work of the community court, which otherwise could be deemed distant or too difficult to access. There are also complex connections between formal units of the local state in the urban downtown and the minor state in the periphery of the city. Sometimes the community court, submitting a legal document, can also refer a case to the police station or to the formal "official" state district court.[3] Other times, different types of cases mark the complex disconnections between the court and other local forms of conflict resolution. For instance, even if sorcery accusations are brought to the court, in line with the previous Socialist policy against the customary, the community court, along with the neighborhood secretary, merely organizes ordeals that will require bringing diviners from a faraway area and organizing the ceremony of ingestion of *mwekathe*, a magical substance made of cereal that is supposed to unveil the guilt of sorcery. The judges will not ponder abstract questions of invisible worlds or consider magical issues as a legal matter; they pass judgment or suggest reconciliation only when there has been a confession that can be taken as actual material evidence. For instance, in May 2005, a block secretary ("Communal Unity Minuapala," 17 blocks, 5,275 inhabitants) attended the court's sessions to solicit the judges to speed up the resolution of a sorcery accusation that had been presented to the court two years earlier. The case had stalled, and the two sides were about to resort to physical attacks. The judges refused to preside over the case and demanded several times that the secretary raise the money needed to organize the sorcery trial, bring expert sorcerers from another district, and so on, but he had not done so.

In July of the same year, the court was asked to organize an ordeal following a sorcery accusation. Once again the judges delegated the authority over the case to the neighborhood secretary. The judges demanded that "results" should be obtained through healers from a distant district. The family demanded that the accused people "pay the bill" and give some monetary compensation for this offense and also that they move far away from the neighborhood. The court contacted an Administrative Post (formal local state unit) in a nearby district to arrange the move.

When a case finally arrives at the community court, the procedure is as follows: Three days a week (the days on which the court works and one other day), the "prosecutor" Hernando receives complaints and gives the litigants a white paper with a blue seal, which has a written appointment summoning the person to appear in a few days' time before the court, along with the other party, usually accompanied by several relatives of each. The plaintiffs must fill out a small form with their names and other data and pay a 20,000-meticais fee (almost one US dollar). They also give a succinct oral account of the case, from which the prosecutor produces a written report that the judges will take into account when the case is heard. Sometimes both parties involved arrive together at the court to fill out a complaint. More often, it is one of them—the plaintiff—who files a case. He or she must ensure that the other party—the defendant— appears at the time of the hearing. I was present on two occasions when something somewhat extraordinary occurred: before the offended party approached the court, the defendant filed a case that would be pursued against himself.

A few days later, the same people will be standing outside the court, waiting for their case to be dealt with. Their opponents—neighbors, friends, relatives—will be standing a few meters away from them, whispering, looking at the floor or gazing into the distance.

At about eight o'clock one morning, the judges themselves tidy the room in which the sessions will be held. The attorney Hernando helps them and then rapidly goes back to take up his post, ushering people into the house. He hears complaints, narratives of quotidian dramas of pain, violence, theft, or debt, which he writes down on small cards. The president of the court suddenly stands up from his seat inside the room, walks around with abrupt movements, and orders that the people involved in the first case and their families be brought in. The second judge in the court's hierarchy steps out of the house, to the shadowy verandah in front of it, calls in a loud voice the names of the people involved in the case, and asks them whether it is a "complete" case, that is, whether everybody involved and their families are present. The ceremonious movements of the judges exaggerate a solemn formality that imbues the small court, alternating statements and silences as if to consolidate an effect of legitimacy.

The door opens and everything starts once again. People enter the room silently. With minimal gestures the judges indicate to them where to place themselves. As they sit one by one, it becomes evident that these are people who are undergoing complex and sad situations. They occupy their places with expressions of deep melancholy. Serious, looking at the floor, most of the people involved in trials at the court give the impression of being under duress, experiencing tension and fear in the face of a state institution and the obligation of exposing their anxieties and conflicts.

The president-judge leads the session. He begins by asking the complainant her version of the facts and expectations. Time and again he inquires about the truth. "Is that true?" "Is she speaking the truth?" The labor of the judge involves constructing a certain truth from many perspectives and reasons, with plural causes and effects. A negotiated truth emerges out of the witty rhetoric and theatrical gestures of the judge and the calculated way in which he addresses in turn the different participants of the trial.

The statements succeed one another: accusations, defenses, shortcuts, detours, and returns. The procedure resembles that of a trial at a state court, albeit several steps—interrogations, depositions, agreements, and sentences—are conflated into a single one. The discussion of each case takes about one to one and a half hours. Normally, a case is solved in one meeting, although sometimes the judges will summon the people once or several times more to the court, until the case is finally resolved, which in general means that the litigants have reached an agreement.

During the hearing of the case, the president-judge will lead the session in which he and the other judges interrogate those involved in the conflict; one by one, everybody—litigants and their relatives—will be asked to give their point of view. The two parties involved in the quarrel will speak of their particular concerns with respect to the case and the, material and immaterial, values included in the dispute. The relatives will inexorably engage in argumentations that exceed the individual perspectives of the two people involved in the case and will refer to a wider moral economy linked to kinship structures and ritual practice. Within the intricate folds of the case under scrutiny, what emerges is the imbrication of individual quandaries and dyadic relationships with larger moral obligations. These subjective aspirations and predicaments are articulated with a collective normativity defined by the judges or the families attending the trials as "our tradition."

The legitimacy of the law's rulings is also constructed through the ceremonious ways in which people conduct themselves during the trials. Everybody is told to act reverentially within the court. Besides body language, postures, and gestures, such as sitting still, this deference is enacted through orality, in the way the allowed, proper, words are uttered. The language used must be respectful, extremely polite, according due respect toward the legal ritual held at the court.

The litigants speak only when summoned to do so, as the court's rules do not allow them to talk to each other. If asked, they might speak several times, and after everybody involved in the case—litigants and their relatives—have spoken, it will be the turn of the judges. The president-judge, as the master of this juridical ceremony, addresses the other judges and invites them to interrogate the litigants and offer their views on the case.

## The Place of the Law

Throughout Nampula Province, twice a week at the same time, a plurality of spaces, be they old, small, settlers' houses, or some clearing in the woods under a tree, become spaces for the adjudication of justice. The community court in Khakhossani hears cases every Tuesday and Friday beginning around eight in the morning. The judges explained that in the early eighties the FRELIMO state had demarcated days, times, and modes of working at the court that continue at present.

On a Tuesday morning, with sunshine falling on this side of the neighborhood, there are teachers standing outside the school waiting to begin classes and kids running around shouting. In a few minutes they will be heard singing the new national anthem and reciting in a very loud collective voice the day's history lesson. And a few steps further on, people linger in small groups whispering, pausing, waiting for the court to begin its work. Inside the humble, decayed house, which bears no official symbol whatsoever, the court occupies a spacious quadrangle. It is almost in ruins, its dirty walls covered with damp stains.

It is 9 a.m., at the community court in Khakhossani. On the right of the hall, a cracked wooden door that does not open all the way leads into what is pompously called the "Room of Audiences and Trials," where the court holds its twice-weekly sessions.[4] It is a square room with two windows. One overlooks the white wall of the neighboring school, and for months, a small bench will always be set in front of this window for the anthropologist and his assistant, as part of the usual theatrics of the court sessions. The other window is located on the wall opposite where the judges sit and overlooks a larger portion of the landscape lying beyond the courthouse's front: the beginning of a road, houses and huts, trees. The ceiling is falling down in places, the walls are dirty and stained, the paint aged and cracked. Large spider webs are the sole ornament in two of the corners.

Many smells mingle within the darkened room. The scent of humidity from the walls meets that of the old, rotting wooden benches and mixes with a strong odor of sweat. There is a wire hanging from the ceiling, a power installation that does not work. There are two small tables and some precariously built wooden benches, with nails emerging underneath. In one of the corners, the attorney sits behind a table and receives complaints and cases from people. Within the four walls of the room, somehow justice arrives,[5] as do the silent, morose neighbors involved in small dramas and the jovial judges, stepping slowly over the dirt floor, full of particles of cement and dust that have fallen from the old ceiling. There is a charged ambience inside the room, where moments of extreme tension mix with times of general hilarity or joy and where, sometimes, after a discussion has ended and an agreement has been reached, the judges will invite the fierce opponents to shake hands and hug each other.

The Room of Audiences and Trials is a site of a theatrical performance of slow movements, routinely bureaucratic as well as delicately stylized. As the law itself, it articulates in one object an abstract universal and a concrete particular.[6] Sitting inside this room by the window, which lets in the sunshine, the hot breeze, and the noise, one can see five judges sitting, chatting and consulting each other, in front of a small group of people in silence. There are two wooden tables, a larger one for the president-judge and three other judges and a smaller one for the judge who is in charge of the written files. This judge, sitting to the side, is the adjunct or deputy president, the one who writes in the registers and is second in the hierarchy of the court after the president, or chief justice.

Next to the judges' table, a box holds pieces of evidence from several cases. Another table, next to the door, is the site of writing, where the adjunct judge sits alone, taking notes, registering the proceedings. Scattered across his table in an organized disorder are notebooks, folders, copies of legal codes, laws, issues of the *National Gazette*, colored pens, and endless sheets of paper. Behind the table where the judges work are benches and small tables with piles of aging, yellowed folders containing hundreds of dusty pages, records of cases that have been tried in the last few years.

Against the wall with the window, are several small benches for the relatives and neighbors, eyewitnesses of crimes and disputes, ad hoc judges, as
well as warrantors of future agreements.

Facing the tables, two rows of unevenly built wooden benches have
been placed as though mimicking the setting of a formal state court. The
two people involved in the trial will be seated in the first row. The positions are deemed important for the adjudication of justice. One day the
president-judge told a sheikh who did not want to see his authority diminished by his being involved in a case about land that "the community court
is the place where you sit side by side with your enemy."[7]

At 9:20 a.m. the door opens and everything starts. Two people come in.
The woman is dressed in a ragged yellow T-shirt and a bright green skirt
that has imprinted on it a large image advertising a national cell phone
company. The man has no shoes, only old, dirty brown pants and a white
shirt. His head is very small and round. Behind them appear five or six
persons, led by an older man wearing a colorful hat. In a matter of minutes I will learn that they are relatives from both families. It is a divorce
case. Two weeks ago the wife had destroyed the place of her husband's
lover. She burned the small shack and most of the mistress's belongings
after confirming that her husband had spent the previous day hiding there.
Discussions of adultery, sexuality, and domestic violence ensue. While this
case unfolds behind closed doors, outside the house handfuls of people
linger, sitting on the dirt or on the few half-destroyed steps leading up to
the house's small veranda, waiting for the slow, ceremonial court to con-
clude its deliberations.

When the court is in session, people sit outside on the veranda, waiting in small groups from the early hours of the morning. The door is an
interface between the inside and the outside of the law. The dirty, cracked
wooden door used to be green at some point in the past but is not anymore.
In decay, as is the rest of the house, it closes only by means of a small nail
with a twisted end. During working hours the door opens several times,
and through it enter the two or three people involved in a case and their
families. The spatial figure that emerges is repeated time and again; the
ritualistic recurrence plays a role in creating the effect of the law.

## The Future

Inside the house, a young, bearded man is sweeping the floor, as if engaged
in a grave dance. His face congealed in a serious expression, he moves

around the ample space of the main, central room, with a straw broom in hand. To the right, three older men sit, chat, occasionally making ironic jokes about each other, like mild blows: the judges also wait. Speaking at length with the judges about their work, regional politics, or their perceptions of the local people, one gets the impression of a never-ending opening toward the future, as though the Socialist ethic still lives on, and the post-independence project will one day achieve some of its promises. But sometimes through phrases or short remarks denoting despair or tiredness, they also convey the idea that, perhaps, the future already lies in a distant past.

The judges are sitting at their post, biding their time, waiting for another judge to arrive, waiting for nine a.m., to begin their work. They are placed on a sort of juridical stage, in which the community court erects its legitimacy around humble, almost minimalist paraphernalia that allude to an imagination of the state. Next to the table is a pole that used to have a national flag wrapped around it. Presently, two small banners hang from it, one white, one yellow, forgotten propaganda of the ruling party from the last elections, five years ago: "Together, toward a better future."

Beyond the slogans, during the work of the court itself, the allusion to state power and legitimacy is also patiently constructed through rhetoric: an interplay of verbal and written words that, whether during the unfolding of a trial or in the subsequent record of it, has multiple intricate layers. This may take place through the constant invocations of an ideology of the state that the judges make throughout the sessions ("this is the house of the government"; "the state does not approve of what is going on with these families") or through the handwritten headings, signatures, and formulaic phrasings, reminiscent of official state discourse, in the written case record.

The banners, the sign of sovereign power over a territory, of its limits and its exclusions, illustrate the continuity between the previous regime and the current democratic one. The national anthem and other symbols have been recently changed, but still today, both in the decrepit house that hosts the former People's Tribunals and in the palatial buildings of the capital ministries, the sovereign banner rises high. The Mozambican flag that was conceived in the Socialist period is still the national icon of the new democratic state, which has ceased to be a "people's republic." Still at present the flag portrays the AK-47 rifle and the plow, evoking the emancipation of rural work from corvée labor, a nascent nation of peasant-workers' power, and the violence of anticolonial struggle (turned the violence of civil war). Their silhouettes loom large upon the current dispensation and its promise of emancipation.

While the national flag is, indeed, usually present alongside the portrait of the national leader in most courtrooms (such as the other main one in which I conducted research, located in nearby Nakasiki neighborhood), the Khakhossani court's mast lacks the symbol of the nation. The black-and-white portrait of the president of the Republic, however, fiercely stares at everything, as though controlling every move in the room. It is the same photograph found everywhere in the nation-state. The eyes of the president seem to be looking over the horizon, or into the future, as though the time alluded to in the pennants is still looming. But time is running out and the future of that photograph taken in the early eighties is today.

Another case of conflict and debt between neighbors is being discussed. Meanwhile, a judge calculates the days that have passed since it was first presented to the court, as they decide that it will be continued two weeks later. He verifies the exact number of days and weeks of payments of installments of a debt ("they paid one hundred thousand meticais on the fifteenth") with the help of a calendar that is a sticker with FRELIMO electoral propaganda.

The ritual of justice that takes place inside the space of the court is akin to a politics of anachronism. If temporality is always a crucial feature of justice—as the president-judge often reminds the people at the community court—the time of the law in this case is a chain of disjoined moments. It adjudicates justice as though it existed in two phases of history, in two political eras, in two different spaces at the same time: the present democratic time, with its liberal institutions and its rule of law, and Socialist time, which unfolded between the moment of the anticolonial armed struggle (and the law of its liberated zones) and the zenith of Afro-Socialism, with its system of popular justice.[8] FRELIMO rule encompasses both juridico-political eras.

## The Ritual of Justice

"What? Repetition!" shouts the judge, when the members of a family leave the courtroom at the end of a case, only to enter again a few minutes later to participate in a different case, where they are once again accused of doing sorcery. The main accused person, the son of one of the women, is not present. "We will let him rest for a week, until the eighth, due to a death in the family."

Afterward, when the president-judge admonishes the neighbors, he enacts a pantomime by the way in which he moves his hands, weaving a choreography in the air with the firm movements of his hands that later will include his gaze and the words he utters. It is a pedagogic theatrics: "The tribunal entails an education," he affirmed a few times during sessions. There is a theatricality at work in the community court aimed at cementing the legitimacy of its position and the efficacy of its rulings. It takes place through a certain staging of the sessions, the movements of the judges and others, the set places that each person must occupy, and the order in which they speak. The reverential way in which people are expected to act within the court is part of this most austere scenery.[9]

At 11:35 a.m. the door opens and a new group of people enters the room. The adjunct judge solemnly asks them whether this is such-and-such a case and whether they had reached some agreement among themselves as the court had suggested two weeks ago (it is a case of theft among neighbors). Silently, with eyes fixed on nothing, they take their seats as they are ordered. Each of them, according to their connection to the case, occupies a specified place on the various benches that the judges have diligently polished and set up earlier this morning. A juridical script that structures the work of the court organizes the positions, the gesticulations, silences, and turns to speak according to a hierarchy among characters. The relatives from both parties involved in the trial play the role of witnesses, warrantors, auxiliary judges, and even jury. The families perform not only economic or juridical functions but also religious ones in the many cases involving the performance of ceremonies or dealing with various spirits (as in cases of sorcery or divorce). Day after day the judges perform the same moves and deal with the cases submitted through a system that prescribes improvisation within a fixed set of rules. The repetitive dynamics of the court involves almost scripted movements, steps, and gestures. This libretto, in which the norms of state law and customary law are entwined, prescribes the discourse and staged positionalities of the people present. The president-judge functions as the director at this theater-courthouse, coordinating the choreographies, dictating the allowed movements, and organizing the scene.

The judges wander about the room while the plaintiffs enter and occupy their places. The president-judge stands up abruptly, walks a few steps, looks around in all directions, and then disappears into the next, larger room. All these moves create suspense: it is a play with time, which becomes elastic—now slower, now faster—and in the process contributes to the theatrical weight of the law.

Rhetoric performs a central role in the work of the court. The judges' voices—representing the speech of the state, or jurisdiction—play with different tones, inflections, modalities. The voices are alternately amicable, inquiring, severe, or punitive according to the moment and the conversation. The way in which words are spoken is as important as what is actually being said.

The judges utter words that try to create an aura of ideological legitimacy of a distant government. These are voices of authority ordering the theatricality of the court and its fictive way of constructing a reality, channeling the circulation of a certain substance of justness. This is the space of the *spirit of the laws*: a promise, a hope, the intuition of an arrival, or the adjudication of an impartial and fair present.

That distilled element circulates endlessly throughout the courthouse, from word to word, gaze to gaze, from the portrait of the president to the same portrait stamped on the skirt of a woman. That metaphysical particle cements a social relation, a sense of belonging in a state. This spirit animates the functioning of the miniature theater of justice through circulation and repetition. The timing of the ritual shows the cyclic interruption of a certain order and its precarious restoration through an entwinement of law and custom, of official norm and kinship rules, or writing and orality.

## Letters

The court holds, piled against a wall, hundreds of files filled with miniature handwriting that patiently recount, in page after page, the deeds, the offenses, the debts, the promises, and the deceptions of the people involved in court cases. The court, as archive of sorts, gathers the registers written by the judge who, absorbed in a mechanic endeavor of transcription, seems to hold the key meaning of that writing. This writing adheres to the formalities of the invocation of state sovereignty. And yet, for whom is it written? In which economy is accounted the saving of that record?

This writing records the unfolding of conflicts over time. During a trial the president-judge admonishes a litigant, showing him the importance of the pieces of written evidence and the registers from previous sessions on the case. It is through writing that the exact nature of the court as a state unit is revealed. Beyond symbols or rhetoric, the handwritten headers of the file encapsulate each case, miming the language of an official record, such as those produced in state district courts, establishing the state's juridical sovereignty.

The headers record that the process has taken place in the "Republic of Mozambique" in the "Province of Nampula."[10] More specifically, the following header reveals the juridical location of "Tribunal of Khakhos-sani neighborhood," and this court is introduced under the sign "Ministry of Justice." A sign of a mimetic justice, the registers produced at the community court—an interface between "formal" and "informal" law—imitate the forms, procedures, and discourses of more institutionalized forms of state justice. The central state's ministries and courts located in the capital are a machinery of writing that projects its imprinted legal discourse throughout the nation—in laws, decrees, national gazettes, regulations, and myriad juridical documentation.

In the northern provinces, the handwritten pages of the files at the community courts, yellowed by the passage of time and the effect of humidity, constitute a writing on the margins. It is a calligraphy annotated at the frontiers of the nation-state, and at its juridico-political limits, where state sovereignty weakens, where its services are almost not present. In places such as this provincial court, a blurred governance and a different sense of citizenship begin to take effect, constructed out of disjoined political temporalities, out of the localized blending of state law with the norms of the customary.[11]

The records of the processes involve an encounter between calligraphy and cartography. The file is also a virtual map of the trajectory of each case since its inception and through all the micro-juridico-political institutions that it encountered until its arrival at the court. Each space leaves a trace behind, a written page that is incorporated into the final record: the registers from the local secretary, the police station, other courts. Pieces of evidence are also sometimes included, such as a declaration of good faith, a signed "act of commitment" toward the payment of a debt, or a "talisman" written in Arabic that contains astrological-magical signs, evidence in a divorce case involving sorcery.

The judges seldom invoke precedents, and yet there is an ad hoc use of previous similar cases in the way that the judges affirm to strongly take tradition into account for the resolution of cases. Customary law and state law, oral and written norms, blend in a commonly shared feature once again through the judges' respect for legal precedent.

Although the judges rarely invoke precedents, the written record is available to be consulted in future cases. In fact, after the day's load of

cases had ended, I have often seen the judges busy discussing among themselves the file of a previous conflict. The record is available for future in-
spection not only by some more or less abstract external officer but also
by the parties involved in the dispute, people who have agreed to obey the
court's mandate and to honor their enforced agreement.

## Another Writing

Within this legal field where state juridical practices mingle with customary norms, there exists as well another, parallel type of writing: a system
of inscribed signs that refer to other spirits, other laws. I had already heard
allusions to this scripture, usually in relation to local manifestations of
political power in which the occult had played a role. But the first time I
had the opportunity to observe this writing, it appeared in a startling yet
prosaic way.

I was flipping through the pages of a file when I encountered a minute
piece of paper holding a type of writing that, while belonging to a different
kind of law, was included within the registers of the legal case. Earlier, I
had accompanied the judges as they walked through the neighborhood in
order to take measures—literally—in relation to a divorce case. Indeed,
besides hearing once again the endless testimony of the involved parties,
the judges had to measure the piece of land, the dimensions of the house,
and various belongings that had to be divided between the spouses. The
kernel of the quarrel was the wife's intention to separate from her husband because he had allegedly performed sorcery against her with the
aim of murder.

We were all sitting outside the house in the blasting sun; the couple and
some relatives were sitting in the dirt, but the several judges, the neighborhood secretary (who had been asked to participate, in an out-of-the-
ordinary gesture), and I had been offered wooden chairs. While the judges
interrogated the couple and relatives once again, I studied the file with the
register of the case.

In a morose way, the spouses were discussing the violent events: the
woman wanted to get a divorce because she thought her husband wanted
her dead. And yet they were still living together while the separation was
being arranged and the belongings divided. I was leisurely turning the
pages and reading carefully, in order to understand more clearly the vicissitudes of the case. Suddenly, I found a little piece of paper, written in

fluorescent-gold ink, that had a circular drawing, a spiraling figure, and other small drawings in each corner and various sentences written in what might have been Arabic. The paper constituted a piece of evidence that the wife had submitted to the court as proof of the misdemeanors of her husband. Thus, among the several writings related to the conflict, the file also contained this other piece of magical writing, a talisman, by means of which, allegedly, the man had attempted to bewitch—and kill—his wife.

This piece of writing underwent several readings. At the beginning, the woman had found the paper in the home and had taken it to a sheikh, who was also a diviner, for him to examine. He had determined that it was a means for the husband to bewitch her, yet merely "in order to make her leave the house," according to the confession produced by the husband once his intentions were exposed.

I examined the talisman after the judges evaluated it. But yet to read does not always mean to understand the meaning of what is read. I was merely admiring the elaborate drawings without being able to decode the phrases supposedly written in Arabic. It exuded a peculiar aura, intended to achieve an intervention in the world by means of an invisible force. It was a performative language, inscribed on paper in order to produce an immediate effect, from a distance.

The talisman was included within a file that held several folios narrating the various trajectories of the conflict—from the home and the family to customary figures of power such as diviners and then to the local state, and within it from one legal and political authority to the other. Located within the labyrinth of those several juridical writings, the talisman also shed light on similitudes that existed between itself and a legal document, or between custom and the law. Indeed, performativity worked behind all these various legal writings. The talisman was a metonym of all those folios produced by various legal authorities, with their dutiful protocols and pompous handwritten headings, evoking the nation-state, also talismans of sorts; writings that produced effects of power, miming the language of the central state.

A case file is like a collage of a variety of pieces of paper, enclosing different documents, which bring together two types of writing. The talisman that bewitched the woman and the sentence regarding the man found guilty of the crime of commissioning that once-hidden document are instances of two metaphysical systems of writing aimed at producing effects on real lives.[12] The court had admitted the written talisman as evidence after a local sheikh had deemed it real, holding the fetish of magical writing to be a legal matter. Once again the orientation toward a modern spirit of the laws embraced within itself the dictates of other spirits, the rulings of other laws.

## The Archive

That other type of writing also has its place of documentation. The fourth judge does not fit at the table where the others sit. His desk is a very old trunk. It even bears the remains of an old sticker, almost completely effaced, possibly an advertisement or travel destination. The origins of the old dusty case are uncertain. Perhaps it had been there since the Portuguese settler owned the house, some forty years ago or so. It is not just an old suitcase or piece of furnishing. The judge sits there because he is in charge of this wooden case, which serves as the archive of the court.

I learned about its existence one morning after a day in which I had not attended the trials due to a slight illness. My assistant related to me the events of a case of divorce and domestic violence that we had been following for three weeks. She told me that the "evidence" from that case—a pair of dirty, ripped, gray trousers and an old, dirty shirt—was being kept by Judge Nipante in a wooden box.

Indeed, when I inquired about the peculiar box cum table, Nipante informed me that it was, in fact, the court's archive. He explained that, for obvious reasons, the evidence that was the centerpiece of certain cases had to be kept for a whole year after the cases had been adjudicated. He signaled the tattered clothes: "These were damaged by a woman who was jealous of her husband." Then he referred to a "drug" that he was keeping inside the archive, the term signifying the substance through which sorcery was done.

On a clear morning, sitting next to him (I always sat beside him, my back to a glassless window) half an hour before the work of the day started, I observed that Nipante had opened the archive and was organizing and classifying its contents. I wondered whether he had opened it, in a matter-of-fact way, just to show it to me. By that time, we had become somewhat closer, and as there was more trust between us, Nipante was more loquacious and explained many more things to me about the court and the judges' experience.

That time, as he took out all the objects one by one, I saw, as in a mad collector's album, the archive's interior.[13] There were clothes, pieces of paper, a pipe, small glass bottles. One particular thing struck me. He showed me the "drug" involved in a sorcery case. It was not a substance to be

consumed—liquid or otherwise—but a garment, a colorful one, in bright
purple and yellow. Even though the drug or substance of black magic that
was being referred to was no doubt immanent within that piece of cloth-
ing—drenched in it or otherwise—the quality of the concept of "drug"
had been concretized in a double move: from "spirit" (sorcery force, being) to substance (drug) and from this to "thing," a most sensuous thing, a
brightly colorful silky cloth. He also showed me another drug. This time it
was a small green handkerchief that was folded in a knot and held something inside.

The archive that Nipante held accommodated not letters but things.
There were, indeed, dozens of dusty files with written registers of cases
piled against the wall, on benches, behind the place where the judges sat.
But there was in this case a mimetic use of signs and names from the imaginary of the state. Within that frame, the concept of "archive" was reserved
for that compendium of objects.

If an official archive is always a metonym of the state, if its collections
aim at coinciding in an imaginary, ideological way with the state's territory,
what was the relationship between this box full of objects and the state
component of the community court? If the archive is always intended as
a miniature of the history of the state, what did this small box of fetishes
stand for?[14]

The house, which represented a vanished state that still lives on in a
kind of afterlife, kept (besides the written files) in its "archive" a different
kind of historical evidence. It was the history of a condition that blended
official law and other, local, traditional norms, inscribed on things, among
which the "drugs" clearly stood out. That substance-object, the drug, held
the key to the mystery of the archive and, in a sense, to the functioning of
the court. Not only did it crystallize an underlying relationship between
magic and jurisprudence, between the occult and legality, but it also represented a larger process that took place within the tribunal: the way in
which abstract concepts became concretized.

In the judge's words, a drug had been materialized in a thing that could
be *worn* instead of in a substance that could be *inhaled or ingested*. This
local customary logic sheds light on the functioning of state law. Indeed,
within the court, a spirit—the supposed force of evildoing—became materialized in an object, in the same way as the ethical substance of justice
allegedly becomes the state[15] concretized in the material spaces of state
units, as the spirit of the laws.

Thus, the wooden box of the archive is a cipher of the court as a historical product of this region, as an institution reproducing customary citi-

zenship of oral and written norms. Besides the box, there are hundreds of written cases, stories, depositions, affidavits, and sentences. A large archive in itself, the court holds files, cases, juridical writings, remembrances, registers of small dramas and quarrels, arranged and worked out through various kinds of norms. The court constitutes, through constant performance, both the abstract space and time of justice and its concrete location.

## A Matter of Time

Everything seems to stand still, immobile. The judges and the people seem to represent already-predetermined roles within empty positions, as though we were inside a miniature theater where the individual spaces of the judges, plaintiffs, and witnesses, although unique, have been organized before and act in quotidian dramas that unfold without reference to the various subjectivities present. The sessions at the courthouse are not the final staging of a play; they are, rather, an endless series of rehearsals. Within this delayed temporality, the law and sociability seem to stand still.

It is Tuesday, 10:30 a.m. A case has just ended; the people are slowly exiting the courtroom, one by one—first one family, then the other one. Now the door opens and the protagonists in another case enter the room; they all look very serious, almost sad, as they take their seats, guided by the judge's gestures.

Each case takes, on average, about one hour. That time includes the declaration of each person involved in the quarrel and two or three contrapuntal dialogues between judges and claimants. After each of the judges has stated his point of view, the testimony of the relatives (five or seven from each family, though sometimes not all of them speak) is heard.

There is a precise timing at work within the performance of justice. Each person must speak, one at a time. First are the declarations of the people involved in the case and their answers to the questions of the president-judge, who is always the first to speak and who determines each person's turn. Then, the relatives speak. Afterward, a general question-and-answer session takes place between the judges and all the people present.

It is crucial for the adjudication of justice to establish certain measures of time, regarding the exact dates of the beginning and the end of relationships, conflicts, debt. For instance, at the unfolding of a divorce case, both the troubled couple and their families are asked to provide exact dates of marriage, the duration of the prenuptial period of acquaintance, the times when the couple consulted with both families, and the length of the sacrificial ceremonies held before the "traditional wedding."

At 11:30, a woman gives her testimony in a case regarding the theft of a scale. The president-judge carefully takes notes as she states the dates on which the relevant actions took place. The judge then compares these dates against the memories of the man accused of the theft.

The movements are slow and words are uttered in an unhurried manner. The time of the law unfolds in this small room as in a theater but also as in a bureaucratic office, where a routine-like schedule takes place, day after day, hour after hour, through which the time of the law unfolds inexorably through meticulous acts. Hour after hour, the cases follow each other in a slow—at times tense, at times joyous—way. The normal workday extends from eight in the morning until one or two in the afternoon, sometimes ending earlier if there are fewer cases. The judges do not call it a day until all cases are resolved.

On a Friday afternoon, after a day of work, evidently tired, speaking slowly, one or two of the judges would point toward the road and beyond it, toward the neighborhood, and they would call it "the factory," meaning that although the day's caseload was completed, during the weekend the neighbors would patiently construct violent struggles and intricate arguments for the judges to deal with the following week. Sometimes, for one reason or another, a case is postponed for a week or two. If so, the president might realize with frustration that the case has reached a dead end and abruptly summon the people to the court the following Friday, at eight in the morning. Sometimes cases are postponed until all the relatives are in town and are present at the court, or until the parties involved "reflect" upon the agreement offered by the judges. In these somewhat extraordinary cases, the temporality of the law and, in a sense, its routinization— the bureaucratization of "informal" justice—are starkly apparent.

And yet, the judges explained the work of the court, its efficacy, in terms of its celerity. In conversation, various neighbors who had taken their cases to the court also affirmed that, in contrast, the official district court (in the few instances in which they were familiar with its existence or work) was absolutely beyond their means. They explained that they did not possess the resources, including money for fees or lawyers or legal knowledge, to be able to take a case to the local state tribunal in the city's downtown. Besides, at the community court, neighborhood dwellers can be certain that, somehow, their case will be solved that same day or at least within a couple of weeks, while the time of the law in the state court system was much slower. It would take months, if not years, for these very same cases to get resolved within those legal labyrinths holding hundreds of files and involving the work of the few trained attorneys and prosecutors in the provincial capital.

## Languages of Time

During the hearings of a case, people and judges speak in Makhuwa, and apart from certain key political terms, such as "police" or "behavior," the only words uttered in Portuguese are those referring to time or number. Thus, within long speeches in Makhuwa the exact date or hour in which a certain event took place are instants that stand out, pronounced in the colonial language ("on Monday," "during a whole month," "at ten in the morning," "two weeks ago"). Magnitudes, quantities, and dates are defined in Portuguese ("in 1969," "four hundred"). Makhuwa measures and conceptualizes time differently from Western ideology and taxonomy.[16]

During one case discussion, an old woman speaking in favor of her daughter in a divorce case referred in Portuguese to moments in time ("since 1997," "on the eighteenth of March"). This situation, repeated innumerable times at the tribunal sessions, shows that colonialism installed a version of the passage of time that governs ritual and the law. On Tuesday, at ten a.m., a man narrates to the judges a story about the pain he is currently feeling. He starts speaking slowly in Portuguese: "It happened two weeks ago, on Friday, at nine in the morning . . ." Then, he finishes his declaration in Makhuwa.

The legal deployment of language at the tribunal is shaped by the historical transition between colonial and postcolonial regimes. The colonial regime imposed a hierarchy of political and linguistic grammars in which Portuguese occupied the top echelon and various local "dialects" were placed at the bottom. This hierarchy of languages mirrored the structuring of the colonial society in terms of space and rights. The customary was the oral register of the rural and of those noncitizens/workers who spoke indigenous tongues and inhabited the spaces that surrounded the city of political inclusion, Roman law, citizenship rights, and the Portuguese language. Policies of assimilation bestowed the alleged blessings of colonial education, modern ethical edification, and European-language skills on selected, restricted sectors within native society; these sectors were then entitled to certain restricted rights of citizenship. This background history still influences the scope and form of national citizenship at present, as observed in the community courts.

After independence, as a means to promote national cohesion in the new, free nation-state beyond the divisions brought about by ethnic, tribal, and clan structures enforced by the colonial regime, the new Socialist government endorsed Portuguese as the sole national language, prohibiting any other vernacular tongue. The proscription of local languages was part of the ban on the customary, its authorities, rituals, and beliefs. In the first decade of the twenty-first century, during the democratic transition, at the hearing of every case at the community courts, this politics of language reemerged as versions of different juridical regimes expressed in both Portuguese and Makhuwa. One judge admonished a young man accused of being married twice and enacting violence against the second wife: "If you were my nephew, I would whip you (*dar chimbocadas*). . . . You have not acted according to our traditions. . . . You only have your Portuguese culture."

In a way similar to the linguistic entanglements, different temporalities both conflict and coalesce in this seizing of life by the law. The time of customary law and that of state law differ. "Custom" (past-oriented sanction) conflicts in its perspective with the future-oriented normativity of state procedures. Individuals or couples present their cases before the court when the time of the family has run out. The urgency of customary law and kinship rules informs the work of the community court, where magistrates often boast about their high rate of solved cases per day.

Following a given case throughout several weeks, it becomes evident how life and the juridical procedures that attempt to capture and regulate it function along parallel tracks, at different velocities. The wounds caused on a pair of wrists by the extended hanging of a man from a chain while detained at the local police station are very conspicuous at the first hearing of the case. But they heal slowly but steadily, and when the hearings of the case are continued three weeks later, the scars are much less prominent. A similar thing happens to the wounds on the face of the woman who was beaten by this man, resulting in his punishment.

On Tuesday, at 12:30 a.m., the second hearing of a case concerning a conflict between two military men, both friends and neighbors, begins. One of the men has been seeing the other's wife. They have tried to settle the issue within the families and then through several visits to the police station. The relatives want the two couples to be physically separated, and so they ask the judges to decide who is going to continue living in this neighborhood and who is to leave. The president-judge states, "We are going to give ourselves some *time*. Let us reconvene this Friday, the fourth, at 8:30 a.m. Meanwhile, you must think deeply about what you are going to decide." Another judge, speaking about a similar case three weeks later, refers to the regular schedules, the routines, in terms of the efficacy of the court's legal mechanisms beyond the mere use force: "We are here on Tuesdays and Fridays. The rest of the time is the time of the police."

The work of the community court shows that temporality is crucial to the effective enactment of any law. Whether in regard to customary or state law, a fundamental lapse of time exists between the transgression of a norm or breaking of a custom and the moment of its legal sanctioning. The textures of this temporality are felt during the court's procedures. The dialogues, the interrogations, create a texture where the problem analyzed and the lives involved mix with the performance of justice. According to the judges, time and reflection should bring about justice. In the restricted space of the court, the corporeality of a life appears as a legal matter worked by the spirit of the laws, or the abstract of time of the juridical.

## The Form of Law

Along with the files holding transcriptions of cases, the tribunal held another subtly encrypted narrative of a disjoined temporality. In 2004, the community court no longer had an official existence and was just a vestige of a political epoch that had ceased to be.[17] The joint democratic transition and neoliberal restructuring of the economy had left the former popular courts outside the state system of justice. Claiming a legitimacy built upon the memory of the previous Socialist state, the court still aimed at providing justice and order out of quotidian conflict. At the scale of the neighborhood, this situation reproduced a wider process taking place across the country, in which various temporalities of law and politics complicated the distinctions between past and future, subsuming both into a deep present.

Inside the small white building, judges and neighbors carried on with their labor. One morning, the president-judge reformulated the recent past by saying to a group of neighbors: "This is the House of Government. You must know that the state is like God on earth. In the heavens there is God, but here on the earth the state is the authority." His words bounced off the dirty walls of the small room. High above the minimal staging of a theatrics of justice, the president of the Republic, in representation of the entities that the judge had evoked, stared at everything from a photograph that depicted him in his youth, soon after the revolution took place, as if authorizing the session.

Inside the courtroom, images and objects materialized the abstract concept of a state. A poster, a pennant, a piece of paper, a typewriter, these were humble things aimed at representing a large political structure. The ritualized use of letterhead paper and typewriters within a context of illiteracy and orality and the deployment of icons and flags summoned the distant "government."

As one came along the dirt road, beneath the foliage and beside the uneven line of houses, the courthouse stood out, darkened under the blasting sun, magnetically attracting groups of neighbors who took their conflicts to a building they defined as the "house of the government's law." A process[18] that was only partially explained by the force of law took place at the courthouse, which was larger than the space that encompassed it. In conversation, the judges themselves admitted that their legitimacy was compromised with regard to portions of the population. The legal monopoly on violence was complicated by the fact that this minor state represented a real institutional space and a parallel, bypassed one.

What led the members of the local population to submit their quarrels to the minor state? What was the force that made them acquiesce to its decisions and to honor the pacts it arranged? Local legal agents constantly needed to negotiate various situations, solving local conflicts by means of an articulation of coercion and consent, played out in a context of ambiguous struggle for power. Fear and deception, resentment and suspicion, these emotions still dominated the political relations between the "state" and local populations. In a region that for decades had opposed the FRELIMO state, the ex-Socialist judges performed their duties in a context of relentless opposition from many local dwellers, RENAMO agents, chiefs, and religious leaders.

## Thresholds of Justice

In the mid-2000s, while a small minority of the population had access to the mechanisms of the urban official judiciary, the vast majority of the population in rural and periurban areas was both included and excluded from national citizenship, through the enactment of localized forms of rights, which blended official state and customary norms. The forms of law, or jurisdictions, were replicated in spatial and territorial terms.

In legal terms, the community court's understanding of jurisdiction encompassed a modernist Western genealogy of colonial Roman Law, Socialist regulations, and liberal conceptions of the rule of law, as well as local tradition. Invisible jurisdictions, related to other spirits of the law—ancestors, the dead, the not yet alive—also emerged at the tribunal's sessions, whose practices at times accommodated other life-forms and otherworldly belief.

In spatial terms, the peripheral neighborhood was a buffer area between the distinct spaces of the "city of cement" and the peripheral "city of straw." It also mediated between the different juridical regimes being enforced in the region, linking the city center (its boulevards and buildings, its official bureaus, and its small, dilapidated shops) with the countryside, the rural villages, and the scattered markets along the road. It constituted the elusive borderline between the modernizing, stylized cultural forms of the lettered city and the resilient, yet constantly changing customs and kinship rules of the rural areas.

However, the threshold was just a spot along a continuum. The socio-spatial logics of the area showed that the neighborhood constituted the forefront of the countryside wedged at the heart of the city. A scintillating quotidian collage of economies, legalities, corporeal practices, rituals, beliefs, and languages constantly unsettled the political distinction between urban and rural, recasting in new and different ways the village-city links.

Everyday dynamics in the neighborhood indicated how the customary was slowly reconquering spaces that had been colonized earlier by the state. The neighborhood court illustrated how customary citizenship, a blend of official rights and local norms, was enacted through rhetoric and theatrical modes, as a field constituted by demands from local dwellers and maneuvers of articulation conducted by the state. The work of the community court exemplified ways in which life—local conceptions of the body, sexuality, kinship—at some point, at least momentarily, might capture the law.

# Next of Kin

This chapter analyzes how the former People's Tribunals set up during the early Socialist regime to advance modern law and oppose "obscurantist tradition" presently enforce an amalgam of official state law and customary law and kinship rules. Relatedness is here a local inflection on national forms of belonging and rights, which reproduce customary citizenship.

In 2004, after decades of violent political and social transformation, the dynamics of kinship among Makhuwa people still bore a resemblance to descriptions offered by classical ethnographies of the area. Materiality and spirituality were entangled within the logic of matrilineal clans ruling everyday sociality through personal and collective names. In that context, *nihimo* represented the spirit of a lineage and the place of origin to which all its members belonged. *Nihimo* constituted a matrilineal clan, founded by a matriarch, reproduced through exogamy, and rooted in places designated as sites of worship and invocation of ancestors (*nifulo*). Members of each *nihimo* shared a mythic founding ancestor, and they observed similar taboos (*amuiko*) regarding animals, plants, or places, in particular rites and beliefs with respect to the birthplace.

The subject was included in the world of adults by means of initiation rites, through which perennial debts to the dead ancestors were acquired. Through these rites mothers transferred the spirit of the *nihimo*, transmitting a new personal name chosen by the uncle and godfather, thus solidifying the authority of a lineage, placing the subject (whose previous name became taboo) under the jurisdiction of its spirit.[1]

These and other daily and cyclic ceremonies marked a mode of sociality through which structures of relatedness redistributed the spirit of the clan as a system of credit within a moral economy of debt.[2] The temporality of the cycle of production of domestic communities intersected the time of the family as a structure of debts and delayed repayment. Phases of production and reproduction were articulated with the rhythms of circulation of vestiges from conflicts that needed to be renegotiated and pardoned.

A different spirit of the laws, related to the spiritual structure of the clan, permeates local institutions of justice. The jurisdiction of kinship shapes the way in which the norms of relatedness appear within the legal space of the court. The dynamics of the community court consists of entangled practices of gift giving and debt articulated within a local sense of justice. While the logic of the law establishes equivalences that organize retributions and punishments, local knowledge presents a view of justice as open-ended negotiation and articulation.[3] Whereas a conception of fair justice as repayment for an offense is a widespread trope, in northern Mozambique this metaphor is inflected by a vernacular depiction of relatedness in terms of indebtedness. If the law is an economic circle of exchanges, here justice appears more akin to a gift, whose circulation opens the time of a debt.

In the north, since the late 1970s, Socialist state programs that attempted to erase the customary have been bypassed or contested, blending with regional processes of concealment, co-optation, cooperation, or resistance that produced mixed politico-cultural forms in which a ritual, a belief, or a language continued existing and sheltering the aspirations of a local people. The primacy of kinship in rural and periurban areas also influences the dynamics of the community court, where the temporality of the customary becomes entwined with that of Socialism and current liberal democratic transformations. Countering decades of revolutionary orientation that shaped its logic, the tribunal has become a sphere through which the state attempts to articulate with the customary or community of families and clans to enhance its legitimacy.[4] At some ineffable instant, during the court sessions, the tables—such as the old wooden tables at which the judges sit—are turned, and the court becomes a mere extension of kinship structures; the state apparatus is transformed into a sounding board for the customary.

At the community court, the spirit of the laws encounters the spirits of *nihimos*, as an ethics of relatedness saturates the logic of state governance. Kinship materializes at the tribunal as an assemblage of loose rules and changing categories that prescribe the repayment of inherited debts: a contingent circuit for the distribution of gifts (not merely scarce material goods but also gifts of honor, honesty, and hospitality). Violence both threatens and sustains this process under the guise of a hostile domesticity, the threat of invisible factors, the haunting memories of war, or the force of official law that prescribes physical punishment.

Extended families play a key role in the rituals of justice at the court, as official law attempts to regulate issues of intimacy and desire. Facets of the everyday domestic and of subjectivity—emotion, violence—are harnessed by the imagination of the state deployed by judges. They become the material foundation for the force of law and its expansion over all life-forms, deploying what could be labeled the "intimacy of the state" as a technology of local governance.[5] Gradually, the state seems to become an extension of the malleable networks of kinship, and official law appears to amplify elusive local rules of relatedness. The inner folds of relatedness and the domestic become the infrastructure of the state.

Kinship and personal narratives are the matter on which local juridical authority works. Thus, life, both in its corporeal-biological and in its experiential-phenomenological sense, appears as the foundation of the local implementation of the law, which regulates a split subject—subjected to both official rule and local normativity; subjected to the spirit of the laws as much as to local spirits and norms—entitled to an incipient form of localized citizenship inflected by the customary.

## The Gift of Justice

One time, halfway through my fieldwork, when I invited a young adviser to the governor to attend a session at the community court, desire was mobilized on both sides. The judges and neighborhood secretaries became enthused about the opportunity to obtain some resources for the depleted tribunal, but they were also wary of the impression that the court's endeavors might produce on the state officer. Meanwhile, my acquaintance would show me an unexpected face. After quietly witnessing with a shy smile the trials and tribulations of various neighborhood dwellers, he participated at the president-judge's request in the discussion of a divorce case, interrogating the couple and their relatives, giving testimony and passing judgment on issues of love and hatred, adultery, disease, and care.

Moments later, while walking on the rocky path toward the main road that marks the limit of the neighborhood, he was visibly moved and gravely confided in me. The session at the courthouse had reminded him of his own childhood, of the lively and charged atmosphere experienced in his home when the people of the village came to his father's house to solve their *milandos* (conflicts). His father, a carpenter, had become secretary of the village's dynamizing group shortly after independence. He had been appointed by the local FRELIMO cells because the villagers respected him and despite the fact that he belonged to a family with strong roots in the system of customary chieftaincies. Years later, when People's Tribunals were created, his brother was elected as judge, a position he still occupied twenty years later. But back then, during a transitional political moment that also involved a transformation of legal practices regarding popular justice, it was the secretary's home where local conflicts were resolved.

A brief, yet telling story that the young officer narrated shortly after my arrival in Nampula illustrates intertwinements of national political history and local legal normativities. I later encountered similar narratives in conversations with many other local dwellers, which evoked regional imaginaries that conceived of justice in terms of the repayment of offenses-as-debts, as opposed to an imaginary of instant punishment achieved by means of calculating equivalences.

It was 1976, one year after independence, and in his father's *povoacao* (small compound, a precedent for FRELIMO's collective communal villages) a conflict like so many others erupted. During a fight over a woman, a man wounded another in the leg with a large butcher's knife. Friends and relatives of both men continued the discussion at the secretary's home. The wounded man's supporters wanted to inflict an equivalent injury on the offender. Two men started calculating the depth and length of the wound by inserting a rope into the flesh of the injured fellow, clearly hurting him even more. The secretary was away when they arrived and the group was ushered in by his sons and some official aides. Only after the return of the official authority from the ruling party did things calm down enough to allow both groups of friends and relatives to agree on a less violent solution. An equivalence to the offense was found through a payment in kind: vegetables, grains, and oil in exchange for the wound inflicted during the brawl. The secretary had to combine the new FRELIMO policy regarding conflict resolution and the privileging of communal order with an understanding of local custom and sensibility. The outcome was a negotiation that sought reconciliation through an exchange of equivalences, solving the matter of the offense through a circulation of countergifts.

I later understood better the historical and political meanings of this narrative after conversations with other members of Makhuwa groups who presented me with slightly different versions of a similar conception of justice pervasive in this locality. This view can be summarized by the words of someone who lived in a peripheral neighborhood in Nampula City and who, having migrated years earlier from the hinterland, now had a job downtown at an administrative state office: "A conflict (*milando*) never gets absolutely solved. There is always something that remains; the offense is not repaid in full. That small leftover must be *pardoned*." As though the offense bears a certain interest, the logic of equivalence and repayment can never encompass the whole of the original event. Its subsequent ramifications open up the circuit of debt, which might enable the possibility of sociality itself.

"A *milando* never gets spoiled." That is, a conflict between two people defies the passage of time; it does not get consumed over time. "The one who commits an offense forgets, but the offended one does not." This memory runs parallel to the leftover debt, which cannot be subsumed by the measure of equivalences and the potential exchange.

This conceptual scheme, along with narratives of everyday sociality, fragments of political discourse linked to the local state, and memories of the war and its rituals prevalent in this region, illustrates local forms of circulation of value. What circulates, as the foundation of local sociality, is a kind of gift: an elusive presence or ethereal emotion condensed in an object, in an instant, in a place. It is an indefinable object that circulates continuously—from one person to another, as in a sacred ceremony or in the procedures of a neighborhood court—making itself tangible for an instant, only to disappear a moment later. Donations, objects, money, commodities, and debts circulate, but the present that actually becomes the foundation of the social lies elsewhere. This element, which encloses in itself the mandate to reciprocate, and actually reconstructs relatedness by means of delaying absolute reciprocity and opening up short circuits in the circles of indebtedness, can be called the gift of justice.

Referring to mundane quarrels, people in this area would often declare, "A *milando* never rots." The memory of the conflict has to be exhausted, alongside the leftover of the offense that has to be forgiven. What creates sociability in this region is the remainder that circulates, the spirit of a gift[6] that escapes the absolute closure of the economic circuits of debt and exchange or the social structures of due respect and repayment of offenses. The leftover that evades the suture of the circle, the debt—monetary or moral—that is never paid in full, realizes the potential for sociality. Without debt and its interruption of a circuit, there would exist no social relatedness. The remainder opens the possibility for time to unfold or for life to continue. It is the sign that, despite the violence of war and the force of law, history is still open-ended and unfolds through the circulation of that residue, the matter of local quotidian sociability.

This logic of legal offense and moral indebtedness follows a regional political culture in which the totality of a conflict is never solved, in which the whole amount of the debt that is the offense does not get repaid. A memory persists that generates a need, a disposition, the potential for a shared living-on. This remainder can be an individual remembrance of an offense that, paradoxically, both precludes and produces relationality, or it can be the collective regional memory of a war that, much as in the community court, generates the need for pardon and reconciliation. This remainder constitutes the elusive, circulating matter of a present with which the possibility of a suitable future is constructed.[7]

This circulating gift re-creates sociality, producing tangible effects on people who also circulate through this locality. Stemming from that ineffable leftover, life is constantly reconstituted, in a state of becoming and displacement. Peasants and urbanites travel constantly from one point of the region to another, transporting money, commodities, gifts, and other people. They are "internally displaced people" who return to their charred homes after the war, migrants who move from the hinterland to the coastal cities, or people who commute merely to get by, to perform odd jobs or participate in barter. Quotidian ceremonial exchange with the realm of the dead and the spirits is another reason for regular displacements.[8]

In this endangered, fractured social landscape that encompasses enduring fears from the time of the war, the unreconstructed material effects of its violence, and the dislocations produced by overlapping juridico-political regimes, the surplus product of these social exchanges, a spirit or gift, is a sign of the fragmentariness of local sociality. The circuits that channel the exchange of social value have gaps. In this context, the circulation of the gift of justice is a short circuit. The movement of exchange does not engender absolute reciprocity: in the absence of exact equivalences, the debt remains unpaid.

Government programs and legal reforms mandated by the central state aim at closing the gap and suturing the openings of this fragmented social field.[9] The post-Socialist project and the transnational neoliberal one attempt to implement a social engineering of containment through legal reform to close the circle, to give and take time.[10] Yet their failure is evident, as the work of this gift—justice or kinship—on the politics of everyday life produces an open future. The remainder still circulates as the basis for an everyday sociality that somehow still endures and continues.

## State of Relatedness

Within the social structures of Makhuwa people in Nampula Province, kinship relationships are understood in terms of a logic of debt linking the members of a family or clan. For instance, a person is indebted to his or her spouse; a father or mother, to his or her son and vice versa; there is also the crucial relation of mutual obligation between a person and his or her maternal uncle.[11] By virtue of that "naturally acquired" social bond, the subject is socially included in a set of norms on duties and prohibitions that declare taboos and allow engagements with everyday forms of reproduction and consumption of life.

If we follow community court cases through time and back to the neighborhoods, the specific jurisdiction of relatedness becomes clearer. They also illustrate the history of a particular articulation of citizenship and belonging, in which the force of law and the form of custom coalesce and conflict, and rights enjoyed as a state citizen blend with allegiances to a "traditional" local community. While official institutions link the individual to an imaginary of the central state depicted as the source of the political, the jurisdiction of relatedness refers him or her back to an alleged place of the origin of life.

Social assemblages of kinship loosely condensed around the names of a family or a clan (*nihimo*) disseminate throughout a territory while maintaining a key relation to a specific space of provenance and a particular temporal frame. What is reinstantiated through the rhetoric of kinship, while being displaced with each repetition, is a story of origins, a narrative of a reversal that goes back to the name of a single place, a moment, an individual. Kinship's ritualistic cadences and rhythms constantly refer back to an event and a definitive place. Locality is the "original" site to which everything should return, yet "custom" appears as a mechanism of ritual deferral. "Tradition" gets transformed at each moment of alleged ritual repetition, in courts, chieftaincies, land claims, rituals, initiations, prayers. Kinship is considered here as neither a region of inhabitance nor a place of arrival, but a detour.

Kinship spatializes a genealogy. It commands respect toward those elders who refer their lives and their memories back to a common point of origin. It constitutes an order that sustains a debt owed to everything that has emerged from the same space as one's own life. It is a mandate to return to the place of birth after death.

The formula "next of kin," with its temporal and spatial dimensions, adequately evokes configurations of relatedness in this region, implying proximity and intimacy, as well as deferral and spacing. Kinship constitutes here a form of social experience based upon processes of debt and deferred repayment. Customs of ritualized respect, hierarchy, obligation, and hospitality are immanent mechanisms geared toward delaying the settling of almost insurmountable debts.

"Next of kin" also means that the alleged place of origin is always displaced, moved back or pushed farther away. Hence, a whole organizational chain based on that initial place becomes dislocated, and each structural element—"mother," "uncle," "son," "neighbor," and even "owner" (*dono*)—is constantly deferred in its attempt to designate a certain space of kinship as place-holder of a well-defined identity. Kinship spatializes a dislocated sociality. The jurisdiction of kinship disseminates and defers throughout space the meaning of names and functions of various elements in the webs of relatedness.

In northern Mozambique, kinship structures sociality, alternately expanding and contracting to include ever more members of a community within its segmentary arrangements and contingent networks through rhetoric and ritual gestures of donation. It also reproduces debt, enacting an almost mandatory deferral of its settlement, suspending generalized exchange. Makhuwa segmentary groups keep loose interconnections that establish a moral economy of respect and indebtedness, only to be constantly interrupting it and deferring its final resolution. Through this delay of repayment of a moral or monetary debt, the gift of justice emerges.

This local type of sociality reemerges at state institutions such as the community court, which is the distillate of recent strategic intersections between local and national processes. The community judges explain the logic of their rulings in terms of enforcing "their tradition" and emphasize the importance of being knowledgeable about the region's "customs" in order to gain legitimacy from the people. They refer to this turnaround of a regional political history with ambiguous statements, expressing awareness of the fact that a community court that was originally opposed to tradition functions in an opposite way today. Yet their matter-of-fact references to kinship and custom probably indicate the extent to which undercurrents strongly endured and survived the years of Socialist normativity, paving the way for current forms of customary citizenship.

Kinship functions as a grammar that permeates the court's juridical practices. It constitutes a sort of code in which the signifiers are both attached to a signified and yet open to various articulations that work in a contextual mode, endowing situations with contingent meaning. The meaning of these signifiers, such as "uncle" or "mother," disseminates, creating an unstable network. Kinship is a language that expands onto various adjacent fields, such as the economy, the political, and religious ritual. The moral economy of kinship might include the use of legal or commercial terms, such as "proprietor," or through rituals of marriage or filiation,[12] it might intersect with the field of the political (be it related to party politics and state authority or everyday local forms of power).

For example, genealogy occupies a central space within the dynamics of the court, connecting the time of local ancestry and the national history of the state.[13] The postcolonial state tried first to co-opt and then to obliterate kin-based authority and social patterns organized in terms of descent, through both temporal (law, historical narrative) and spatial (collective villagization, displacement) processes. At present, the region is still ruled by matrilineality, with the maternal uncle occupying a flexible but robust central position of authority. Therefore, the logic of the court always demands the presence of the mother's brother as an ad hoc attorney and guide for the person involved in a trial. The main axis organizing the ruling of a case links the maternal uncle and the main judge.

Walking one day on the dark, winding paths of the neighborhood in the company of one of the judges, I asked him about aspects of kinship that intersected with the functions of the court. Walking quickly ahead of me through the labyrinth of foliage and shadow, he explained how everybody must always come to the trials accompanied by their family. The work in the court assumes a juridical subject always located within kinship structures. A trial cannot take place without relatives of both parties. The closest family members are required to be present as witnesses and even as judges and as warrantors of a future agreement. But the family not only provides certainties about the time to come but also crucially evokes the immediate past of the event and a past located in a previous time of ancestral norms and ritual that constitute the social and discursive context of the subject.

The pairing of state's justice and its counterpart, a local normativity of kinship, creates an impression of equality and tolerance. Yet the court's performative dynamics show how the descending lines of genealogy do not endow everybody with equal rights. Rules have exceptions in terms of gender and generation. Only in very special, infrequent cases may a man attend the trial by himself. Normally, if the person shows up alone, he or

she will be required to come back another day, in the company of his or
her relatives. This was illustrated by the trial of a man, a poor, miserable
drunk, who was dressed in rags and barely conscious during the several
court sessions he attended. He appeared mentally absent throughout it
all, and repeatedly the judge ordered him to come back in two weeks' time
with his uncle.

On a dark, stormy morning, when few cases were heard and the judges
and I were chatting together in the Room of Audiences and Trials, the
president-judge confided to me the crucial fact that nobody was allowed
to attend the court sessions without being accompanied by relatives. He
nuanced this general rule: "A man can perhaps, exceptionally, attend the
session without his family. Only *confusos*[14] come alone, like that drunkard
who comes often and we always have to tell him to go and look for his
uncle. A woman can never attend unaccompanied. Her case is absolutely
different. If she came to the court by herself, she would not be heard.
Women are weaker." Pointing out the window, at a little black bird that
sang outside the house on the branch of an old tree, he stated: "A woman
is similar to that bird over there. She has a very low voice. She cannot
speak by herself at the court. For her to be heard, she must attend with
the family."

Kinship terminology, grammars of gender and generation, organize
modes of address at the court, a fixed yet flexible taxonomy that provides a compendium of names for legal subject positions. "Is this true,
my mother?" one of the judges asked a lady whose daughter was involved
in a divorce case. This customary form of address, deployed within the
dynamics of a case, is charged with a juridical surplus. The calculated use
of kinship terms establishes a sense of familiarity and confidence, which
enhances the aura of legitimate authority patiently constructed by the
judges, and which ultimately will create a breakthrough for the resolution
of the conflict.

Regional dynamics of kinship are reflected within the restricted space
of the court—for instance, in the way people of the same age group are
subsumed under a single common term in order to create intimacy and,
therefore, a contracted obligation of exchange and return. The judge calls
all elder females "mother," a term flexible enough to encompass every
married woman, even very young ones. Yet in certain circumstances,
"mother" can become "daughter," just as a young man can be labeled
"son" and then, more importantly, "nephew" in order to evoke a symbolic
surplus of authority.

The judge is a public functionary located at an interface between community and state.[15] His authority derived from invocations of kinship is superimposed upon his legitimacy as official adjudicator of justice and punishment. Although he is endowed with a legitimacy that stems from his belonging to the central structures of power, in order to reaffirm that legitimacy, he must resort to a common feature of moral sociality in the region, the use of terminology and forms of address rooted in kinship norms. The community judge's reasoning becomes legitimate also because he is seen as an older uncle or paternal figure who participates in the practices of local tradition.

The labyrinthine moral economy of kinship—production, circulation, and consumption of desire—is a canvas for the imprinting of bodily and affective forces. It constantly opens and closes inner hallways for normativity and exchange, invoking a past tradition that is constantly being reshaped under present historical conditions.

Life enters into the realm of the state by means of the intersection between kinship structures and the law. Even at the court, the mysterious effects of evil itself are entangled with rules of kin affiliation. In one case, concerning a grievance between relatives that, unusually, was being argued in Portuguese, suddenly the Makhuwa term *olapha* emerged, a loaded term that evokes the consequences of a witchcraft curse proclaimed by a family member. The judges, perplexed by the fierceness of the accusation but perfectly knowledgeable about its logic, were compelled to conduct interrogations about an evil wish that was circulating among relatives. Through this verbal exchange the court legitimized a private agreement sanctioned within family structures as well as the invisible effects of evil processed within kinship rules. At the court the rules of intimacy of kinship become the logic of the immanence of the state.

The fact that the local state becomes an extension of family structures shows how the state can be conceptualized as a relation[16] and not as an apparatus. Kinship relations articulate with multiple local political and juridical modalities forming a minor state that enforces customary citizenship.

## Filiation: Properties of Kinship

The entwined praxis of customary and state laws enforced by the community court links social obligations to a moral imagination of debt. For instance, beyond the more evident cases of indebtedness or the evaluation

of property in certain trials, questions of filiation and reproduction connect moral and social value. On occasion, securing children's well-being in
the process of granting a divorce is included within a general process of
evaluation.[17] In this case, kinship and filiation are linked through genealogy and inheritance to the calculation of a moral and economic value.

When dealing with divorce cases, the community court deploys its true
nature as a state institution through its attempts to provide for the children
of the separated couple. The securing of their subsistence signals the program of administration of a population, evoking the collective and individ-
ualized management of life by the state.[18] If kinship can be thought of as
symbolizing the desire to manage the children's future lives,[19] this situation
also marks a continuity between kinship and the state apparatus, where
filiation forms the basis of citizenship and belonging in the nation-state.
The claim on the management of children's future lives and their registration as citizens with official agencies are points where kinship structures
and statehood merge, showing a field of contention that, beyond the state's
co-option of the local, illustrates strategies of relatedness constituting the
field of the everyday political, saturating official and formal mechanisms
of legitimacy and control.

"Community" and domesticity (a more private space) are realms of
mutual engagement in surveillance and proprietorial control, as the family knows and observes the life of each individual in detail. Relatives have
decision-making power over their kin's lives. A marriage, for instance, is
a node in a network of social relations. Through dynamics of rumor and
threat, as well as the moral authority of the maternal uncle, the families
on both sides enforce "customary jurisdiction" on the unfolding of the
relation and on the offspring.

The court functions as a sort of public theater for the expression of
the "private" realm of the family, reproducing its authority over family
members. Here, the distinction between the notions of public and private
applied to state agencies and family structures does not hold, shattering at
the same time the division between state law and customary law.

During the discussion of a divorce case at the court, members of both
families confronted a young couple in conflict who were seeking to separate. The young couple had moved in together without asking for permission from the parents and uncles, and hence without performing the
usual ceremonies of propitiation and purification. At the court, during the
hearings related to this conflict, the families showed their resentment and
acrimoniously complained about what they saw as the current, negative
effects of those past incorrect actions, which had produced an unhappy

marriage. This case illustrated a generational gap increasingly deepened by current social trends prevalent in periurban areas, such as the transformation of values through modernization and the liberalization of norms due to processes of urbanization and the dissemination of media images. These processes alienate the youth from their elders, as older rules of matrilineality, location, and habitation are weakened.

The logic of the court establishes a dialogue between the judges and the family elders that takes place beyond the particular perspectives of the litigants. In this case the court became a political space for the reinforcing of a tradition that the elders in the family saw as being bypassed by the married couple seeking a divorce. The court was seen as a space where the law, custom, kinship structures, and the state apparatus mingled their imaginations and practices in an effort to achieve normativity.

As often happens, the people involved in this case were sent back home to reflect further on a potential decision and agreement. A few days later I interviewed members of one of these families, and we discussed what had happened earlier during the case discussions. The man's uncle made a striking remark, given the court's political history, when he affirmed that he was happy with the way the case was proceeding and, indeed, with the general work of the court. He said that the tribunal was a good place for the family to be heard and to address the youngsters' issues. He found particularly rewarding that, at the court, they met the members of the family of his nephew's wife for the first time, and now they could agree on a common path. In the views of several relatives I contacted afterward, the community court was understood as a political site for kinship structures to reproduce their norms.

In another divorce case, during a preliminary interrogation conducted before the other judges arrived, the deputy president of the court asked, "Is this your wife by law?" He wrote down the man's personal information (his name, his father's name, where he was born). The law was thus invoked when the man was asked about the nature of his link to the woman, since the question concerned the official sanctioning of a marriage by the state. Divorce cases represent the majority of conflicts submitted to the court, including both legally sanctioned marriages (certified by a state unit and official, formal law) and traditional marriages (de facto unions validated by customary ceremonies and sanctioned by kinship rules in consultation with the families).

The woman, who was in a state of advanced pregnancy, gave her own version of the case, speaking for several minutes without any interruption. Meanwhile, the deputy president took notes on what she said. She spoke in Makhuwa, but referred to all measures of time in Portuguese: "On Monday," "for a month," or "during a whole week." The four judges scrutinized her while she spoke. But she did not look them in the eye. She spoke, as others do at the court, as though seeing through them, looking in a fixed way at a point beyond them.

The divorce case revolved around issues of filiation. The husband wanted to have a child and therefore took his wife to a healer. But then, apparently, he suddenly changed his mind. And when she got pregnant, he wanted her to have an abortion. "The doctor at the hospital told me that he contaminated me with a disease." Now the man was living at his uncle's home. The woman claimed that he took with him 50,000 meticais (about two US dollars) that he had not yet returned. The case included a component of actual monetary debt, which at various points during the argument seemed to alternate between being the source of the attempt at separation and a mere effect.

When the husband was summoned to speak, he agreed that he owed her the money. Nevertheless, he claimed that since the beginning he had told her that he had no means to raise a child, and he never wanted her to get pregnant. The president-judge, in the metaphoric way of speaking that the judges often employ, asked: "But you knew that the factory of children had its production organized around the sexual relation. Why did you marry this woman if you did not want any children?"

An invisible force was invoked, as another source of evidence: "The spirit of the house in which we used to live did not allow her to get pregnant. But when we moved to our next house, the new spirit made the pregnancy possible." "But the accusation about the abortion is based on lies. There was no attempt at making her have an abortion," added the man. "And the clothes that I took with me were mine." Afterward, the woman claimed that the man tore apart some of her clothes and stole others.

A new discussion ensued between the couple and some of their relatives, and then the man even denied having taken the 50,000 MT. He had not seen that money, he said, visibly distressed: "I did not take anything." At that point, the judges also got upset as the case became confusing. "Are you a criminal?" asked Adelfo (the judge-sheikh) in an outburst of fury. Suddenly Judge Ignacio interjected: "He is a criminal, like everybody from Angoche and Moma." Then, speaking to the man, he declared: "You contaminated this woman with the disease to go marry a woman from Angoche."

The state, suddenly, passes judgment over bodily matters, such as health, illness, and its potential causes. The argument began revolving around death. The judges warned the man that he must take the woman to the hospital in order not to be indicted for her and her child's death. It was a theatrical performance staged to frighten the man and make him provide for the woman's health. At the hospital, the doctors told them that they needed 300,000 MT for medicine and treatment at the primary-care unit. The judges reprimanded the man for not even attempting to gather half that amount. The performance of anger and authority continued. The president-judge inquired: "Now, tell us what you are planning to do. Because you know that if this woman dies, you will not lose anything. It is her family that is going to lose. Tell us what you are going to do, to sort this problem, so we can resolve this case. Say what you will do, for this relative of hers to hear."

The man had fallen silent, showing signs of feeling suddenly beleaguered. Then once again "kinship" framed the temporality of the law. The president-judge asked him about his kin, "Do you have a family?" and more specifically, "Do you have an uncle?" Then "this case is going to be continued next week. You will have to call your uncle in order to attend and participate in all these discussions." The president-judge turned to the deputy president and declared, closing the case for the time being: "The uncle will hear the interrogations on Tuesday." Another judge said: "Now you can leave, and go to the hospital in order to heal this illness through public health; or, otherwise, heal it in a traditional way. Do something about this disease."

Friendship and close links between neighbors also might evolve into relations considered to be kinship. A case of adultery that was presented to the court illustrates the interchangeable nature of these bonds and the ways in which, in their flexible choreography, they organize everyday sociability across grief, hurt, and subsequent salvage. The two men involved in the event were indistinctly labeled brothers or friends. During the procedures related to this case, the aggrieved husband related how he had spoken with his wife's lover about the pain and damage he had suffered. The lover offered to pay him some money. The two men used to be close friends. "I do not want money," said the husband, "but our friendship has ended."

This had happened three weeks ago. This morning the three of them are seated in the court. The woman is giving her convoluted declaration, which touches upon a series of intimate details about both of her relationships. The word "whore" arises during the interrogations and discussions with the judges. She claims that her brother-in-law (and lover) pursued her and harassed her. Immediately afterward, when the judges allow him to speak, he defends himself: he has not assaulted the wife. He can pay some money in order for all this to end.

The woman is sitting between the two men. She wears a yellow shirt and a long, ragged black skirt. Her husband, a young man dressed in a yellow Brazilian football T-shirt, holds a little girl in his arms. The daughter is a privileged spectator at the trial, hearing firsthand every single word coming out of her parents' mouths while playing with the hem of her minuscule dress. The woman's lover is sitting to her right. Behind them, on the bench for the families, sit silently five quite-imposing men, dressed in dark jackets and wearing Islamic caps (*khoffias*). To their right are two women, one of whom is breast-feeding a baby. Without uttering a sound, out of respect for the courthouse, these seven people patiently listen as the woman gives her anguished deposition.

"Thanks" is the last word that the woman pronounces, closing her speech in the same, barely audible tone in which she has given her emotional version of the facts. The air inside the court is charged. The accusations and responses are intensely moving; the three people involved appear strongly affected. The lover, a tall, strong, handsome man, has listened to the declaration while sitting with his head in his hands, looking at the floor, his elbows on his knees, appearing exhausted and overwhelmed.

Following the conventions of the court, everybody listens to each person's statement without interruption, and only afterward do they reply to their arguments. Thus, after the woman ends her speech, the lover begins his own, gesturing as much as talking, moving his hands in a very rapid, nervous way. One of the judges admonishes him: "It is not allowed to speak by means of gestures. If you continue doing so, you will have to pay a fee." As soon as the man starts gesticulating again, his own relatives stop him. Then he crosses his hands on his lap and resumes speaking in Portuguese. For the next twenty-five minutes, he gives a very long, intricate account of the facts, filled with details and twists. Progressively, the categories of friends and neighbors (the two men had been very close friends, which implies various bonds of solidarity) become entangled with that of brothers-in-law. "Are you done?" asks the third judge and moves on to question the intimate details of the story. "The concrete fact is that you have been with this lady." "And what about you, lady, have you been only once with this man?" An argument ensues, about who seduced whom, or who went into whose house. It is clearly evident that the man cannot stand what the woman is saying, let alone her tone. Helpless, he smiles ironically, making most of the people in the room burst into laughter. From behind, a relative disapproves of his attitude: "Behave yourself; you are in the presence of the *responsables*," using a common popular term for political authorities to refer to the judges.

Intersecting fragments of memory, mixed with strategies of truth telling and deception, slowly clarify the narrative about this conflict and its characters. The chorus formed by the family members offers more precision: They are both military men, comrades-in-arms. The two couples got married at roughly the same time. And here is where the categories of kinship and the rules derived from them intersect the flow of their lives. They consider themselves in-laws due to being close friends and neighbors; they even moved to Beira at the same time. The judges need to disentangle the accusations of adultery, apportion guilt, and pass judgment on a potential agreement. More information is needed, as the case proceeds very slowly. They try a different approach and decide to show the woman that they do not trust her: "Mother, why don't you accept your sin?" asks the president-judge before reciting a series of traditional proverbs in Makhuwa. It is the beginning of a small performance of sorts, as he all of a sudden verbally punishes the woman, raising his voice and seeming to grow angrier and angrier; he gesticulates and even shouts. While the echo of his voice still resonates off the walls and ceiling, the president-judge walks out. He will wait outside for a while. Another judge takes over the interrogations.

The case is complex, the narratives are contradictory, and the whole process is taking too long. The witnesses are brought in once again, and with their declarations, new aspects of relations of kinship, friendship, and locality emerge as yet other legal categories, illustrating their pragmatic flexibility and their a role in the potential resolution of the case. The family of the lover (they are originally from Nyassa Province), including his mother and brothers, declare that they consider the husband to also be their relative, because his family is originally from the same district as them. Locality-as-kinship is deployed here in the attempt to build trust and engineer an agreement. Then the brother of the woman's lover is interrogated: "The events took place in Maputo a while ago but still continue today, here in Nampula." The two men have been transferred to the same destinations three different times; thus, the parallel relations have continued.

In a few minutes time, the court will attempt to provide a solution to the quarrel. But before that, a subtheme emerges, a slightly smaller side path, running next to the main road of the argument. It concerns, as the procedures of the court often do, connected matters of debt and offense. The tension in the room increases by the minute. Now speaks a woman who has kept silent all along, sitting in a dark corner at the back. She is the wife of the accused lover, and enraged words come out of her twisted mouth, her face showing barely repressed fury: "This man owes us." She has now become a fourth party in the conflict, as she refers to the husband of the first woman—the one who initially brought the complaint—as somebody who is in fact guilty, as his wife has seduced her husband. For her, this is the root of the adultery case, and she claims that the tribunal must order the man and his wife to pay something to her and her husband. New folds of the conflict emerge, doublings and redoublings in which the offender suddenly occupies the role of aggrieved person.

Judge Ignacio declares: "The friendship does not necessarily end here, but neighborliness must end. You two must live separated from each other by at least a kilometer." Hearing this, the relatives look at each other happily, with notable satisfaction. A cousin says: "Yes, the court can decide this. It has the authority to enforce this decision, because these two are military men, they carry weapons, and there is this woman in between them, who is a carburetor, mixing their forces, and they are going to kill each other." Afterward, everybody is absorbed in the discussion about who should move and where to. Everybody mentions the men's trajectories, and they all laugh at the fact that the two men are from Nyassa Province and are married to two women from Beira, finding it hilarious and referring to local humor about regional variants in customs and manners.

As the lover was the first to move to the zone in which they live now, the court asks Vasco, the husband, to move away. At this point, they have begun to sort things out. Humbly, with a melancholic expression, Vasco calls the other man "my friend, my brother." He says: "I never wanted him to pay me. Now I ask him to leave." The discussion between the two men about who must move away goes on and on, seemingly endless. Judge Adelfo looks at the woman fiercely, blaming her: "This whole discussion between these two men is absolutely your fault." Then, in the face of the impossibility of an agreement, a suspension of temporality and the law occurs. The president-judge declares: "We are going to give ourselves some time. Let us reconvene on Friday at 8:30 in the morning. You must think very well among yourselves about what it is that you are going to decide. You are all very nervous. You must think everything over quietly and only then come back."

At the community court, filiation and kinship blend with the political under a single genealogical register. The court, situated on a borderline between state and community, responds to demands from both sides and often blurs their distinctions. One morning, while Judge Nipante and I were sitting outside the courtroom, waiting for the sessions to begin, he spent several minutes in silence, looking at the poster hanging on the wall. It was an advertisement for the upcoming general elections, calling the people to register to vote. Later that day, after the sessions had ended and we were heading back to the city in an old van, I asked him about the way in which the judges evaluated conflicts concerning marital separations. Within a series of generalities, he said in an offhand manner: "There was a divorce case a few months ago. It did not move forward because the father had not registered the children." The judge used the word *recenceo* for registration, a term used to refer to voter registration, whose meaning people extend to the notion of any kind of official record of identity. That terminology exemplifies ways in which the political—suffused by state ideology—saturates the everyday practices of relatedness and desire.

In divorce cases, besides fulfilling demands from the couple and their families, the tribunal focuses prominently on securing the registration of the children at the proper office. This process includes strong pressure on the parents from the judges. They place the identity and citizenship of the couple's offspring above the well-being of the parents. As a laboratory where "life" is processed into juridical matter, the court is an instrument of the state engaged in the registration of its citizenry and the regulation of its future life.

"On Tuesday you will present to us the registration forms of your children; have you understood, or do I have to send some force, like a police force?" At yet another divorce case, the judges admonish a man. He has two sons and the court wants him to come to some agreement with his wife about "mechanisms" to provide for their raising and feeding. The force of law is invoked, as a threat, as a potential fulfillment of a legitimate right to punish, aimed at enforcing a divorce and the reproduction of filiation. A relative of the man speaks from the dark depths of the room, adding pressure from the family: "This man is very much my partner and friend, so I want to advise him that he should not lie to the court; that he should not hide anything and should abide by the law. He has to register his children so they are forever his sons." "The problem had been solved on our very first meeting," says a judge. "The only thing remaining was to register the children and then the court would have signed the divorce papers."

The wind slams the door violently. The judge asks: "Who is the evildoer, you or your wife?" "I am," says the man, and pointing to an old lady

in the back, he adds: "If you allow my mother to speak, she will explain."
"No, of course, your mother will never condemn you. The problem has
already been solved and there is the sentence. We are not going back to
it again. We will resume from the point at which we had arrived last time.
Again, why did you not register the children?" The judge then launches
into a long digression that links the national history of the state and the local history of this neighborhood to the everyday realities of these families.
Through his own testimony, the judge encompasses several roles: educa-
tor, priest, psychologist, as well as prosecutor. His speech is a whole detour
into parables and history devoted to educating the man as a responsible,
independent citizen, as a subject of the court, as a Makhuwa man.

"We are not going to allow this thing to happen, that you do not register
the children. Just so you know that you are in the Republic of Mozambique and that there is a government in this country. You thought that at
the provincial court they would oblige you to do this but not here at the
community court, and that is probably why you came here. But you must
know that there is a government in this Republic and that you have responsibilities for having married the daughter of this *dono* (owner, gentleman)." The mention of this word, from a repertoire of both property and
kinship terms, locates a discussion about relatedness (couples, offspring)
within a broader frame of economic relations. *Dono* (with its ancient link
to *don*, "sir," and also to owner of a *don*, or "gift in land") is reminiscent of
a metonymic scheme that relates kinship relations to landownership and
the distribution of authority among kin.

The term, used within local schemes of kinship, also implies a colonial
history superimposed on a precolonial, customary base. The Portuguese
term "*dono*" has become a synonym for many different Makhuwa terms.
During case proceedings a husband might be called the *dono*, or owner,
of a woman. Owning property also means responsibility for and authority
over a place or people. This term that kinship borrows from the economic
field has also acquired political features. For instance, once I accompanied
one of the judges to another court from which the president-judge had
been long absent due to illness. Afterward, the judge reported back to
his colleagues that we had attended the tribunal's session but "the *dono*
was not there." Similarly, on a week in which FRELIMO held its national
meeting of the Central Committee in Nampula City, another judge, in
conversation with neighbors waiting outside the court, said that the
city was full of people due to the arrival of "all the *donos*." On another
occasion, in a case over money owed for the rental of a house, *dono* referred to the person who was renting, that is, the actual occupant at the

time, and not to the owner of the house, so the property relation implicit in the term implies a degree of contingency, as kinship terms also often do, referring to context and the pragmatics of a given situation and the interests of the people involved.

That which is proper to "kinship" eludes us. The networks of relatedness in northern Mozambique constantly expand and contract, in a contingent choreography. These movements reflect the properties of kinship: modulations that the participants in its rituals (ceremonies, rules, practices, prescriptions) obey and share through their belonging to a certain group or lineage. They shape a regional landscape of networks of belonging and debt, of ownership and rights of use and hospitality.

The concept of *dono*, or "owner," bears a primordial meaning associated with the possession of an object, a place, or a person, but this sense is often transformed into one related to kinship terms, in which the idea of kin relatedness seems to imply debt, obligation, and property. As such, the term emerges often in the court's procedures, during discussions of offense and conflict that recurrently involve aspects of kinship, both in their knotted entanglement and in their elastic resolution. This social context begs the question of value—social, moral—and of the economic worth attached to those relations of familiar authority. The next two sections illustrate examples of cases of kinship as a system of debts circulating monetary and moral value.

## Debt and Money

The dynamics of monetary debt among friends or neighbors illustrates, in all the splendor of its minimal, yet dramatic contours, questions of conflict and reconciliation concerning moral indebtedness, history and memory, official state law and local custom. The case file that I will now discuss begins with a statement of jurisdiction. Written in tidy calligraphy, in dark-blue ink (the record has a number written in red on the first page: "Number 70/2004"), the case is duly placed in the "Republic of Mozambique, Ministry of Justice, Province of Nampula, Community Court Khakhossani neighborhood." The file begins by stating:

> Declarations of the Plaintiff.
>
> On the 7th of May 2004, at this community court, located in Khakhossani neighborhood, in the presence of elected judge XXX, compeared before me

the national [citizen] named XXX, from Rebozo, age 40 years old, son of XXX and of XXX, from the district of Micoboalas. Inhabitant of the neighborhood of Montanha, house number XXX, who presents a complaint against the citizen who calls himself XXX, who on 4th of July 2003, asked Mr. XXX for a monetary value of 5,200,000 MT, alleging that he would use cement blocks to finish the construction of his house, promising that he would pay him back on the 15th of July 2003. According to what is stated in a document annexed to this legal record, after the declaration of the accused person XXX . . .

The key term at the beginning of the file is "compeared." This ancient legal category for presencing refers to the appearance of a person before a court of law. Compearing indicates communal relatedness between persons or between institutions and authorities that act as individual legal subjects. There is a communal element in jurisdiction that brings together a group of persons related by the performance of the law.

After having his depositions acknowledged by the notary public of the Civil Register in Nampula City, the debtor declared that he was going to settle the debt on 27 April 2004, at 3 p.m., adding that he really wanted to fulfill his commitments. "So that this becomes known, I inscribed this act. . . . Nampula City, 7th May 2004." Following this are the signatures of the declaring person (plaintiff) and the judge who received the legal complaint.

This formulaic legal narrative translates everyday parochial dialogues into a positive discourse of the law that references a minor interruption of time through debt. It is a case of a delayed transaction, in which the debt is never repaid so the deferral is extended, prolonging the conflict.

This monetary agreement or scene of indebtedness is representative of the more expanded landscape of sociality in this region, one permeated by an imagery of the subject as both individual and "multiple," of social relatedness as built on a conception of owing (respect, hospitality, provisions) and obligations. A case of monetary debt in which the settlement is constantly deferred functions as though repayment was deemed ultimately impossible and yet would constitute the new beginning of a quest for justice. The legal language, the back-and-forth dialogues in absentia between the litigants invoking honor and obligation, point toward the seemingly perennial circulation of an obscure share, always on loan, overdue. What is this debt?

The case record shows how the circulation of this small debt intersects various jurisdictions. The second page of the case record is a handwritten page produced by an officer of a nearby police station. It establishes that the case of debt has been brought there, and the policeman (acting as a first judiciary instance) submits it to a "community center" in the neighborhood. This one-page document bears the red-ink stamp of another "community court," which has produced the final record.

After the first two handwritten documents, a third page presents a short statement typed out at the same police station. It is a "declaration," a short, bland note. A man, stating his name as XXX, and his identity card number, declares that he has "contracted a debt" with Mr. XXX for an amount of 5,200,000 MT to be paid on 15 July 2003. In the last sentence of this cursory legal note, truth and contingency are entwined, as a legal acknowledgment of a debt, the simulacrum of an oath: "Because this is true and because of motives found convenient, I state the present declaration, signed by me."

A blurred Xerox of the original handwritten note is also attached to the file. Next in the case file is a small piece of paper, written in both red and blue. It is a "Message of Notification." Citing articles from national laws and penal codes, the officer at the police station notifies the national (citizen) XXX to compear before the authority of the police. An element that keeps reappearing throughout the file, to the extent that it slowly takes over as the main thread in the scattered narrative that the record represents, is that each and every document in the file establishes a delay in the repayment of the debt. Dates are amended by the authorities and the litigants; various declarations postpone the settlement; a constant deferral of agreement interrupts the granting of a grace, the satisfaction of some form of justice. The next document states the declaration of the accused person acknowledging his deeds, his compearing before the law merely prolonging the delay in repayment.

A case always states its spatiotemporal coordinates: "On May 11th 2004, compeared before this Community Tribunal of Khakhossani Neighborhood citizen XXX, Resident of (Neighborhood, Street, House Number). Identity Card Number . . ." The file includes a photocopy of an identity card, issued by an official state agency, which bears a name, date, numbers, along with a photograph and a fingerprint. A person's identity card gives legal testimony of a singular life. The document exemplifies how a citizen is one and multiple, a singular case and a universal type.

The declaration adds the element of accrual of debt. Monetary relations usually involve this aspect of chrematistics. The accused person states that he originally (in May 2003) had borrowed 2 million meticais, but the original loan carried a stipulated interest rate of 40 percent, which after a few months had already increased significantly the amount of the original debt, because of which the accused person had agreed to pay back the debt in installments of 1,300,000 MT each. Acknowledging the debt, stating installments and dates for repayment, the declaring subject closes his deposition and signs it, along with the judge.

The last document in the file is an intricate declaration, full of bureaucratic data: names, locations, places, dates, civil status, identity card numbers, file references. Its object is to appoint two "representatives" to whom the plaintiff gives "powers and rights" in order to proceed to collect the debt owed by Mr. XXX. They will "represent him in all public offices, police entities, tribunals." The file closes with the statement of place, date, and the signature of the plaintiff.

Amid the proliferation of technical data related to numbers, names, locations, and agreements of representation and negotiation, what emerges is a scene of constant deferral. The contingent nature of a case sheds light on a more widespread form of sociality, one composed of delay and postponement, of constant awaiting.

Indeed, in a region ravished by material destitution and scarcity, "kinship," as a political and economic scheme of social relatedness, is a technology to manage the seemingly provisional nature of life, where sociality is understood as life-in-waiting. Unfinished, interrupted projects (governmental, local, personal) linger on and preside over these decaying places, those eroded memories and corroded socialities, yet they are also entangled within many minor, emergent processes, within a life unfolding as a constantly delayed circuit of unpaid debts.

Cases such as the one just outlined allow a broader understanding of sociality in this region, in which an element is presented as always being owed, circulating, building a precarious sociality. In this fractured social landscape, what seems to suture the open-endedness of the social is the promise of the arrival of justice, at the level of interpersonal relations. It is a gift of justice, circulating as a mechanism channeling the interrupted event of repayment, alternatively administered in a legitimate way by official law and the customary.

What slides between the lines of the law's discourse and practice is the elusive yet firm presence of customary forms and values. The force of "honor" emerges powerfully, through a promise to fulfill the law by settling a debt, and the mysterious cadence of "other motives also found convenient" appears adjacent to the lawful exigency of "truth." What might this parallel truth be? What are the values attached to "other" reasons that intersect the law of the state?

The norm loosely holding together these "communities" is the circulation of a debt. It is the collectively shared acquiescence to an original debt without origin, owed to another, to a lineage and its spirit, to the dead ancestors. Periodic initiation rituals and everyday practice reinstantiate the circulation of an ineffable, immaterial gift that, since the moment the person was born into its circuits, has opened the time of a debt and its impossible repayment. A case of debt is but a local echo of the resonances of legal jurisdiction and reflects local dynamics of indebtedness, materializing a customary citizenship, or dual form of social belonging.

## Debt and Time

On any given morning, before the sessions at the court begin, Hernando, the "prosecutor," receives complaints about cases of both material and symbolic debts. Today, it is a small scene of three people, taking place in the dark, central room of the house, where the feeble daylight from the back door forms shadows and wrinkles on the three faces as they argue politely but firmly about debts. A young man, dressed in very old and dirty white pants and shirt, refuses to sign a document that stipulates his debt if he is not allowed to read it first. The debt amounts to 2 million meticais (around eighty US dollars). He is sitting at the table in front of Hernando, who threatens him with prison. Beside the table, with an expression that combines boredom and rage, stands the man who claims the debt, an older, bearded, obese fellow, dressed in a white shirt and a *khoffia*.

People involved in another case of debt wait outside the house. A moneylender, whom I had met a few weeks ago at the first meeting of a case of debt, is waiting outside the house. A man who had borrowed a certain amount of money had lost his job four months ago when the factory in which he worked closed, a situation that had affected many others in the outskirts of this city. Since then, the man had been postponing making payments and had been asking to reschedule his debt, which was agreed upon at a session in the court. But this time the debtor has not shown up to pay this month's installment, so the court will pursue him to make him comply. To refer to this, as in many other cases, the judges use a formalized bureaucratic language: "The court will *notify* the person, and if he does not attend, we will produce *other intelligence*" (meaning having recourse to the local police or other public authority). Meanwhile, the lender tells me that these days there are not many outstanding debtors (at other times, they abound). He usually sends the police to look for them and force them to pay, but today he has brought the case to the court.

These are two examples of cases of actual monetary debt, in which a sum of money has been borrowed and its repayment has been delayed, resulting in the accrual of interest. There are related cases in which the court estimates the approximate value of an object in dispute, most often the belongings of a couple who are divorcing, such as the house in which they live and the land on which it is located. The judges might travel on those occasions to the site of the household.[20]

Another case involved an amount owed for the rent of a room. The case continued for three weeks. After the first session, the judges went to evaluate the house and the fairness of the price of the room. The *dono* (owner) was requesting supplementary interest on the original price of the rent because he had undertaken improvements on the place. "Now the court can see that you were lying. You have not made any improvement to the house. Moreover, this young man was paying regularly and you had not arranged a fixed price to begin with." It turns out that the youngster is the son of a printer who used to produce the "official" letterhead for the tribunal. This fact seems to have influenced a change in the evaluation done by the judges, who were initially favorable to the man claiming the debt because they had confirmed that the young man had not been paying rent. The president-judge declares: "Both men are guilty. The *dono* lies and this young guy lies as well." He admonishes his "nephew," telling him he should listen to the advice given to him, and orders him to pay a sum in three installments. Several kinds of debt thus intersect at the conclusion of this case: the monetary debt to the owner of the house, with interest; the symbolic debt of the judges to the recently deceased father of the young man, which prompts the judge to call him "nephew" and hence to include him in a network of kinship and debt; and, finally, the debt owed to the spiritual realm, that of the dead, since the young man states that he will not be able to repay the debt soon because he has to go to Molocue District to conduct ceremonies following the death of his father. He has already paid for the construction of the tomb and the gravestone, but he has other expenditures for rites in honor of the spirits of the dead. A date for the first payment is agreed on by both parties and the president-judge signs the record of the case.

Other kinds of interest arise from various tactics of pressure, distraction, and punishment enacted within the time of a debt. Those conflicts produce obligations of symbolic debt that a person owes somebody else by virtue of their particular social relationship. For instance, during a divorce case involving domestic violence, two litigants and two relatives held a loud discussion among themselves at the back of the room. The case revolved around an unpaid debt: for the divorce and as reparation for the aggression against his wife, the husband had been told by the court to give her 300,000 meticais, a small radio, and a few other items. This conflict is an example of a composite case in which debt is conceptualized simultaneously as both monetary and moral, involving an abstract relation of indebtedness due to a structural (marital) bond of kinship.

## Life as a Legal Matter

Life itself enters the courtroom in the form of small quotidian dramas. Through the procedures of the community tribunal, issues of subjectivity or intimacy that originated in the home or the family become legal matters. The concealed life of a person, a private dispute, or a secret ritual is transformed into a public issue where a bureaucratic element shapes the intimacy of the state.

The law aims at capturing the life that unfolds within the court as intimacy, desire, or the body.[21] Temporality makes law and life coalesce and collide. Biological time and juridico-political time, or parcels of life—bodies and a body of law—become contiguous at the instant in which the force of law takes over. Yet over time, life and the law will inverse their relationship.

The very existence of the law and its legitimate enforcement depend on the experience of subjects. Conflict resolution amounts to the submission of "life" not to the court of law but, on the contrary, to the very materialization of the law by that "life," which is the source from which it extracts its legal force.[22] Local life shaped by the customary constitutes the foundation of the state in this region, while the force of law imprints its effects of desire on the subject's body by means of sentiment as much as by means of legal enforcement.

During a case of adultery and domestic violence, one judge said: "We should have started by discussing the issue of jealousy, but as these people committed a crime, jealousy is now underneath and the crime moves on top of the issues." This assertion also refers to the only distinction the judges, who hear and decide all kinds of cases, make between "social cases" and criminal cases. These different aspects are permanently intertwined: a divorce case that began as an argument about various perspectives on marital responsibility suddenly became an acrimonious debate over the body, intimacy, and desire, as both spouses exchanged bitter remarks on their sexual behavior, genitalia, and disease. This exchange was addressed to the judges, for them to evaluate the depth and the truth of those offenses. In this way, the judges become an interface not only between a husband and a wife, whose most intimate dispute is thus mediated by the state, but also between the private realm of the family and the home and the public domain of the law and the state.

Within the practice of the community court, kinship constitutes a circuit for the exchanges of a moral economy, a device to secure the future interests of a debt, as can be observed in the concern and responsibility the state takes in the reproduction of a population or in recording its genealogies. The tribunal, harnessing traditional rules and relations, provides justice following a double-entry book of debt and repayment that blends the state's codification of the private lives of subjects as a system of equivalences with a local imaginary of sociality as indebtedness.

The analysis of legal cases in the locality's expanded social context shows that debt—from loans, to fines, to "due respect"—constitutes the general form of the economic logic of the law. Often, at the court, the legal processes aimed at reconciling the parties end in a calculation of monetary compensation subtly engineered by the judges, who, it is acknowledged, can compensate for only a minor share of the offense. This staged exchange—a blend of legal logic and rules of kinship understood as a system of credit—is akin to the donation of a "gift of justice."

The gift of justice, represented by the interrupted exchange that takes place at the court in the form of staged arguments and performed promises and settlements, is a condensation of various entangled regional forms of sociality. The simple objects or small sums of money that circulate through various kinds of agreements are but the material support of the actual gift that is exchanged. This gift consists of a shared idea of fairness linked to the pardon of a remainder or surplus that stems from a conflict. It is not a conception of the gift as an object of perfect reciprocity. Rather, it emphasizes its agonistic aspect of subsumed conflict and a loss that dissipates with each transaction. It is a gift that is abandoned or lost rather than given and returned.

This type of post-Socialist custom found in northern Mozambique at the beginning of the twenty-first century is the historical product of the confluence of different trajectories. It shows the imprint of Socialist forms of deferral of violence and punishment that were present in precolonial forms and that the revolutionary regime tried to temper. It also maintains the original aspect of a search for an equivalence to the offense or transgression present in regional customary law (as recorded through fieldwork and archival data) but acknowledges its impossibility: the exchanges of actions, things, or currency are intended as mere staged acts in a double movement of acknowledgment of a debt and the indefinite postponement of its repayment. This performance, made patent in the court's procedures, opens up an enlarged time where the emergence of the social or the reconstitution of sociality is possible.

The forms of the gift of justice organizing the resolution of conflicts at the court constitute a new manifestation in a history of local justice: as novel iterations of the entanglements of law, ethics, custom, and kinship rules in precolonial and colonial customary courts as well as renewed versions of the popular justice of the former People's Tribunals. In the context of neoliberal juridical and economic reforms, the forms of conflict resolution practiced at the community courts and the contemporary variation of custom here defined as "gift of justice" might work well, from the viewpoint of state reformers, with new global forms of legal mediation and with the prevalence of norm and normalization over the strict sovereignty of the "law." The articulation of regimes of law and custom produced at the court gives rise to customary citizenship and a specific type of subject who claims it.

# CHAPTER SEVEN

# Subject: To the Law

This chapter explores how, in northern Mozambique, entangled re-gimes of subjectification enforced by custom and the law produce a citizen-subject shaped by a double bind of post-Socialist communal ethos and kinship rules. At the community court, this individual uses reason in public and enacts entitlement to rights mandated by the nation-state while also being constituted by ritual norms and kinship. In the following sections, I will explore questions of memory, reason, desire, and the body, which constitute the materiality of a truth-telling citizen who performs civility while also being attached to structures of tradition and relatedness, embodying forms of customary citizenship.

## Matrilineal Rights

The file of a legal case includes a photocopy of an identity card issued by the City Archive of National Identification, stipulating the citizen's name and bearing his or her signature. The photograph and fingerprint are images equivalent to the calligraphic imprint of the name and reiterate the identity of the subject determined by the state. Although the document is indispensable in order to file a complaint at the community court, the law does not constitute the sole framework that channels the court toward rendering a sentence or effecting a "reconciliation." At the court the legal identification of the subject takes a detour through the customary, as the orality of tradition intersects the official imprint of citizenship.

The judge addresses a plaintiff: "Next week, you must bring your ID. It is very important. These papers are like your uncle." Locating the state at the same level as the customary and linking national belonging to local kinship hierarchies, the judge's commandment is subtly stating the primacy of relatedness over official law.

The speech of official jurisdiction has been echoed by the local voice of the customary. In reality, what determines the subject's identity is matrilineality, a flexible system of protocols for placement and indebtedness. The state officer equates this system to citizenship, addressing a subject who is a product of multiple entangled historicities and juridical regimes. The state articulates with locality and its tradition in order to shape the subject, invoking kinship to address a citizen thus mediated by the community. Acquiescing to the customary in the form of kinship structures or ritual belief, the court illustrates local variations of the current national context of "recognition," as custom blends with official law and expands the restricted sphere of democratic rights into a localized version of national belonging. This local form of jurisdiction shapes citizen-subjects through customary citizenship.

As illustrated by the daily practices performed at the tribunal, the state takes over the familiarity of the everyday and harnesses the trust of kinship. To be perceived locally as legitimate, the state must become something akin to a relative and perform its duties. The judge's metaphor, as a local undertone of national jurisdiction, is based on local conceptions of legitimate authority, which make reference to the concern and control that a mother's brother ought to fulfill vis-à-vis his nephews. The judge's reference to official identity cards and kinship implicitly traces an analogy between the modes in which the state ought to provide, advise, and shelter its subjects and organize the mechanisms of inheritance through which value circulates and the ways in which an uncle should act vis-à-vis his sister's progeny.

The detour of citizenship through kinship bespeaks a regional history of past antagonisms and current articulations of the state with the customary, acknowledging the demise of key aspects of the postindependence project. The erasure of the customary undertaken by the postrevolutionary regime finds its counterpoint in today's official invocation of the precolonial moment for the reconstruction of the nation-state. If the early Socialist regime vowed to "bypass the tribe in order to construct the nation," today at locales such as former People's Tribunals, customary norms are being enclosed by the law, harnessed by a movement of sublation enforced by the state in the localized version of a politics of recognition. The postponed postindependence goal of autonomy and emancipation of the subject encounters the ceremonious deferral of kinship, where every single case of relatedness is located within a descending scale of displacements that never fix the exact meaning of a term and always accommodate one more category or mandate hospitality for a new stranger, ever generating proximity and intimacy.

Two different jurisdictions collide within a multiple field of legal norms producing a citizen-subject, an individual bearing several names. When an individual crosses the threshold of the court and enters the realm of the law, she is first interrogated about her identity, and her proper name and filiation data are established. The name of the subject is usually a combination of Makhuwa and Portuguese terms, just as the language in which the disputes are argued switches from the regional language to the official national one, reflecting entwinements between the state and the customary. Names recall a recent history that conflates several legal and political layers,[1] in the same way as the names of the People's Tribunal and the People's Republic have been transformed by the democratic transition.

Names need to be stated, and thus, it is the event of a signature that marks the limits of the temporality of the law. The text of a finalized case file will be piled upon other files against the wall of the courtroom as an attestation to the passage of time, including a unique signature that signals acquiescence with the sentence. Each page of the file and each declaration are signed at the bottom, while the final signature of the judge authorizes the whole record, which covers the event up to its legal solution.

Most people in the neighborhood are illiterate, and sometimes, instead of each page being signed, the litigant's fingerprint replaces the signature on the last page of the file. Once, at the end of a divorce case, the question of the signature was slightly displaced. When the couple about to separate were banned from living on adjacent pieces of land, the man agreed to leave the house he had built to his wife but insisted on taking with him the front door, which was, so he claimed, a magnificent piece of wood. At the court session, the woman's elder son, aged eighteen, signed the act of divorce on behalf of his mother, who was illiterate. He inscribed her name on the page, while her first husband (his own father) and her current spouse also signed, as witnesses.

## The Intimacy of the State

Following the era of the party-state system, which had suffused all dimensions of the social, the state was, still in the mid-2000s, a vector present throughout the social field. At the community court, life, understood as

intimate aspects of embodiment and desire that exceed political distinctions between private and public spheres, was transformed by the state
into a legal matter in an attempt to attain legitimacy.

The door of the courtroom opens and everything starts again. Enter a
case of adultery. A man and two women walk in slowly, with somber, fearful expressions on their faces. The man sits on the bench in between the
two women, looking sad and dismayed. One of the women, who carries a
baby tied on her back with a bright-red piece of cloth, begins to speak. She
narrates events of aggression and violence that have occurred between
herself and the other woman. By chance, due to a random encounter
with acquaintances on the street, on an afternoon when she was not supposed to leave her home, the woman had discovered the liaison between
her husband and the other woman, who is now seated on the other side
of her husband. She narrates the subsequent events, which involve physical assaults and arson.

In a case of adultery, the court's aim is to determine culpability, eval-
uating the emotions and calculations that locate love outside the law.
First, the court wants to elucidate who seduced whom. In this case it is
quite difficult to establish an orderly account of the facts from the disparate, uneven chains of images and stories that crisscross in the litigants'
depositions. A single label begins to emerge from amid the counterpoint
of aggression and accusation: the term "whore."

The wife had gone to the lover's shack, and finding her alone, she had
beaten her with her bare fists, then with an iron tool she found lying on the
floor. The other woman fought back, attempting to whip her. The fight had
ended with the shack being set on fire. The flashback of memories produced by the trio of lovers stalls time and again, hitting a word, as though
it were a stone: "whore," "whore." The label summarizes the aggrieved
words, the resentment, the hatred wrapped in the remaining effects of
petty violence. The judges will soon join the litigants in a discussion of the
word's reach, as hatred, love, and sexuality will be put on trial through a
dialogical exchange of flowery admonitions and indictments.

"So, this is, then, how this case was born," said the president-judge, in a
solemn manner. "Lady, is it true, what this woman is saying?" The woman
announces she will speak in Makhuwa. Halfway through her declaration,
with the help of my whispering assistant, I understand that the case actually centers on the accusation of aggression (blows, wounds, and the burning of the shack) against her. The narrative of infidelity and betrayal that
we had heard before is merely the background of the acts of violence.

Her lover's wife has called her a whore. She replies that the man had been married before, that he has another wife and four small children elsewhere. In reference to the current wife, the lover accuses: "She is the actual whore. She stole the man before from that other woman, destroying that household." Suddenly, a new layer of the conflict unfolds, which makes the arguments more heated, the resentment more flagrant. A new life is brought into the dispute, as the lover reveals that she is pregnant, which motivates a thorough philippic addressed by the judges to the man.

Paulo, the second judge in the hierarchy, compares this heated case to the ongoing war in Afghanistan, the violence unleashed by the US bombings and the resistance. "You are the Bin Laden in this case." And then he adds an unfinished sentence, as a verbal punishment carrying a neologism: "Those things related to *loverism* . . ." "You say this is your wife and that is your lover. If you were to get married, everything would be different, but as things stand now, you have committed adultery. What do you have to say?" The man replies in a near whisper: "I don't know what leads me to do these things."

The two women attempt to resume speaking. The president-judge shuts them up, telling them: "You have already talked too much. This has been all nullified; it brings no result whatsoever." The president-judge then adopts a pedagogic tone toward the lover, referencing "traditional" marriage custom. "You should have gone to see your parents and told them, 'This man is coming after me, wants me, I do not know whether as friend, lover, or wife.' "

"What is your preference, to be a married man or an adventurer?" This time, it is Ignacio, another judge, interrogating the man about his future plans. The lover replies: "My dream was to get married after beginning to work. I started seeing this gentleman when I was still in school. This man charmed me, but I did not know that things would end up being like this. It is what they usually call 'involuntary acts,' that is, when one is not conscious of performing them." The judge questions her again: "Why did you use to ask him what you would do if you became pregnant? If you wanted to get married, you should have not done all this. Whether this hurts now or not, you accepted then the evil."

The controversy returns once again to the issue of the lover being a "whore." The wife adds: "This woman lives with another man, named X." "Do you have evidence of that?" the president-judge asks her. And then says, raising his voice: "If so, we are going to notify this man and call him to appear before the court." An aunt of the lover tries to say something, but she is ordered to remain silent by a judge, because she has not been called upon to speak yet. Meanwhile, the wife accuses the lover, who defends herself by evoking the man's underhanded maneuvers: "Months later, after I had been seeing this man, when I was living in Natakane, his first wife warned me that he was married twice. I am not married now; a few men visit me only every now and then."

The judges clarify matters. Ignacio (very serious, frowning) declares: "A man is never a whore. A whore is only a woman that accepts someone else's husband." Paulo (authoritative and playful at the same time, smiling) adds: "It is in the dictionary of science at a global level . . . a whore is a woman who sleeps with any man, a policeman, a professor, a mason. . . . But by definition, the man cannot be a whore." The president-judge interjects: "This case has entered into crime, according to what we, the men of the law, determine. This was a mere social case, but now it is a crime that must be judged! [He is now shouting.] We have to gather matter for this case. We have seen how the social case occurred, but later on a criminal case ensued, with the burning of the house. We are going to examine all the evidence, summon witnesses to study the process. Do you understand, Mr. Luis, Ladies?! It is a criminal procedure!"

Amid these discussions on violence and deception and guilt, the court aims at performing its role as warrantor of life and of the accounting of a population. The president-judge asks: "Who is going to be responsible for this pregnancy?" Both families start a discussion, raising their voices. The judges raise theirs even louder: "We want the person that got her pregnant!" The wife whispers at her husband's ear, apparently telling him what to say. The man affirms: "I am going to assume the responsibility I owe to my wife. I was the one who got this woman pregnant." The president-judge and Ignacio get very angry at the way in which the woman now manipulates her husband. They reprimand her: "You attacked this woman; you wanted to burn her house. You could even go to jail." Ignacio unpacks the logic of their thoughts: "The serious problem here is not that this man sees two women. The problem is that this one wanted to burn her house. If we go to the PIC [police], they will go to jail."

While the judges discuss whether to summon the other man that has been mentioned or not, the lover, with a fearful tone, says that she wants the court to be the warrantor of whatever agreement is decided upon, because she is afraid of being attacked and her house burned once again. Also, she expresses that she wants the man, who got her pregnant, to provide for her and her child. The president-judge declares: "You must come back next time with male relatives, because this lady, your aunt, will very soon back out." The aunt complains. The young lover asks that the case be continued at the next session of the court or at some other day, but always on a Friday, so she can attend with male members of the family. A few minutes afterward, they are all summoned to return to the court on Friday, 4 June.

Three days later, in conversations held near the court, two judges explained to me: "Polygamy is allowed within our culture, and not just in Nampula. A man can have, for instance, three wives and introduce them to each other. The woman's polygamy must be secret; if the husband discovers it, there will be problems. The codes do not allow it."

## Desire and Violence

At the court personal experience encounters the emotions of the state, wrapped in the court's rationality. The procedures of the modernist tribunal, inheritor of the enlightened project of the Socialist state, process desire through argumentative logics. This section and the next explore the two-sided logic of force and rationality expressed in the court's work.

The man sitting at the bench carries signs of violence imprinted on his arms. The skin of his wrists has been torn. Purple, bloody areas surround the large wounds in which his veins are visible. The flesh has been turned inside out. He has spent the last night at the police station, and now his face shows a calm anxiety that paradoxically accompanies and opposes the trembling flesh of his arms.

Relatives of his wife had gone the previous afternoon to the local police station in Natakane neighborhood to denounce him for having beaten her up badly. A small police squad had caught him at a friend's place, where they found him half drunk. To punish him, and as a warning, the policemen had hung him all night long with ropes from the window of a small cell. The man looks as though they had also beaten him up. Now he is shaking a little and his mood exudes fear and anxiety. The teary eyes are reddish; his gaze is lost, lifeless.

Early this morning the police had released him and sent the case to the community court. The violence that the man inflicted upon his wife, as well as the violence that he suffered during the night he spent at the police station, forms the context and foundation for the legal deliberations that will take place today at the tribunal. The wounds that his fists inscribed over that woman's body on a night of anger and alcohol have found an echo in the marks left by the hands of the policemen and the ropes. The allegedly lawful violence of the police was at first intended to provide a legitimate response as an equivalent to the original violence.

To what extent is there a continuity between both instances of violence, lawful and unlawful? Even the force of "community" law carries the potentiality of a punishment upon which its legitimacy is founded. The agreement reached in this divorce case will be shaped by an initial punishment already enforced at the police station, which occurred without any legal restraint whatsoever and which threatens the subject with future violence. This case illustrates the way in which "community justice" can be devoted to reconciliation, but its final outcome is predetermined by the institutional network of formal and informal spaces of law and violence in which the court is inserted. In the midst of discussion about the divorce case, the president-judge says to the wounded man: "From now on the case is in justice's hands. Justice does not search for color or race; it looks only for proof of evidence. You have to answer to justice, or else, this case can be sent to a superior agency. Come back on Friday with your wives."

The case was interrupted after the first session, when the involved couple and their families were not able to arrive at a settlement. The man was told to go to a local, rudimentary primary-care unit. When the case was resumed a week later, the general mood of the man seemed less somber as the wounds in his forearms were slowly beginning to heal. Two parallel processes of healing took place, as the temporality of the law could be discerned in the healing of his scars and physical injuries.

As shown in the previous section, the conflicts examined at the court bring emotions to the fore. The tribunal passes judgment miming the state's management of its population's passions. The pedagogy enforced by the judges is also a sentimental education; the rationalization of life by the law is not a legal resolution of conflict but an intricate counterpoint between reason and emotion. Intimacy and subjectivity are at stake as the court deals with conflicts among kin. Cases of adultery or divorce often disseminate into subsidiary issues of the body, its fluids or organs, sexuality or disease. Life, both in its biological sense and as desire, becomes a legal matter within narrations of conflict and truth.[2]

Life enters into the space of the courtroom under various forms of desire or bodily experience often linked to intimate violence exerted upon close kin, which is incorporated by the court within the fabric of the law. The legitimacy of the law, based on its potential enforcement through force, is related to the social violence that it harnesses from the conflicts brought under its jurisdiction. The violence that a husband inflicts upon his wife or his children, the violence of a man against his neighbor's son, punishing him for repeatedly stealing from his farm, the violence of a mob that visits an old lady accused of occult practices, or the implicit violence enclosed within the harshness of a sorcery accusation—all these everyday forms of violence are reflected in the mirror that is the law, which cancels it and lifts it up, restoring order by both displaying and concealing the violence that the conflicts enclose.

The enforcement of the law at the court is a compromised historical issue. On occasion, the president-judge referred to the lack of a police force at the tribunal and compared this situation with that after independence, when militias were available to protect the members of dynamizing groups. During the first years of the court's work, policemen were present at the sessions. Often the president-judge evoked another epoch, the Socialist past, when a general atmosphere of apprehension pervaded society vis-à-vis the state and reinforced the authority of the court. "With the peace accords everything changed. . . . We used to have the authority to send people to jail. . . . Now only rarely can we submit a case to the city court."

Once at the beginning of the court hearings, the new person in charge of the community police force housed at the court was publicly introduced and thanked for his willingness to collaborate with the tribunal, even though these small platoons were increasingly known in the area for their excessive use of force, not always for legal purposes. The court shows that "official" law co-opts the violence that it is supposed to constrain or rule out. Beatings, rape, and physical or verbal abuse were forms of domestic violence often discussed at the court. Signs of force imprinted on the body were considered evidence of "legal matter," a term that evoked the concreteness of violence being judged beyond the abstraction of the law.

### Reason: True Memories

The logic of the court opens a space for the public use of reason, where issues of truth and memory are fundamental for the emergence of justice. According to local knowledge, conceptions of justice imply a double dynamics of remembrance of conflicts and forgetting or pardon of a remainder. Toward the end of many discussions of cases, the judges insist on elucidating whether the offended party has "pardoned" the "adversary."

Memory plays a crucial role in the unfolding of the law, as litigants and witnesses summoned to the court must give a truthful account of themselves and their divergences. Afterward, the judge deploys a mnemotechnics to register the disputations. Oftentimes the resolution of a case is postponed from one week to the next. Then, memories are measured against previous declarations, becoming evidence as testimony, or embodied in objects such as a piece of cloth or a talisman.

The plaintiff is at pains to remember what he is being asked to remember by the judge. The witness attempts to help with her own recollections but fails, as she is evidently falsifying the narrative. Truth, memory, and norm collide in the midst of a case: "Is this the truth, Mother? Is it true?" the judge inquires, as the discussion stops and starts. Even in this precarious setting where orality is prevalent, cases are evaluated according to precedents of previous quarrels. The community court replicates in miniature the archival and monumental mechanisms of memory of the state.

At the tribunal, memory links the individual and the collective community, acknowledging that individual memory is also the reflection of collective narratives, practices of remembrance and forgetting enacted by families and lineages. Within the dynamics of the court, which blends the work of the judges and that of families, the subject's individual memory blends with kinship's machinery of memory, a register of gifts and debts, accrual of interest and repayment obligations.

Alongside the exposure and judgment of desire, the court constitutes a place for the public use of reason[3] and presentation of truths, practices that were banned during colonial times and through which, along with their body language and rhetoric, the subjects of rights invoke a kind of dignity that must be officially recognized. At the hearing of a case, a man with a fierce, angry visage keeps repeating, almost screaming, to the judges: "She is just saying destroyed words!" "This doesn't mean anything at all. . . . These are merely destroyed words!" He means that the woman who is accusing him of serious misdeeds is plainly lying. The legal dynamics in place here imply that at the court the individual is a subject only insofar as he or she establishes a secure relationship with the truth.

The court functions as a lie detector, a machinery geared toward the production of a truth.[4] Its representation of the good citizen is a subject who speaks the truth. "You are lying, you are lying, criminals!" says the judge to accused members of a family. It is an ethical quest to restore order through a performance of veracity, the remains of a Socialist project to transform subjects, which is at odds with the context of a locality where the everyday textures of the political are understood as being enmeshed in simulacrum and secrecy.

"Is that right?" "Is it true what this person is saying?" are the recurring interrogations that the judges address to the conflicting parties. Then a confessional mode ensues that is so vivid, regretful, and penitent that it seems as though giving an account is already part of a painful punishment.

The court's obsession with a metaphysics of truth expresses the legitimacy of various political and religious local authorities. Within a secularized context, sheikhs, elders from Christian churches, local political functionaries, traditional healers, kinship figures, and others are called upon to offer counsel, pass judgment, or guarantee agreements. Through this localized politics of recognition of pluralism, vestiges from a diverse array of theological and political traditions enhance the court's force of law, transformed into an amalgam of imaginations, from politics, religion, or custom, that compel the subject to speak the truth.

This exercise of truthful rhetoric is shaped by elements of respect and fear that coalesce in the legitimacy of the community court, stemming from the invocation of the aura of the state. However, this respect, claim the judges, is merely a diluted version of what used to be a real feeling of fear vis-à-vis the state. One judge recalls a time when the force of law was linked to a general condition of fear stemming from the authoritarian rule of the Socialist regime. "In that era, back in the day, there was real respect," the president-judge said to me when we were tracing the local history of the court. "There was reverence because there was fear. People dreaded the government. Right there, there was always a policeman. You see how people act nowadays in the court. There is no respect. They do not show good manners. They do not remain silent. It was different at that time."

Decades after independence, there was in place a laborious pedagogy of questions and admonitions through which the judges attempted to shape the subject's behavior as a truth-telling subject. In the mid-2000s the court's force of law stemmed from the assemblage of the new politico-economic coercions of the liberal democratic regime, the remains of apprehension and mistrust toward the Socialist state apparatus, and the social effects and aftershock of the civil war.

At the tribunal, reason and memory blended official law and customary law. Performing at the same time both as a citizen and as a subject, the individual enacted private aspects of subjectivity—linked to desire as well as to the public use of reason prescribed by the legal belonging in a nation-state.

The possibility of a self-determined subject, its dignity, was at stake in the procedures of the tribunal, which performed the postindependence promise of state creation of a fully self-possessed postcolonial citizen. Yet in 2004, in the northern regions, local state institutions acknowledged that this emancipated subjectivity still implied a previous precolonial and colonial subjection, illustrated by forms of indebtedness mandated by customs channeled through kin-based structures.

## Debt and Sorcery

The woman, slim, her head covered with a yellow scarf, her legs crossed under the bench, is testifying before the judges, giving her version of the painful facts that prompted a conflict. It is a case of sorcery in which she is accusing other people, sounding furious, deeply hurt, and yet, somehow, managing to maintain a calm tone. Her statement, mostly referring to death, lasts for about twenty minutes. The woman wears a bright-white shirt and a skirt with slogans that celebrate the anniversary of the National Women's Association (a FRELIMO organization) and a photograph of a national heroine, a Mozambican female athlete who has established records in the Olympic Games. While she presents her recollections, she eats sugarcane and breast-feeds her baby, who is wrapped in a colorful cloth bearing the face of a local politician. Speaking about death while giving life appears as a delicate dialectics of invisible forces that might nurture or destroy the body. The legitimacy of the court's legal work also seems founded on those modes of becoming, of entangled life and death.

The cascade of her words is clear, and yet no one can discern truth from nonsense in her rushed speech as yet. The way she speaks about the invisible forces that have harmed her body sounds exaggerated, too extreme. The woman she is accusing of invisible misdeeds is sitting not far from her, wearing a T-shirt with the image of a prominent local politician.

When the first woman finishes giving her speech, the president-judge and another judge look at each other and smile sarcastically and turn toward the other litigant, a man, and ask him about his wife's whereabouts. Before he can answer, the wife starts an agitated speech from her place near the rest of her relatives at the end of the room. After a while the president-judge interrupts her: "I already understood one phase of the problem." Then another judge speaks for about ten minutes. The first woman, with a melancholic expression, listens to the judge's interpretation of the action of invisible forces that have caused the misfortune of a couple and a deep crisis in her extended family.

Sorcery accusations in which the offended family asks that an ordeal of ingestion of *mwekathe* be conducted are common at the court. Often they are connected to cases of divorce and accusations of adultery, the kinds of cases that are seen as variations on the theme of indebtedness between people who owe each other respect due to kinship.[5]

The president-judge goes in and out of the room. When he returns, he pretends to be taking notes as he interrogates another "mother" to obtain the name of a female sorcerer involved in the accusation. He shouts: "You are all criminals; this is pure deception! You cannot remember the name of the woman at this 'hospital' that you visited so many times?" A tense, violent moment ensues as he continues screaming, demanding names so that he can "notify" them and send them to the police station.

After the hearing of the accusations on divorce and sorcery, another judge affirms: "This case of adultery and bigamy is finally solved; the couple will continue living together; we achieved *conciliation.* Now we have to pass judgment on the man's attempt to strangle her with a rope." The judges leave the room, returning ten minutes later, along with the couple involved in the case. "This, in any tribunal, would mean a prison sentence because you did it on purpose. But here, in the community court, there will be only a fine. You will be *amnestied*; we will not send you to the police or the district court. We will not call the ministers of the church to show them how their Christians behave in their homes." Everyone is silent, and we hear the voice of another judge solemnly reading the sentence: "Nampula Province, June 4. . . . Disrespect toward his wife and toward the whole of society. . . . A fine of 150,000 meticais." The president-judge announces: "You have three days, until Friday, to pay; otherwise, we will submit the case to a superior court." Within the framework of the law, measures taken against a moral offense or a crime relate a loss to the estimated potential means for recuperation. In this juridico-economic calculus of social relations, transgression is analogous to indebtedness, and repayment is conceived according to a logic of punishment.

While the law constitutes an economy of calculation of equivalences and exchange of sanctions for transgressions, the dynamics at the community court reveals a different logic. The modality of conflict resolution enforced at the court is strongly permeated by widespread regional patterns of sociability that conceive of the social bond not as exchange but as debt. The community court enforces a sense of the law mixed with customary perspectives that present communal sociability not as a closed circle of reciprocity but rather as open-ended, based on the deferral of exchange and of repayment of morally sanctioned debts, implying also the postponement of violence and punishment.

First, the judges calculate the just compensation—objects, money, or actions—for a given offense. Second, the remains of a Socialist communal ethos and the resilient customary conception of the social as mortgage intervene to interrupt the actual repayment. Even if some monetary value or object is exchanged, the most important aspect of the agreement, or "reconciliation," has to do with another, more abstract question, the "spirit" of that gift, representing the remainder that cannot be forgotten or erased and needs to be pardoned. The object exchanged as gift is not strictly material but, rather, a local conception of justice.

Beyond bequests and loans through which objects circulate, life itself conceived as biology and as intimate experience is considered to be on loan. Customary law is a compendium of strategies of borrowing and repayment. Obligations acquired by means of kinship bonds, a physical aggression that requires punishment, or the malicious dealing with property or money, its theft or destruction, connect the intrinsic economic value present in the disputed object with the moral value of norms and duties and punishment dictated by the law.

## Self-Possession

The court constitutes a threshold between a private and a public sphere, shaping citizen-subjects along entwined issues of rights and subjectivity.[6] The ex–People's Tribunal illustrates the trajectory of postcolonial subjectivity, the free subject of rights whose autonomy was still shaped by articulations of law, kinship, and custom. At the court the subject had its autonomy compromised by the double bind of the requirements of state law and customary law. The neighborhood tribunal was located in a liminal space between "popular justice" and the "rule of law," referencing the ideology of a predemocratic moment that equated court, state, and political party.

Modern political thought conceives of the modern subject in reference to the figure of the legal subject. The liberal notion of the rule of law, inheritor of the Enlightenment's spirit of the laws, posits that the legal status of the subject, as an individual citizen signatory to a social contract, precedes all other forms of subjectification. "Subject to the law" is the formula that constitutes the fundamental matrix of modern subjectivity.[7]

The dialectics between the juridico-political identities of citizens and subjects in contemporary Africa is related to the double meaning of the concept of subject, as the product of both subjectification and subjection.[8] Present governmental practices and legal regimes shaping the postcolonial subject still show the imprint of colonial legacies—for instance, in the persistence of aspects of colonial bureaucracies or the importation of custom into local governance.

At the court, where the subject acts out the double guise of her subjectivity—as a private subject and a public citizen—her intimacy becomes the intimacy of the state itself, through technologies of the self that provide an education in the ritualized imagination of the state and its discourse of government. They represent pedagogic practices instilled in the individual so as to make of her a self-possessed legal subject. From the viewpoint of the court, the person is at the same time a self-possessed individual and also superadequate to herself. It prescribes techniques of the self[9] and techniques of the body (including modes of conduct at the court) that give her a surplus of meaning, which transforms the person into a legal subject.

During the court procedures, intimate desire, the exterior skin surface, and the organs of the body often constitute the objects of dispute, putting the body at stake. The community court rules upon the embodiment of biological life; the body's marks, gestures, and emotions are presented as evidence and witness. Becoming juridical matter, corporeality—scars, wounds, bodily fluids—intersects with issues of sexuality, pregnancy, reproduction, illness, or death, constitutes the foundation of the law, and relegitimizes the work of the court in the eyes of sectors of the population.

Modern democratic theory defines the citizen as self-possessed, which also means owning her body. This has consequences in ethico-political terms (the freedom to reason in the public sphere) and economic terms (the freedom to sell her own embodied labor power). Yet at the community court, the individual constitutes a citizen-subject also shaped by the kingdom of custom, whose rights are constrained by socioeconomic destitution and by the normativities of relatedness, recognized by official state justice.

While the Western subject is a tragic figure that bears a metaphysical face and an immanent face, the two corporealities of the African postcolonial citizen also form a duplicitous transcendental-empirical figure. It articulates the abstract body of the citizen and its universal rights, allegedly located above historical difference and local variation, and a singular body materialized in the flesh of the subject of custom.

## Debt and Freedom

The woman remains silent throughout the hearing of the case. It is not about her life, her deeds, or her sorrows that the men are arguing. She apparently listens as though it is all a distant background noise, indistinguishable words, unclear claims and rebuttals. She is sitting at the bench, alongside the men who argue, but it is not clear at first who she is. The discussions are about debts, petty violence, work not performed, disrespected ceremonial procedures, and more. Then, suddenly, slowly, a new argument emerges. As the heated back-and-forth exchanges unfold, the life of the woman begins to be referenced. Absent from the quarrel until a moment ago, she becomes centrally entangled within narratives of recrimination and damnation, of an economic and spiritual conflict that mars the lives of these families.

In the narratives of the conflict the woman appears to occupy a central role, yet her actual presence seems to be strangely displaced. The statements show that she is but a looming shadow, threatening in a way the men do not describe explicitly, yet evidently subdued within the structure of the family. The case revolved around the woman's unstable but permanent role within these family structures. The issues of debt and deferral that were being disputed involved property, money, and two locales. Yet the case's framing and object were not the most relevant issues. Rather, as the narrative of the case unfolded, the role of the woman within the dispute evolved, from marginal to central. Her manners and desires, her movements or lack thereof, and the possibility of her life itself were not thought of as a gift this time but almost as a commodity. During that first session (the case was discussed at the court over three weeks), the references to her life, her position, the chores she performed, and her liberty to move about began to shed light on the peculiar situation of this woman's life—not the properties of a life but life itself as property.

Relatedness evokes different questions of ownership. Local languages and memories intersect with the question of appropriation, of the curtailing of freedom. The woman was the wife of the young man involved in the quarrel, as well as the sister (or first cousin) of the other young man, the other party in the conflict. She lived with her husband at the house of his parents. She "labored all day," she "worked for others," she alleged at the second session, "without receiving anything, neither money nor a dress, nothing." Neither could she leave the house freely.

From my reflections about the history of the area and the practices I had observed or that elders had recounted in our conversations, I gained some inkling as to how the figure of this woman echoed a distant past. Later, my assistant would confirm my intuition. "She is a slave," she told me, as she briefed me about a court session that I had not attended because of illness. We were in the dark living room of the old house where I stayed. The word reverberated, as though bouncing back from the decrepit walls. The nonchalant, yet loaded tone of my collaborator added nuances to the many deep connotations of the term within the political culture of the region. Local testimonies I collected, admitting to semisecret practices, informed me that this was a singular sign of an extended set of practices of kinship understood as property, strategies that connected relatedness with capture, possession, and control.

The presence of the so-called slave at the tribunal, not as a citizen but as a subject, questioned the modernity of law and the legacies of the independence project in the contemporary rural north. In early modern liberal democratic thought, the citizen is equated with a proprietor, yet today at the crossroads of law and custom a slave reemerges as the citizen of a postcolonial democracy, much as the subjects of chiefs who regain state recognition. The subject of kinship structures that provide security and allow for reproduction, as well as for surveillance and servitude, is a citizen-subject. The two corporealities entangled in one individual are the sign of a pervasive customary citizenship, a condition of subjectivity and subjectification inflecting at the level of the local and the singular body the alleged universality of democratic rights.

## Civility

Each person enters the building of the court under a double appearance. First, as subject to the law, the scope of her individual rights should coincide with the space of her body, according to the restricted sovereignty that liberal juridical regimes grant to a legal subject of rights and her emancipatory potential. Second, she is also a communal subject located under the rule of various traditions and customs. Crossing the threshold of the law—metaphorically, the doorsill of the courthouse—the subject trespasses a limit between a private space analogous to the field of the customary and the public realm of state law.[10]

Can this movement be solely understood within the logic of the liberal democratic regime? Can the sphere of the private, supposedly located beyond the public realm of the state, encompass the practices of custom and kinship ruling over the intimate life of desire, thought, and bodily practice? The articulation of legal regimes at the court puts in question the current developmentalist *doxa* that considers the terrain of the customary as coextensive with the space limited by the normative concept of a civil society.[11]

Contemporary policies reify the colonial juridico-political distinction between the space of the customary and territories practicing modern forms of sociability, which since occupation have been ruled by European juridical regimes. Yet the community court constitutes an interface between state law and customary normativity in a neighborhood that also functions as a liminal border between the modernizing, stylized cultural forms of the city and the enduring, yet changing customs of the rural areas.

Thus, the concept of "civility," etymologically linked to the city, acquires a particular political resonance. The procedures of the periurban court show how, within the transition from a civil war to a civil state, the old division between city (as site of civil law) and countryside (as space of customary law) is still enforced. Within the elites' political discourse, the customary maintains traces of that allegedly uncivilized state of nature that colonial governance had associated with indigeneity. The register of civility signals everything that within modern citizenship is related to techniques of the body and the shaping of subjectivity, as an ethical and aesthetic adequacy of the person to perform the identity of a subject of rights. Through manners, movements, speech, and so on the materiality of embodiment and desire at stake at the court illustrates the articulations and confrontations between citizenship and civility.

The actual implementation of official policies of recognition of the customary in community courts and chieftaincies illustrates to what extent the postcolonial subject—the new democratic citizen—is also constituted by the temporality of custom, spirituality, and rules of filiation. The legal performances of the court present overlapping aspects of colonial and postcolonial juridical regimes meeting the resilience of custom and kinship, shaping a subject through the mandate to become a citizen before the law.

## On the Citizen-Subject

Anastasio Moculiba was born in a rural district in the hinterland of Nampula Province. Like most people from that area, he is a Muslim. In 2005 he lived on the outskirts of the provincial capital, although every year, like many other dwellers in the periurban neighborhoods, he worked for three months in rural areas four hundred kilometers north of the city. His family owned a small *machamba*, or field, behind the two large shacks made of mud where they lived. Only one member of his extended family had a somewhat stable, albeit intermittent job related to the "formal" employment sector, working sporadically for a provincial ministry in the downtown area.

After Anastasio's uncle passed away in 2001, he became the main actor in the extended family. A few years later, a bitter dispute with a cousin over a small piece of land that the family cultivated had unsettled relations among his closest kin. His cousin had spread nasty rumors about him in the neighborhood, which damaged Anastasio personally and forced him to seek a settlement through mechanisms beyond those of his family.

As his cousin was close to RENAMO, he took the conflict to local party officers, who transferred it to a chief living on the eastern outskirts of the city. Meanwhile, Anastasio consulted with a local sheikh, who gave him advice and put him in touch with a FRELIMO block secretary, also a Muslim and from the same home district, as well as being the cousin of a powerful figure in a semisecret group of Muslim authorities in that rural area. Members of this semisecret local elite spoke with RENAMO authorities working at the office of the district mayor (formerly a FRELIMO officer). These officers contacted RENAMO personnel in Nampula City, who spoke with the chief in charge of the case in his informal customary court, and together with a FRELIMO neighborhood secretary, they all agreed to take the case to the community court, where a deal was brokered to settle the land dispute between Anastasio and his cousin.

The entanglement of juridical regimes and local political struggles present in this case reference a broader political context of fragmentary state agencies and norms and official authorities, mixed with religious and customary structures. Here, the recourse to official tribunals is out of the question. Personal relations and semisecret networks involving religious authority mediate interactions with state politics. The periurban citizen achieves access to "justice" only through the maze of political networks involving party officers and customary authority.

The individual who approaches the court seeking justice is a concrete subject of rights and also an abstraction: the citizen of a republic. At present the court addresses her as a member of a "community," whereas in the recent Socialist era she would have been considered an individual element of a collective people. Today, in the postcolonial periurban areas, the subject is haunted by an uncanny historical figure. Through current political practices of subjection, the figure of the slave reappears folded within the emancipated democratic citizen.

At present, an African citizen is a nonsubject, a free individual emancipated from being a forced laborer and an object-commodity alienated from itself. As a product of the entangled histories of citizenship and subjecthood in Africa, today the citizen is a twofold entity that articulates two jurisdictions within a single self. As a mix of local and national entitlements, customary citizenship illustrates what could be defined as the two corporealities of the postcolonial citizen. Whereas an older political theology spoke of the king's two bodies,[12] at present in the postcolony the double embodiment of the citizen-subject secularizes that ideology into the split condition of postcolonial subjectivity. This legal subject performs customary patterns in the "private" sphere of relatedness or of being a subject to customary authority and also exerts its legal rights in the sphere of civil society. Customary citizenship is the juridical condition of the subject's two bodies.

The trajectory of citizenship in postcolonial Africa has produced a variant of the universal definition of the subject, which modern political philosophy defines as subjected. The paradigmatic figure of the modern subject is the legal subject, a reasoning individual exposed to sovereign power. Subjecthood anticipates subjectivity; the subject as politically subjected entity (*subjectus*) anticipated the *subjectum* of rational cogito. The two subjects are related by the question of rationality. The subjectivity who derives its being from rational thinking—"therefore I am" (*subjectum*)—is also the one to whom the Enlightenment acknowledges the right to the public use of reason (*subjectus*). The modern subject historically prefigures the citizen.[13]

African historical experience puts in local perspective the alleged universality of the Enlightenment's political narrative by showing its

fragmented, derivative trajectory in the (post)colony, where the historical sequence that goes from subjecthood to citizenship was tragically reversed. The movement that occurred in Western political philosophy, in
which the subject returns in the citizen, is duplicated in the African postcolony through the return of the precolonial and colonial subject within
the emancipated citizen.

In rural areas ruled by chieftaincies or in the periurban neighborhoods
and their courts of law, the current configuration of subjectivity is that of
a citizen-subject, which departs from the history of its counterpart in the
West. The subject reappears in the permanence of layers of subjecthood
to local sovereignties (chiefs, customary law, relatedness) and subjectification through traditional "technologies of the self" imbricated with the
alleged emancipated subjectivity of the democratic citizen. The issue of
freedom that was located at the center of postindependence reforms is
contested by the duplicitous corporeality of the citizen. The oppressed
subject returns within the liberal citizen, still enclosing the figure of an
enslaved being. Let us examine another figure of this predicament.

When I spoke with Nereida Mambalane outside her house, located not
too far from the community court, we were sitting with a few of her relatives. They nodded and intervened with tangential stories of their own,
alternately clarifying and obscuring the main aspects of her narrative. I
had to talk at length with several of them in order to be able to exchange a
few words with the woman. Nereida was born and raised in Khakhossani.
A victim of repeated acts of domestic violence, a year earlier she had separated from her husband and gone to live with her elders and her uncle's
family. The uncle put her in touch with a FRELIMO neighborhood secretary, who got her a job cleaning rooms three days a week in the downtown
office of a private company.

For a few months, her husband tried to get back together with her.
These attempts had been alternately amicable and menacing. His threats
also involved their two children and one older son born before they were
married. The source of the deep disagreement was related to questions of
birth and ritual. Around the time her second child was born, when misfortune struck her household and neighboring households with whom they
cultivated some land and engaged in minor economic activities, sorcery
accusations were exchanged between her husband's family and nearby
neighbors. The ritual cycles of ceremonies had not been followed, some
argued. The sacred taboo on the place where the umbilical cord was hid-
den had been broken, replied the others. The future life of the child was

placed at the center of these acrimonious disputes. Soon after, her husband's violent behavior toward her began.

Around the time of our interview, her case, submitted by the elders in
her own family with whom she had sought refuge, had been discussed for
the second time at the community court. At the court, she was quiet most
of the time, ostensibly grieving. When she attempted to present her own
version of the facts, it was through short, marginal remarks. Her attempts
to communicate failed time and again, as the two factions involved—her
elders on one side and the family of her husband along with neighbors on
the other—slowly began weaving the beginnings of an agreement.

The discussion of this case had become long and convoluted. At the
end of the second session it was increasingly evident that the two families would succeed in arranging for the woman to return to her previous
home and her husband. In this case, the authority of the elders imposed
constraints that the subtle maneuvers of the community judges could not
overcome. Contrary to many divorce cases, the acts of domestic violence
never became the object of discussion. Some among the neighbors had
acquaintances within the lower ranks of the system of secretaries, a fact
that neutralized the preeminence that the local state institution could have
over the subjects.

I could exchange only a few words with Nereida, under the vigilant gaze
of some of the elders in her family. Her uncle was away, working at farms
outside the city, and that situation somehow encouraged me to approach
her. Nevertheless, it was not easy to speak with her in the context of her
household. When I asked her if she was happy with the agreement they
had reached, she answered with evasive, meandering words. She affirmed
that she was pleased by the way the tribunal had worked, that she saw justice being done through the combination of different political authorities
at the level of the neighborhood, which found its final resolution through
the mechanisms of the "government" (meaning the neighborhood court).
Instead of asking her whether she was satisfied, and whether or not the
agreement involved curtailing her freedom, I asked her about the ways in
which the court could guarantee or at least oversee that the agreements
were honored later within the families. She responded that the elders were
doing what they thought was best for her in her situation, and she was glad
to be reunited with her children.

In fact, Nereida was once again almost shackled to the bonds of kin
and the labor of custom, which made her both a wife with regard to her
estranged husband and a domestic servant for the elders in two related

families. Her offspring were almost like hostages in this arrangement, sanctioned by custom and enforced by the law. Loose structures of relatedness, understood as a system of deferral of debts, located Nereida within a normative framework that stripped her of her will and bestowed upon her a different kind of value. The woman herself was a debt, a subject shaped by the materiality of the time of indebtedness opened by the delayed reciprocal exchange between families from both lineages.

The customary practice of considering a subject itself as debt was tolerated by the mixed juridical regime of law, ethics, and norm that was implemented at the community court. The woman was entitled to the rights and bound to the obligations of various aspects of customary citizenship, with its complex, hazardous entanglement of freedom and coercion.

As in the previous case concerning a captured woman, in this case in which a woman was again at the center of a legal quarrel, the body was not hers. She could not dispose of her corporeality, of her self, of her freedom to move, to work, or to love as she wished. Various historical and social forces shackled her. The current figure of the female domestic slave, trapped within structures of kinship and ritualized custom, is a memory trace referencing social contexts that questioned the discourse of postindependence emancipation and democratic freedom. This singular case shows the fragility of citizenship in the postcolony, haunted by the figure of the subject as forced laborer.

The universal rationality of the individual citizen and the desire channeled through kinship networks are two jurisdictions that produce the embodied reason of the citizen-subject. The edifice of postcolonial politics rests on this fragile figure, which still bears the mark of the local sovereignties that the state had claimed to suppress. In contemporary Africa the subject returns folded within the modern citizen. This is a split subject torn between the demands of the state and the community, an individual self that is autonomous only insofar as his "identity" takes a detour through the communal realm.

The court's procedures materialize forms of customary citizenship that in the everyday life of the neighborhood appeared blurred. At the tribunal the subject returns to itself through the family and the lineage. The policy on "community justice" implicitly recognizes this detour of the social, as the deferral through community and kinship of a postcolonial subject that challenges autonomy by constantly negotiating the limits of its freedom.

The subtraction of the past from the political present produces a remainder, which is the postcolonial subject. This citizen-subject is the

sedimentation of a political history, the remains of a succession of temporalities and legal regimes that have produced, alternatively, a colonial subject devoid of rights (available for forced labor, taxation, and other forms
of servitude) and a contemporary subject of rights (an individual member
of a liberal democratic citizenry, with alleged entitlements to elect those
who govern him, to work freely, and to live and work throughout a national territory).[14] The rationality of the colonial subject was constrained
by the arbitrariness of colonial law, the force of custom, and the authority
of chiefs. This former slave, later a "free" yet forced worker, constituted,
through a history of colonial occupation, concessionary capital, and metropolitan annexation, the juridical template for postcolonial citizenship.

At present, the community court addresses local dwellers through a
double bind, passing judgment on them as both citizens of a liberal republic and as subjects, members of a local community. The citizen materializes
at the intersection of the interpellations of different jurisdictions of law
and custom, between the demands of the state and those of the community. The mechanisms at play in the court implicitly assume that the person
who appears before the law is not a single individual but rather a multiplicity processed by official and traditional norms. The citizen is a split
individual[15] that relates to itself only after a detour through kinship rules.

# Conclusion

"We made a terrible mistake." This statement was often heard in Maputo in the early 2000s, repeated by high-ranking state officers from the local development industry, consultants from transnational teams working on juridical reforms, and organic intellectuals. The words referred to the decision taken by FRELIMO immediately after independence in 1975 to extirpate tradition and custom from the new nation-state and dismantle the colonial system of customary authority.

Political discourse in Mozambique is manifold. Each main concept or analytic assertion contains several layers of meaning, historically constructed and entangled in contingent factional struggles. They are situational and performatively staged according to the surrounding environment and the specific interlocutors.

The above statement expressed at least two central meanings: the adherence to either one or another vector within the ruling political bloc depending on individual political positions vis-à-vis the recent history of relations between state and customary. On the one hand, the statement was a way of acknowledging a miscalculation of the Socialist regime's capacity to efface "obscurantist" traditions and authorities. On the other hand, for many important members of FRELIMO, the acknowledgment of a crucial error in the policy on customary authority also implied that they had misjudged the historical relevance and the deeply embedded local legitimacy of the field of the customary. The phrase recognized that the nascent revolutionary party-state system had not properly evaluated the force of local formations of power and symbolic, spiritual practices.

The crux of this book turns on the effects of these two meanings. Revealing the resilience of the customary in an African context, the book has explored the effects of its materiality, sedimented in the practices of local juridico-political institutions and embodied in the corporeality of the citizen-subject. Where public discourse often presents the field of the customary as archaic, immutable, and immemorial, this study reveals the specific contours of its historicity, illustrating its capacity for simultaneous transformation and permanence. While changing forms and names (*regulos*, "chiefs of production," "community authority," "customary law," "community justice" "communal forms of land tenure"), the customary persists, through the violence of colonial repression, Socialist ban, or civil war, as a central field of power in the locality.

My fieldwork uncovered a multiplicity of "customaries" beyond the officially sanctioned realm of the local and its traditions. This is manifest, for instance, in the limited, sporadic knowledge of the customary and local juridical regimes held by the officers and consultants of the "state of structural adjustment" producing policy in these fields. The crucial role of the moral economy of relatedness embedded in loose structures of kinship is seldom mentioned in developmentalist studies and reports. The violence and sacredness of the customary are downplayed or ignored by secularizing, liberal reforms of the rule of law.

From the genealogy of an official "customary" juridically demarcated by the state, the narrative reveals how other forms of life in the locality—relatedness, spirituality—are intricately linked with local state structures, as shown in the current analogy between post-Socialist forms of "custom" and neoliberal "norm." Yet the historicity of other, subtler, more invisible forms of customary local power, located beyond the state's surveillance and definition, remains to be explored.

The analysis of the dynamics of citizenship in the difficult context of the "return" of custom illuminates the quandaries of sovereignty in the continent, as well as of its compromised juridical foundation, made increasingly visible over the past two decades in the paradoxical attempt to restore the foundations of sovereignty through legal reforms of the state. Hence, the book engages with the unfolding of the spirit of the laws, or the dominant juridico-economic ideology of governance in an African postcolony at the beginning of the twenty-first century, an era marked by the profound effects of the neoliberal restructuration of the state.

The concept of the spirit of the laws deployed in this study encompasses meanings that range from local conceptions of normativity to conceptions of the state as a unified apparatus consolidated around legal jurisdiction. The most significant of these is the groundless foundation of the law, which supports an ideological legitimation of disparate forms of power allegedly articulated in the state form. The ethnography has shown how the spirit of the laws informs the performative practice and rhetoric of a state in search of renewed legitimacy, both at the "central" level of executive and legislative powers and in a faraway semirural customary/post-Socialist tribunal.

The spirit of the laws represents the enchantment of an imaginary of the state materialized in the law, which reveals its true nature in the moment of recognizing other spirits: in the articulation with traditional norms and authorities and with otherworldly belief and ritual. In postcolonial Africa, this ideological formation is experienced by local people as a new expansion of the juridical into quotidian life-worlds, in the form of the legal configuration of "community" and the reappraisal of "customary" law and traditional authority within the new juridical framing of the state.

Yet at the level of the local, the all-encompassing future-oriented framework of this epoch encounters the temporality of multiple normativities that contest, resist, or resignify its aims and designs. One of the central local formations analyzed in this ethnography has been conceptualized here as the gift of justice. This conception of justice found in rural and periurban northern Mozambique is an example of post-Socialist custom, insofar as its logic of delayed equivalence and pardon has replaced more straightforward measurements of offenses and punishments that before independence often involved the enactment of violence. At the same time, its customary logic of deferred repayment and staged agreements that go beyond the evaluation of offenses and the sanctioning of transgressions articulates well with a dominant modality of norm and normalization that replaces an earlier, stronger logic of the juridical in contemporary forms of state governance.

At the turn of the millennium, in the wake of mass violence and in the absence of official programs of reconciliation, the fundamentally agonistic dimension of this gift rescripted conflict toward a reconstitution of everyday sociality and a solidarity based on sharing what is divisive or the object of struggle. This gift, beyond actual objects that support it, is an ineffable sign of excess that dissipates and escapes with each symbolic transaction or delayed exchange. Local sociality is based on the circulation of this element, which does not create closed forms of reciprocity but rather forms bonds through loss and deferral. The prevalence of such a form of justice propagated by formations of kinship and ritual and permeating the work of former local state institutions supposedly operating under different logics raises the question of the types of law enforced by these agencies and the scope of citizenship rights in the north of the country.

The trajectory of citizenship in postcolonial Mozambique is a singular case, one that allows us to observe the progress and pitfalls of democratization in the broader African context. If we trace the historical shaping of citizenship rights from colonial to postcolonial times, we can see the definitive inflection that "custom" produces upon citizenship rights in the contemporary moment. The view from the level of the local illuminates aspects that remain occluded from the perspective of the central state and the transnational networks that trespass it. The "law" and "life" appear entangled in crucial and complex ways in the political everyday of the locality.

Thus, the former People's Tribunals constitute a prism for observing the status of democracy at the local level. The juridical reforms that recognized chiefs and customary law acknowledged that the postcolonial citizen had not absolutely effaced the subject of precolonial and colonial regimes of subjection. The individual person who entered the community tribunal raised the question of citizenship as well as the question of subjectivity.

Postcolonial democratic reforms in Africa have been unable to fully transform the juridical space of locality inherited from late colonial regimes. The local politics of recognition shows that "civil society" in contemporary Africa is a space trespassed by the codified ambiguity of custom and the falsified complexity of tradition. It is a dynamics of social inclusion and exclusion that transforms the category of "rural civil society" into a contradiction in terms. Close study of this condition in periurban Mozambique shows that these spaces are key for observing the emergence of rural juridical and political dynamics within the scope of the city. As during colonial times, the urban is the space of a "civil society" that forms the apex of legal reforms of governance.[1] The observation of the prevalence of kinship, custom, and ritual in the community court demonstrates that full modern citizenship, as the legal status of a subject of rights that belongs to the city, is still denied to vast portions of the rural and periurban population.

Thus, in 2003–4, in the jurisdictions of rural chieftaincies or periurban community courts, citizenship rights were being implemented with large deficits, due to the blending of state law and customary law. The subject of rights was the product of senses of justice that originated in anticolonial struggles (popular justice) and postcolonial (Socialist or neoliberal) programs that, thirty years after independence, still appeared as an effect of a colonial codification due to the centrality of the customary and the permanence of old Portuguese codes within the neoliberal rule of law.

Yet beyond the evident biopolitical codification of life and its coloni-
zation by juridical regimes designed in the capital by experts, what the
ethnography in northern Mozambique uncovered were forms in which
"life" could momentarily, precariously, capture the law. This can be seen
in circumstances such as the prevalence of kinship rules at a community
court of justice, the acquiescence to spirituality by local state agencies, or
the materiality and corporeality of customary authority and ritual practice
strongly permeating and shaping dynamics of governance and rights.

The genealogy of customary law in northern Mozambique shows the
vectors of government, violence, and local practice that have collided to
shape its current contours. The historical and political study of customary
citizenship unveils it as an implicit juridical and economic category of governance that operates through the simultaneous inclusion and exclusion
of populations. The ethnographic analysis shows that it also constitutes a
politics of life, a resilient space of demand and contestation that breaks
open the current predicament and the future potential of democratic politics in Africa.

# Acknowledgments

During the process of conducting field research and the several phases of writing this book, I received many gifts and I incurred innumerable debts. I am grateful to the following people for intellectual guidance and moral support in the last few years.

Sections of this book were originally part of a project carried out at Columbia University. My adviser, Mick Taussig, was always a great source of inspiration, encouragement, and a sense of purpose. His work on the state, magic, and negative dialectics has been very important for me since I was a young student in Argentina. Mahmood Mamdani was deeply influential on my thinking about certain political and epistemological commitments in relation to the study of state and citizenship in Africa. Gayatri Chakravorty Spivak's teaching and friendship have been key to the orientation of my work. I also experienced the epiphany of attending some of the last seminars taught by the late Edward Said. At Columbia's anthropology department, Nicholas Dirks, Brinkley Messick, Marilyn Ivy, John Pemberton, and Rosalind Morris offered outstanding mentorship and support. Elizabeth Povinelli offered generous and brilliant critical advice, first at Chicago and then at Columbia. Conversations with Partha Chatterjee were most illuminating. Timothy Mitchell generously discussed with me issues related to state and capital. The friendship and support of Joyce Monges were crucial.

Columbia's anthropology department has been since the late 1990s an incredible space for transdisciplinary work, historical approaches to ethnography, postcolonial theory, and critical continental thought, within an urgent sense of the political, made more acute after 2001. I acknowledge the companionship and intellectual comradeship of Nauman Naqvi, Nermeen Shaikh, Nathaniel Roberts, Serguei Oushakine, Deirdre de la Cruz, Daniella Gandolfo, Richard Kernaghan, Suren Pillay, Ruchi Chaturvedi, Narges Erami, Antonio Tomas, Poornima Paidipaty, Emilio Spadola, Antina von Schnitzler, Lisa Mitchell, Mateo Taussig-Rubbo, Rachel Moore, Yukiko Koga, Stuart McLean, Krista Hegburg, Paul Mendelsohn, Lea Mansour, and Ramah McKay.

Within the Africanist academic community, I owe a lot to the guidance and advice of many great scholars. I am most grateful to my dear mentor and friend Peter Geschiere, without whom this project could not have been realized. My friend Ruth Marshall has been inspirational through her own research and her careful critiques of my ideas. Achille Mbembe, as mentor, friend, and host is always a crucial axis of reference for my research. Jean Comaroff has provided profound intellectual guidance from Chicago to Cape Town and beyond, as well as exceptional moral support through thick and thin. John Comaroff, a towering figure in the fields of law and the customary in Africa, has been a very generous guide and interlocutor. Other scholars dedicated to the subcontinent whose work and friendship have guided me are Sarah Nuttall, Ian Baucom, Alcinda Honwana, AbdouMaliq Simone, Mamadou Diouf, Ato Quayson, Mariane Ferme, Harry West, Peter Pels, James Ferguson, Charles Piot, Brian Larkin, Anne-Maria Makhulu, and Kelly Gillespie.

In Mozambique, I'm extremely grateful to all the many individuals and families in Maputo and Nampula provinces, too numerous to name, who were kind enough to help me, host me, and speak to me at length about their ideas and experiences. I am grateful to Francisco Ussene Mucanheia's brilliant insights and warm hospitality, as well as to his family in Nampula and Angoche, especially Momade. In Nampula, Ilda Silva was an outstanding research assistant and friend. I am grateful to the community judges in Nampula City who spoke at length with me and let me attend court sessions, especially the judge-president, the four community judges, and the neighborhood secretary in the peripheral area I call "Khakhossani" in this book. I thank the mayor and local state officers in Mogovolas District. The faculty and students at the research group on citizenship at the Catholic University in Nampula City in 2003–4 provided a warm welcome and intense debates.

In Maputo, I am grateful to João Carlos Trindade for his wisdom and hospitality at the Center for Judiciary Training and Andre Cristiano Jose and the team of researchers at the center. Thanks also to Isabel Casimiro, Teresa Cruz e Silva, João Paulo Borges Coelho, Irae Batista Lundin, Alfredo Gamito, and the many academics, politicians, businessmen, lawyers, consultants, and experts who agreed to discuss their views on past and current sociopolitical processes.

Arjun Appadurai's work on global economy and transnational culture has been fundamental for my thinking and I am thankful for many illuminating conversations with him. I had the privilege to discuss *Provincializing Europe* with Dipesh Chakrabarty during a quarter in Chicago, when the book had just come out, an experience that was central to my intellectual training. Appadurai's and Chakrabarty's texts have deeply influenced this book. Also at Chicago, conversations with Marshall Sahlins and the late Michel-Rolph Trouillot were influential in the inception of this project.

I am grateful to Mike and Kim Fortun, whom I had never met and who were very supportive and insightful on a long piece that I produced in very difficult personal conditions and that they published in *Cultural Anthropology*.

In the last few years the anthropology department at Johns Hopkins has constituted a vibrant intellectual space to rethink issues of state, law, locality, and relatedness. I am grateful to my friends and colleagues in the anthropology faculty, Jane Guyer, Naveeda Khan, Niloofar Haeri, Aaron Goodfellow, Anand Pandian, Clara Han, and Emma Cervone, for creating a very stimulating space to work on ethnography itself as a form of theorization. I am particularly grateful to Veena Das and to my dear friend Deborah Poole.

Also at Johns Hopkins, I have greatly profited from conversations with Gabrielle Spiegel, Jennifer Culbeit, Sara Berry, Pier Larson, and my colleagues at the Arrighi Center for Global Studies, especially Siba Grovogui, Beverly Silver, Kellee Tsai, and Ali Khan.

The JHU anthropology department, which had been an immensely stimulating intellectual place, also became in 2008 an amazing space of ethics, care, and kindness that has humbled me and transformed my life. I am most grateful to the Johns Hopkins anthropology staff, faculty, and graduate students who created an incredible network of support for my family and myself during those extremely harsh times. My thanks also to Bhrigupati Singh, Prerna Singh, Gerardo Renique, Ranendra Das, Bernard Guyer, Sanchita Balachandran, Maarten Ottens, Bob Leheny, Hent de Vries, Adam Falk, Neena Mahadev, Sameena Mulla, Citlalli Reyes, Thomas Cousins, and Lindsey Reynolds.

I am eternally grateful and in debt to all the friends and colleagues mentioned here and to others throughout the world who provided exceptional moral sustenance in 2008 and ever since then.

At Johns Hopkins, I am also most grateful to Drs. Judith Karp and Douglas Smith and their teams of physicians, as well as to Audra Shedeck and Valerie Ironside and all the nurses at IPOP.

The final version of this book was produced in 2012 while I was on leave from Johns Hopkins as an ACLS fellow and associate researcher at the Mahindra Center for the Humanities, Harvard University. I thank Homi Bhabha, the center's director, for hosting me and for insightful conversations. I also thank Steven Biel, the center's executive director. I am most grateful to John Tirman, executive director of the MIT Center for International Studies, for his friendship and for hosting me as a visiting fellow, providing office space and a vibrant intellectual milieu during the final stages of writing.

I am grateful to the staff at libraries and archives were I conducted research for this book: Columbia University's Butler Library and Lehman Library; University of Chicago's Regenstein Library; Johns Hopkins's Milton Eisenhower Library; US Library of Congress; New York Public Library; National Archives in Maputo, Mozambique; National Library, Lisbon; National Archives Torres de Pombo, Lisbon; Arquivo Histórico Ultramarino, Lisbon.

The fieldwork research and writing for this book have been generously funded by several institutions. These are Columbia University's Institute for African Studies, Social Science Research Council–MacArthur Foundation Program on Global Security and Cooperation, and American Council of Learned Societies. Johns Hopkins University has provided a postdoctoral fellowship, faculty leave time, and financial support for research and writing

T. David Brent, executive editor at the University of Chicago Press, believed in the value of this project through its many incarnations, and his vision and support have made this publication possible. Priya Nelson has also been very supportive and helpful at the press. Thanks to both and to three anonymous readers, who offered generous and dazzling critical insight. I thank Pamela Bruton for her excellent and careful copyediting of the manuscript.

Last but not least is my family in Argentina and the United States. To my parents, Susana and Felipe, I owe everything, the spirit and the laws. My blood brother Damian has been a friend and companion throughout our shared lives and has lately saved me and remade me. I am deeply grateful to him and his wonderful family: his wife, Carola, and Jonas, Jade, and Theo. Daniela Procupez has been very caring and supportive in myriad ways, as a true sister. For their love and warmth I thank Analia, Robby, Tobi, Ariel, Valentin, Manuel, and my in-laws Arnoldo and Clarisa Procupez, our aunt and uncle Teresa and Myron Silberman, and our cousins Jennifer Silberman and Josh Bowers.

Friends from Argentina, now scattered throughout the world, who helped me and sustained me intellectually and in many other ways are Axel Lazzari, Susana Skura, Carlos Masotta, Ana Alvarez, Javier Trimboli, Jens Andermann, Gaston Gordillo, Valeria Hernandez, and their families.

My son, Sebastian, is the joy of my life. He makes us incredibly happy, from his early waking every morning and as he unswervingly moves us and makes us proud throughout the day. To my wife, Valeria Procupez, I owe my entire life twice over, and so this book is dedicated to her.

# Bibliography

Abrams, Philip. "Notes on the Difficulty of Studying the State." *Journal of Historical Sociology* 1, no. 1 (1988): 58–89.

Ake, Claude. *Democracy and Development in Africa*. Washington, DC: Brookings Institution Press, 1996.

Appadurai, Arjun, ed. *The Social Life of Things*. Cambridge: Cambridge University Press, 1988.

Appiah, Kwame. *In My Father's House*. New York: Methuen, 1992.

Avineri, Shlomo. *Hegel's Theory of the Modern State*. Cambridge: Cambridge University Press, 1974.

Balibar, Etienne. *Citoyen/Sujet*. Paris: Presses Universitaires de France, 2011.

———. "Foucault and Marx: The Question of Nominalism." In *Michel Foucault Philosopher: Essays Translated from the French and German*, edited by Timothy Armstrong, 38–56. New York: Harvester Wheatsheaf / Routledge, 1992.

———. "Subjection and Subjectivation." In *Supposing the Subject*, edited by Joan Copcec, vii–xiii. London: Verso, 1994.

Barry, A., T. Osborne, and N. Rose, eds. *Foucault and Political Reason: Liberalism, Neo-liberalism, and Rationalities of Government*. Chicago: University of Chicago Press, 1996.

Bataille, Georges. *The Accursed Share*. 3 vols. Boston, MA: MIT Press, 1991.

Batista Lundin, Irae. "A pesquisa piloto sobre autoridade/poder tradicional em Moçambique." In *Autoridade e poder tradicional*, edited by Irae Batista Lundin and Francisco Jamisse Machava, vol. 1. Maputo: Ministério de Administração Estatal, 1995.

———. "Traditional Authority in Mozambique." In *Decentralisation and Municipal Administration*, 33–42. Maputo: F. Ebert Foundation, 1988.

Bayart, Jean-François. *L'état en Afrique*. 2nd ed. Paris: Karthala, 2006.

———. "Foucault au Congo." In *Penser avec Michel Foucault: Théorie critique et pratiques politiques*, edited by Marie-Christine Granjon, 183–222. Paris: CERI–Karthala, 2005.

———. *The State in Africa: The Politics of the Belly*. Cambridge: Polity, 2009.

Bayart, Jean-François, Stephen Ellis, and Béatrice Hibou. *The Criminalization of the State in Africa*. Oxford: James Currey, 1999.

Bayart, Jean-François, Achille Mbembe, and Comi Toulabour. *La politique par le Bas*. Paris: Karthala, 2008.

Berry, Sara. "Debating the Land Question in Africa." *Comparative Studies in Society and History* 44, no. 4 (2002): 638–68.

———. *Fathers Work for Their Sons: Accumulation, Mobility, and Class Formation in an Extended Yoruba Community*. Berkeley: University of California Press, 1985.

———. "Property, Authority and Citizenship: Land Claims, Politics and the Dynamics of Social Division in West Africa." Paper presented at Roskilde University, Denmark, 2006.

Bhabha, Homi. *The Location of Culture*. New York: Routledge, 1994.

Bloch, Maurice, and Jonathan Parry. *Money and the Morality of Exchange*. Cambridge: Cambridge University Press, 1989.

Bohannan, Paul. *Justice and Judgment among the Tiv*. Long Grove, IL: Waveland Press, 1989.

Boone, Catherine. *Political Topographies of the African State: Territorial Authority and Institutional Choice*. Cambridge: Cambridge University Press, 2003.

Borges Coelho, João Paulo. "State Resettlement Policies in Post-colonial Rural Mozambique: The Impact of the Communal Village Programme on Tete Province, 1977–1982." *Journal of Southern African Studies* 24, no. 1 (1998): 61–91.

Burcher, Graham, Colin Gordon, and Peter Miller, eds. *The Foucault Effect: Studies in Governmentality with Two Lectures by and an Interview with Michel Foucault*. Chicago: University of Chicago Press, 1991.

Butler, Judith. *Giving an Account of Oneself*. New York: Fordham University Press, 2005.

———. *The Psychic Life of Power: Theories in Subjection*. Stanford, CA: Stanford University Press, 1997.

Buur, Lars, and Helene Maria Kyed, eds. *State Recognition and Democratization in Sub-Saharan Africa*. New York: Palgrave, 2007.

———. "State Recognition of Traditional Authority in Mozambique: The Nexus of Community Representation and State Assistance." Working paper. Nordiska Afrikainstituter, Uppsala, 2005.

Cahen, Michel. "Mozambique: Histoire géopolitique d'un pays sans nation." *Lusotopie* 1–2 (1994): 213–66.

Capela, Jose. *Escravatura: A empresa de saque, o abolicionismo (1810–1875)*. Porto: Afrontamento, 1974.

———. *O imposto de palhota e a introdução do modo de produção capitalista nas colónias*. Porto: Edições Afrontamento, 1977.

———. *O movimento operário em Lourenço Marques, 1898–1927*. Porto: Afrontamento, 1981.

Centro de Formacao Juridica e Judiciária. *O papel dos tribunais comunitários na resolução de conflitos*. Working paper. Maputo, 2002.

Chabal, Patrick, et al. *A History of Postcolonial Lusophone Africa*. Bloomington: Indiana University Press, 2002.

Chabal, Patrick, and J.-P. Daloz. *Africa Works: Disorder as Political Instrument*. Oxford: James Currey, 1999.

Chan, Stephen, and Venancio Moisés. *War and Peace in Mozambique*. New York: St. Martin's Press, 1998.

Chanock, Martin. *Law, Custom and Social Order: The Colonial Experience in Malawi and Zambia*. Cambridge: Cambridge University Press, 1985.

Chatterjee, Partha. *The Politics of the Governed: Reflections on Popular Politics in Most of the World*. New York: Columbia University Press, 2004.

Chingano, Mark F. *The State, Violence and Development: The Political Economy of War in Mozambique, 1975–1992*. Brookfield, VT: Avebury, 1996.

Clarence-Smith, Gervase. *The Third Portuguese Empire, 1825–1975*. Manchester: Manchester University Press, 1985.

Cohen, David William, and Atieno Odhiambo. *Burying SM: The Politics of Knowledge and the Sociology of Power in Black Africa*. Portsmouth, NH: Heinemann, 1992.

Cohn, Bernard S. *Colonialism and Its Forms of Knowledge: The British in India*. Princeton, NJ: Princeton University Press, 1996.

Coissoro, Narana. "African Customary Law in the Former Portuguese Territories, 1954–1974." *Journal of African Law* 28, nos. 1–2 (1984): 72–79.

Comaroff, Jean, and John L. Comaroff, eds. *Law and Disorder in the Postcolony*. Chicago: University of Chicago Press, 2006.

———, eds. *Millennial Capitalism and the Culture of Neoliberalism*. Durham, NC: Duke University Press, 2001.

———. "Reflections on Liberalism, Policulturalism, and ID-ology: Citizenship and Difference in South Africa." *Social Identities* 9, no. 3 (2003): 445–74.

Comaroff, John. "Reflections on the Colonial State, in South Africa and Elsewhere: Fragments, Factions, Facts and Fictions." *Social Identities* 4, no. 3 (1988): 321–36.

Comaroff, John L., and Jean Comaroff, eds. *Civil Society and the Political*

*Imagination in Africa: Critical Perspectives.* Chicago: University of Chicago Press, 1999.

Cooper, Frederick. *Decolonization and African Society: The Labor Question in French and British Africa.* Cambridge: Cambridge University Press, 1996.

Coquery-Vidrovitch, Catherine. *Le Congo au temps des grandes companies concessionaires, 1898–1930.* Paris: Mouton, 1972.

Cormack, B. *A Power to Do Justice: Jurisdiction, English Literature, and the Rise of Common Law, 1509–1625.* Chicago: University of Chicago Press, 2007.

Coronil, Fernando. *The Magical State: Nature, Money, and Modernity in Venezuela.* Chicago: University of Chicago Press, 1997.

Cota Gonçalves, J. *Mitologia e direito consuetudinario dos indígenas de Moçambique.* Lourenço Marques: Imprensa Nacional, 1946.

———. *Projecto definitivo do Código Penal dos Indígenas de Moçambique.* Lourenço Marquez: Imprensa Nacional, 1944.

Das, Veena. "Secularism and the Argument from Nature." In *Powers of the Secular Modern: Talal Asad and His Interlocutors,* edited by David Scott and Charles Hirschkind. Stanford, CA: Stanford University Press, 2005.

Das, Veena, and Deborah Poole, eds. *Anthropology in the Margins of the State.* Santa Fe, NM: School of American Research Press, 2004.

Deleuze, Gilles. *Expressionism in Philosophy: Spinoza.* New York: Zed Books, 1992.

Deleuze, Gilles, and Félix Guattari. *Anti-Oedipus: Capitalism and Schizophrenia.* Minneapolis: University of Minnesota Press, 1983.

———. *Kafka: Toward a Minor Literature.* Minneapolis: University of Minnesota Press, 1986.

———. *A Thousand Plateaus: Capitalism and Schizophrenia.* Minneapolis: University of Minnesota Press, 1987.

Derrida, Jacques. *Archive Fever.* Chicago: University of Chicago Press, 1998.

———. *Given Time.* Chicago: University of Chicago Press, 1996.

———. "Living On: Border Lines." In *Deconstruction and Criticism,* edited by Harold Bloom et al., 62–142. New York: Seabury Press, 1979.

———. *Politics of Friendship.* London: Verso, 1998.

———. *Specters of Marx.* New York: Routledge, 1994.

———. *Writing and Difference.* Translated by Alan Bass. Chicago: University of Chicago Press, 1978.

Diawara, Manthia. "Reading Africa through Foucault: V. Mudimbe's Reaffirmation of the Subject." *Quest* 4, no. 1 (1990): 74–93.

Dinerman, Alice. "Processes of State Delegitimization in Post-independence Rural Mozambique: The Case of Namapa District, Nampula Province." *Journal of Historical Sociology* 17, nos. 2–3 (2004): 123–84.

Diouf, Mamadou. "African Historiography: Between the State and the Communities." Paper presented at Columbia University, 2000.

Dirks, Nicholas. *Castes of Mind: Colonialism and the Making of Modern India.* Princeton, NJ: Princeton University Press, 2001.

———. *The Scandal of Empire: India and the Creation of Imperial Britain.* Cambridge, MA: Harvard University Press, 2006.

Ekeh, P. "Colonialism and the Two Publics in Africa: A Theoretical Statement." *Comparative Studies in Society and History* 17 (1975): 91–112.

Ewald, François. "Norms, Discipline, and the Law." *Representations* 30 (1990): 138–61.

Fanon, Frantz. *Black Skin, White Mask.* New York: Grove Press 1967.

Ferguson, James. *The Anti-politics Machine: "Development," Depoliticization, and Bureaucratic Power in Lesotho.* Minneapolis: University of Minnesota Press, 1994.

———. *Expectations of Modernity: Myths and Meanings of Urban Life on the Zambian Copperbelt.* Berkeley: University of California Press, 1999.

———. "Transnational Topographies of Power: Beyond the State and Civil Society in the Study of African Politics." In *Accelerating Possession: Global Futures of Property and Personhood,* edited by Bill Maurer and Gabriele Schwab, 76–98. New York: Columbia University Press, 2006.

Ferguson, James, and Akhil Gupta. "Spatializing States: Toward an Ethnography of Neoliberal Governmentality." *American Ethnologist* 29, no. 4 (2002): 981–1002.

Finnegan, William. *A Complicated War: The Harrowing of Mozambique.* Berkeley: University of California Press, 1992.

Fitzpatrick, Peter "The Impossibility of Popular Justice." *Social and Legal Studies* 1, no. 2 (1992): 199–215.

Foucault, Michel. *Naissance de la biopolitique: Cours au Collège de France (1978–1979).* Paris: Seuil, 2004.

———. "'Omnes et Singulatim': Towards a Critique of Political Reason." In *Power,* edited by James Faubion, 298–325. New York: New Press, 2000.

———. *Security, Territory, Population: Lectures at the Collège de France, 1977–1978.* New York: Picador, 2009.

———. *Technologies of the Self.* Amherst: University of Massachusetts Press, 1998.

———. "Truth and Juridical Forms." In *Power,* edited by James Faubion, 6–89. New York: New Press, 2000.

———. "What Is Enlightenment?" In *The Foucault Reader,* edited by Paul Rabinow, 32–50. New York: Pantheon Books, 1984.

Geffray, Christian. *La cause des armes au Mozambique: Anthropologie d'une guerre civile*. Paris: Karthala, 1990.

———. *Ni père ni mère, critique de la parente: Le cas Makhuwa*. Paris: Editions du Seuil, 1990.

Geschiere, Peter. *The Perils of Belonging: Autochthony, Citizenship, and Exclusion*. Chicago: University of Chicago Press, 2009.

Geschiere, Peter, and J. Gugler. "Introduction: The Urban-Rural Connection: Changing Issues of Belonging and Identification." *Africa* (London) 68, no. 3 (1998): 309–19.

Gide, André. *Journal, 1889–1938*. Paris: Gallimard, 1948.

Gluckman, Max. *Custom and Conflict in Africa*. Glencoe, IL: Free Press, 1955.

Goncalves, Euclides. "Local Democracy and the Politics of Recognition: Implications for Land Management in Inharrime, Mozambique." Unpublished manuscript, n.d.

Graeber, David. *Toward an Anthropological Theory of Value: The False Coin of Our Own Dreams*. New York: Palgrave, 2001.

Gundersen, Aase. "Popular Justice in Mozambique: Between State Law and Folk Law." *Social and Legal Studies* 1 (1992): 257–82.

Guyer, Jane, ed. *Money Matters: Instability, Values and Social Payments in the Modern History of West African Communities*. London: James Currey, 1995.

———. "The Spatial Dimensions of Civil Society in Africa: An Anthropologist Looks at Nigeria." In *Civil Society and the State in Africa*, edited by John W. Harbeson, Donald Rothchild, and Naomi Chazan, 215–29. Boulder, CO: Lynne Rienner, 1994.

Hanlon, Joseph. *Mozambique: The Revolution under Fire*. Totowa, NJ: Zed Books, 1984.

———. *Mozambique: Who Calls the Shots?* London: James Currey, 1991.

———. "Renewed Land Debate and the 'Cargo Cult' in Mozambique." *Journal of Southern African Studies* 30, no. 3 (2004): 603–25.

Hardt, Michael, and Antonio Negri. *Empire*. Cambridge, MA: Harvard University Press, 2000.

Harrison, George. *Neoliberal Africa: The Impact of Global Social Engineering*. London: Zed Books, 2010.

Harvey, David. *A Brief History of Neoliberalism*. Oxford: Oxford University Press, 2005.

———. *Spaces of Global Capitalism: Towards a Theory of Uneven Geographical Development*. London: Verso, 2006.

Hawkins, Sean. *Writing and Colonialism in Northern Ghana: The Encounter between the LoDagaa and the "World on Paper."* Toronto: University of Toronto Press, 2002.

Hedges, David. "O sul e o trabalho migratório." In *Historia de Moçambique*, vol. 1, edited by Carlos Serra. Maputo: Livraria Universitária, Universidade Eduardo Mondlane, 2000.

Hibou, Béatrice. *La bureaucratisation du monde à l'ère neoliberale*. Paris: La Decouverte, 2012.

———, ed. "L'état en voie de privatisation." Special issue, *Politique africaine* 73 (March 1999): 137–45.

———. *Privatizing the State*. New York: Columbia University Press, 2004.

Isaacman, Allen. *Mozambique: The Africanization of a European Institution, the Zambezi Prazos, 1750–1902*. Madison: University of Wisconsin Press, June 1972.

Isaacman, Allen, and Barbara Isaacman. *Slavery and Beyond: The Making of Men and Chikunda Ethnic Identities in the Unstable World of South-Central Africa, 1750–1920*. Portsmouth, NH: Heinemann, 2004.

———. "A Socialist Legal System in the Making: Mozambique before and after Independence." In *The Politics of Informal Justice*, ed. Richard Abe, 281–323. New York: Academic Press, 1981.

Jennings, Theodore. *Reading Derrida / Thinking Paul: On Justice*. Stanford, CA: Stanford University Press, 2006.

Jewsiewicki, Bogumil. "The Subject in Africa: In Foucault's Footsteps." *Public Culture* 14, no. 3 (1 October 2002): 593–98.

Kantorowicz, Ernst. *The King's Two Bodies: A Study in Medieval Political Theology*. Princeton, NJ: Princeton University Press, 1997.

Kojève, Alexandre. *Introduction to the Reading of Hegel*. New York: Basic Books, 1969.

Koselleck, Reinhart. *Futures Past: On the Semantics of Historical Time*. Translated by Keith Tribe. New York: Columbia University Press, 2004.

Laclau, Ernesto, and Chantal Mouffe. *Hegemony and Socialist Strategy*. London: Verso, 1985.

Landau, Luis. *Rebuilding the Mozambique Economy*. Washington, DC: World Bank, 2006.

Lazarus, Sylvain. *L'anthropologie du nom*. Paris: Seuil, 1996.

Lefort, Claude. *The Political Forms of Modern Society: Bureaucracy, Democracy, Totalitarianism*. Edited by John B. Thompson. Cambridge: Polity, 1986.

Lemke, Thomas. "'The Birth of Bio-politics': Michel Foucault's Lecture at the Collège de France on Neo-liberal Governmentality." *Economy and Society* 30, no. 2 (May 2001): 190–207.

Lopez, Manoel. *Subsidios para urn código de usos e costumes indígenas nos territories da Companhia de Moçambique*. Beira, Mozambique: Imprensa da Companhia de Moçambique, 1909.

Macaire, Pierre. *L'heritage Makhuwa à Mozambique*. Paris: L'Harmattan, 1996.

Macpherson, Colin. *The Political Theory of Possessive Individualism*. Oxford: Oxford University Press, 1962.

Mamdani, Mahmood. *Citizen and Subject: Contemporary Africa and the Legacy of Late Colonialism*. Princeton, NJ: Princeton University Press, 1996.

——. "Indirect Rule and the Struggle for Democracy: A Response to Bridget O'Laughlin." *African Affairs* 99, no. 1 (2000): 43–46.

——. "When Does a Settler Become a Native? Reflections on the Roots of Citizenship in Equatorial and South Africa." A. C. Jordan Professor of African Studies Inaugural Lecture, delivered at University of Cape Town, 13 May 1998.

——. *When Victims Become Killers: Colonialism, Nativism, and the Genocide in Rwanda*. Princeton, NJ: Princeton University Press, 2002.

Mann, Kristin, and Richard Roberts. *Law in Colonial Africa*. Portsmouth, NH: Heinemann, 1991.

Manning, Carrie. *The Politics of Peace in Mozambique: Post-conflict Democratization, 1992–2000*. Westport, CT: Praeger, 2002.

Marshall, P. J. "The British in Asia: Trade to Dominion, 1700–1765." In *The Oxford History of the British Empire*, vol. 2, *The Eighteenth Century*, edited by P. J. Marshall, 415–39. Oxford: Oxford University Press, 2001.

Marshall, Ruth. *Political Spiritualities: The Pentecostal Revolution in Nigeria*. Chicago: University of Chicago Press, 2009.

Mauss, Marcel. *The Gift: Forms and Functions of Exchange in Archaic Society*. London: Routledge, 1990.

——. "Techniques of the Body" (1935). *Economy and Society* 2 (1973): 70–88.

Mazrui, Ali Al'Amin. *Nationalism and New States in Africa from About 1935 to the Present*. Nairobi: Heinemann, 1984.

Mbembe, Achille. "African Modes of Self-Writing." *Public Culture* 14, no. 1 (1 January 2002): 239–73.

——. "Essai sur la imagination politique en temps de guerre." Unpublished manuscript, n.d.

——. "On Politics as a Form of Expenditure." In *Law and Disorder in the Postcolony*, edited by Jean Comaroff and John L. Comaroff, 299–335. Chicago: University of Chicago Press, 2006.

——. *On the Postcolony*. Berkeley: University of California Press, 2002.

——. "On the Power of the False." *Public Culture* 14, no. 3 (1 September 2002): 629–41.

Medeiros, Eduardo. *As etapas de escravatura no Norte de Moçambique*. Maputo: Arquivo Histórico de Moçambique, 1988.

Meneses, Maria Paula. "Toward Inter-legality? Traditional Healers and the Law in Post-colonial Mozambique." *Beyond Law* 27 (2004): 7–31.

Meneses, Maria Paula, Joaquim Fumo, Ghuillerme Mbilana, and Conceicao Gomes. "The Traditional Authorities." In *Law and Justice in a Multicultural Society: The Case of Mozambique*, edited by Boaventura de Sousa Santos, João Carlos Trindade, and Maria Paula Meneses. Dakar: CODESRIA, 2006.

Merry, Sally Engle. "Courts as Performances: Domestic Violence Hearings in a Hawai'i Family Court." In *Contested States: Law, Hegemony, and Resistance*, edited by Susan Hirsch and Mindie Lazarus-Black, 35–58. New York: Routledge, 1994.

Messick, Brinkley. *The Calligraphic State: Textual Domination and History in a Muslim Society.* Berkeley: University of California Press, 1992.

———. "L'écriture en procès: Les récits d'un meurtre devant un tribunal shar'î." *Droit et société* 39 (1998): 237–56.

Minter, William. *Apartheid's Contras: An Inquiry into the Roots of War in Angola and Mozambique.* Totowa, NJ: Zed Books, 1994.

Mitchell, Timothy. "The Limits of the State: Beyond Statist Approaches and Their Critics." *American Political Science Review* 85, no. 1 (March 1991): 77–96.

———. "Society, Economy, and the State Effect." In *State Culture: The Study of State Formation after the Cultural Turn*, edited by George Steinmetz, 76–97. Ithaca, NY: Cornell University Press, 1999.

Mkandawire, Thandika, and Charles C. Soludo. *Our Continent, Our Future: African Perspectives on Structural Adjustment.* Trenton, NJ: African World Press, IDRC, CODESRIA, 1999.

Monga, Celestin. *The Anthropology of Anger. Civil Society and Democracy in Africa.* London: Lynne Rienner, 1996.

Moore, Sally Falk. *Social Facts and Fabrications: "Customary" Law on Kilimanjaro.* Cambridge: Cambridge University Press, 1986.

Morrissette, Bruce. "Un héritage d'André Gide: La duplication intérieure." *Comparative Literature Studies* 8, no. 2 (1971): 125–42.

Mucanheia, Francisco. "Democracy, Decentralization, and the Customary in Mozambique." Unpublished manuscript, n.d.

Mudimbe, Valentin. *The Invention of Africa, Gnosis, Philosophy, and the Order of Knowledge.* Bloomington: University of Indiana Press, 1988.

Myers, Gregory. "Competitive Rights, Competitive Claims: Land Access in Postwar Mozambique." *Journal of Southern African Studies* 20, no. 4 (1994): 603–32.

Nancy, Jean-Luc. *A Finite Thinking.* Edited by Simon Sparks. Stanford, CA: Stanford University Press, 2003.

———. "The Jurisdiction of the Hegelian Monarch." *Social Research* 49, no. 2 (1982): 481–516.

Newitt, Malyn. *A History of Mozambique*. Bloomington: Indiana University Press, 1995.

Norrie, A. "From Law to Popular Justice: Beyond Antinomialism." *Social and Legal Studies* 5, no. 3 (1 December 1996): 383–404.

O'Laughlin, Bridget. "Class and the Customary: The Ambiguous Legacy of the *Indigenato* in Mozambique." *African Affairs* 99 (2000): 5–42.

Ong, A. *Neoliberalism as Exception: Mutations in Citizenship and Sovereignty.* Durham, NC: Duke University Press, 2006.

Parry, Jonathan. *Money and the Morality of Exchange.* Cambridge: Cambridge University Press, 1989.

Pels, Peter. "The Pidginization of Luguru Politics: Administrative Ethnography and the Paradoxes of Indirect Rule." *American Ethnologist* 23, no. 4 (1996): 738–61.

Penvenne, Jeanne. *African Workers and Colonial Racism: Mozambican Strategies and Struggles in Lourenço Marques, 1877–1962.* Portsmouth, NH: Heinemann; Johannesburg: Witwatersrand University Press; London: J. Currey, 1995.

Pitcher, M. Anne. *Transforming Mozambique: The Politics of Privatization, 1975–2000.* New York and Cambridge: Cambridge University Press, 2002.

Poulantzas, Nicos. *State, Power, Socialism.* London: NLB, 1978.

Povinelli, Elizabeth. *The Empire of Love.* Durham, NC: Duke University Press, 2006.

Ranger, T. O., and Vaughan Olufemi, eds. *Legitimacy and the State in Twentieth-Century Africa: Essays in Honour of A. H. M. Kirk-Greene.* Oxford: Macmillan, in association with St. Antony's College, 1993.

Reno, William. *Warfare in Independent Africa.* Cambridge: Cambridge University Press, 2011.

———. *Warlord Politics and African States.* Boulder, CO: Lynne Rienner, 1998.

Ribot, Jesse, and A. Larson, eds. *Democratic Decentralisation through a Natural Resource Lens.* London: Routledge, 2005.

Riklin, Alois. "Montesquieu's So-Called 'Separation of Powers' in the Context of the History of Ideas." Discussion Paper Series, no. 61. Collegium Budapest, Institute for Advanced Study, September 2000.

Rita-Ferreyra, Alcides. *Povos de Moçambique.* Porto: Edições Afrontamento, 1975.

Roitman, Janet. *Fiscal Disobedience: An Anthropology of Economic Regulation in Central Africa.* Princeton, NJ: Princeton University Press, 2004.

Rose, Nikolas. *Powers of Freedom: Reframing Political Thought.* Cambridge: Cambridge University Press, 1999.

Rose, Nikolas, and M. Valverde. "Governed by Law?" *Social and Legal Studies* 7, no. 4 (1998): 541–51.

Sachs, Albie, and Gita Honwana Welch. *Liberating the Law: Creating Popular Justice in Mozambique.* London: Zed Books, 1990.

Sahlins, Marshall. *Stone Age Economics.* New York: Aldine de Gruyter, 1972.

Schapera, Issac. *Handbook of Tswana Law and Custom.* London: Oxford University Press for International African Institute, 1938.

Schmitt, Carl. *The Concept of the Political.* Chicago: University of Chicago Press, 1996.

Schrift, Alan, ed. *The Logic of the Gift.* New York: Routledge, 1997.

Scott, David. "Colonial Governmentality." *Social Text* 43 (Autumn 1995): 191–220.

Scott, James. *Seeing like a State.* New Haven, CT: Yale University Press, 1999.

Secondat, Charles-Louis de, baron de Montesquieu. *The Spirit of the Laws.* 1752; Cambridge: Cambridge University Press, 1989.

Sen, Sudipta. *Empire of Free Trade: The East India Company and the Making of the Colonial Marketplace.* Philadelphia: University of Pennsylvania Press, 1998.

Serra, Carlos. *Cólera e catarse.* Maputo: Imprensa Universitária, 2003.

———. *Combates pela mentalidade sociológica.* Maputo: Imprensa Universitária, 2003.

———, ed. *Historia de Moçambique.* 2 vols. Maputo: Livraria Universitária, Universidade Eduardo Mondlane, 2000.

Shadle, Brett L. "'Changing Traditions to Meet Current Altering Conditions': Customary Law, African Courts and the Rejection of Codification in Kenya, 1930–60." *Journal of African History* 40, no. 3 (1999): 411–31.

Shivji, Issa. "The Rule of Law and Ujamaa in the Ideological Formation of Tanzania." *Social Legal Studies* 4, no. 2 (1 June 1995): 147–74.

———. *State and Constitutionalism: An African Debate on Democracy.* Nairobi: SAPES Books, 1991.

Silva Francisco, Antonio Alberto da. "Economic Development from 1960s to 2000." In *Law and Justice in a Multicultural Society: The Case of Mozambique,* edited by Boaventura de Sousa Santos, João Carlos Trindade, and Paula Meneses, 91–99. Dakar: CODESRIA, 2006.

Simone, Abdou Maliq. *For the City Yet to Come.* Durham, NC: Duke University Press, 2004.

Skinner, Quentin. "A Genealogy of the Modern State." 2009. http://www.his.ncku .edu.tw/chinese/attachments/article/291/8Quentin_Skinner_A_Genealogy_of _the_Modern_State_.pdf.

Snyder, Francis. "Colonialism and Legal Form: The Creation of 'Customary Law' in Senegal." *Journal of Legal Pluralism* 19 (1981): 49–90.

Sousa Santos, Boaventura de. "The Heterogenous State and Legal Pluralism in Mozambique." *Law and Society Review* 40, no. 1 (2006): 39–75.

Sousa Santos, Boaventura de, João Carlos Trindade, and Paula Meneses, eds. *Law and Justice in a Multicultural Society: The Case of Mozambique*. Dakar: CODESRIA, 2006.

Spivak, Gayatri Chakravorty. *Critique of Postcolonial Reason*. Cambridge, MA: Harvard University Press, 1999.

Tanner, Christopher. "Law-Making in an African Context—the 1997 Mozambican Land Law." FAO Legal Papers Online, 26. http://www.fao.org/legal/prs-OL /lp026.pdf.

Taussig, Michael. *The Magic of the State*. New York: Routledge, 1997.

———. *The Nervous System*. New York: Routledge, 1991.

———. *Shamanism, Colonialism, and the Wild Man: A Study in Terror and Healing*. Chicago: University of Chicago Press, 1987.

Trindade, João Carlos. *Conflicto e transformação social: Uma paisagem das justicas em Moçambique*. Porto: Afrontamento, 2003.

Vail, Leroy, and Landeg White. *Capitalism and Colonialism in Mozambique: A Study of Quelimane District*. London: Heinemann, 1980.

Vines, Alex. *RENAMO: Terrorism in Mozambique*. Bloomington: Indiana University Press, 1991.

Vom Bruck, Gabriele, ed. *An Anthropology of Names and Naming*. Cambridge: Cambridge University Press, 2006.

Wacquant, Loic. "Crafting the Neoliberal State: Workfare, Prisonfare and Social Insecurity." *Sociological Forum* 25, no. 2 (2010): 197–220.

Weber, Max. *Politics as a Vocation*. Philadelphia: Fortress Press, 1965.

Weimer, Bernhard, and S. Fandrych. "Mozambique: Administrative Reform—a Contribution to Peace and Democracy?" In *Local Government Democratisation and Decentralisation: A Review of the Southern African Region*, edited by P. S. Reddy, 151–77. Kenwyn, South Africa: Juta, 1999.

West, Harry. "Creative Destruction and Sorcery of Construction: Power, Hope and Suspicion in Post-war Mozambique." *Cahiers d'études africaines* 37, no. 147 (1997): 675–98.

———. "Govern Yourselves! Democracy and Carnage in Northern Mozambique." Unpublished manuscript, April 2005.

———. *Kupilikula: Governance and the Invisible Realm in Mozambique*. Chicago: University of Chicago Press, 2005.

———. "'This Neighbor Is Not My Uncle!': Changing Relations of Power and Authority on the Mueda Plateau." *Journal of Southern African Studies* 24, no. 1 (1998): 141–60.

———. "Working the Borders to Beneficial Effect: The Not-So-Indigenous Knowledge of Not-So-Traditional Healers in Northern Mozambique." In *Borders and Healers: Brokering Therapeutic Resources in Southeast Africa*, edited by Tracy Luedke and Harry G. West, 21–41. Bloomington: Indiana University Press, 2005.

West, Harry, and W. Gregory. "A Piece of Land in a Land of Peace? State Farm Divestiture in Mozambique." *Journal of Modern African Studies* 24, no. 1 (1996): 27–51.

West, Harry, and S. Kloeck-Jenson. "Betwixt and Between: 'Traditional Authority' and Democratic Decentralisation in Post-war Mozambique." *African Affairs* 98, no. 393 (1999): 455–84.

Wiredu, Kwasi, ed. *Person and Community*. Washington, DC: CRVP, 1992.

Young, Crawford. *African Colonial State*. New Haven, CT: Yale University Press, 1994.

# Notes

## Notes to Introduction

1. See Hardt and Negri, *Empire*.
2. Weimer and Fandrych, "Mozambique: Administrative Reform."
3. For a thorough, learned analysis of the structure and conditions of the labyrinthine judiciary system in Mozambique, from People's Tribunals and the Supreme Court to "informal" justice systems, see the essays in Sousa Santos, Trindade, and Meneses, *Law and Justice in a Multicultural Society*.
4. On People's Tribunals, see Sachs and Welch, *Liberating the Law*. See also Isaacman and Isaacman, "A Socialist Legal System in the Making."
5. The following chapters present an ethnographic study of two types of local tribunals: community courts and People's Tribunals. I understand them—against the grain of FRELIMO's early policy and the legacy of legality implemented during the anticolonial struggle—as contemporary variations (in spatial distribution, juridical form, and rhetoric) of "African customary courts," that is, the precolonial judicial institutions reshaped by the colonial regimes. The classical studies of customary courts are Gluckman, *Custom and Conflict in Africa*; Bohannan, *Justice and Judgment among the Tiv*; Schapera, *Handbook of Tswana Law and Custom*. See also Mann and Roberts, *Law in Colonial Africa*.

## Notes to Chapter One

1. On articulations of violence and reason in the state apparatus, see Taussig, "Maleficium: State Fetishism," in his *Nervous System*. On continuities in the arbitrariness of the colonial and postcolonial African state, see Mbembe, *On the Postcolony*.
2. Hypostasis is understood here as a higher form of reification, one presenting almost ontological contours: *hypostasis as the political modality of the postcolonial condition*. On fetishism of the law in the African postcolony, see the introduction

to Jean Comaroff and John Comaroff, *Law and Disorder in the Postcolony*, and their article "Reflections on Liberalism, Policulturalism, and ID-ology."

3. Throughout this study, I use the term "custom," acknowledging a very complex history of colonial—and postcolonial—intervention, reform, and repression of local ritual, belief, language and forms of authority. On the colonial reshaping of customary law in eastern and southern Africa, see Mamdani, *Citizen and Subject*; Moore, *Social Facts and Fabrications*; Chanock, *Law, Custom and Social Order*; Shadle, "'Changing Traditions to Meet Current Altering Conditions.'" For French West Africa, see Snyder, "Colonialism and Legal Form." On custom, law, and politics, see also Cohen and Odhiambo, *Burying SM*.

4. Timothy Mitchell's approach on the production of a "state effect" blurs received distinctions between "state" and its other, which this book develops in terms of opposition between "state" and "customary," the latter being constantly reproduced locally through ritual and tactics. See Mitchell, "Limits of the State." Similarly, James Ferguson and Akhil Gupta deconstruct a view of the state apparatus as hierarchically situated—in spatial and political terms—above society and as encompassing all localities, which provides a useful way to rethink the nature of the postcolonial African state and its articulations with local polities. See Ferguson and Gupta, "Spatializing States." Partha Chatterjee and James Scott offer two very different approaches on state and political society from the viewpoint of governmentality. See Chatterjee, *Politics of the Governed*; and Scott, *Seeing like a State*.

5. On the state as mask concealing a broader field of the political, see Abrams, "Notes on the Difficulty of Studying the State." On the development of Abrams's perspective in terms of state fetishism and the state apparatus as a fantasy of centralized locus of power, see Taussig, *Magic of the State*. On the work of the state apparatus in terms of its political economy and the excessive symbolic power of its imagination, see Coronil, *Magical State*. On the state as lived in the everyday and experienced in its liminal, juridico-political and (in)visible, (il)legible spaces, see Das and Poole, *Anthropology in the Margins of the State*.

6. Bayart, Mbembe, and Toulabour, *La politique par le Bas*.

7. This conception of the state is derived from the opposite approaches of Foucault and Poulantzas and is already present in Max Weber's *Politics as Vocation*.

## Notes to Chapter Two

1. Chabal et al., *History of Postcolonial Lusophone Africa*.

2. Principal Legislação Promulgada pelo Governo da República Popular de Moçambique (1975).

3. See West, "'This Neighbor Is Not My Uncle!'"; Dinerman, "Processes of State Delegitimization in Post-independence Rural Mozambique."

4. The title of this section is a reference to a Bataillean sense of the economy (and of sovereignty more generally) based on absolute consumption and "unproductive expenditure." The concept aims at implying a political reading of the econ-

omy, linked to the violence pervasive in the last decades in Mozambique. On the concept of "general economy," see Bataille, *Accursed Share*; and Derrida's reading of Bataille's reading of Hegel in "From Restricted to General Economy: A Hegelianism without Reserves," in *Writing and Difference*, 317–50.

5. Cahen, "Mozambique."

6. See Serra, *Historia de Mocambique*, vol. 1, esp. Carlos Serra, "O papel especifico do Portugal na penetração imperialista"; Carlos Serra, "O Estado colonial português em Moçambique"; and Teresa Cruz e Silva, "O imperialismo e a partilha de Africa." On policing, see Dirks, *Castes of Mind*, 149–73.

7. The juridico-political regime of the Indigenato can be situated within an interpretive framework that connects Foucauldian conceptions of power relations with a post-Marxist perspective on the economic. The reference to Bataille's "general economy" should help to expand the field of "political economy." For a frame of reference, see Balibar, "Foucault and Marx." On Foucault / Deleuze / Marx— power/desire/value, see Spivak, *Critique of Postcolonial Reason*. On references to Foucault and codification of desire and the social by capital, see Deleuze and Guattari, *Anti-Oedipus*. For Africa, and a Bataillean conception of sovereignty vis-à-vis production and destruction of wealth and lives, see Mbembe, "On Politics as a Form of Expenditure"; and Mbembe, "Essai sur la imagination politique en temps de guerre."

8. The legal code of the Indigenato must be located within a regime of colonial governmentality understood as state policy enacted upon a "population" of subjects (noncitizens) and encompassing "life," the "body," "health and reproduction," and labor, by means of detailed official calculation and classification. On governmentality, see Foucault, *Naissance de la biopolitique*. Foucault's main lecture on the topic and several critical essays on it can be found in Burcher, Gordon, and Miller, *The Foucault Effect*. On the relation of Foucault's study of governmentality with an emergent neoliberalism, see Lemke, "The Birth of Bio-politics." On colonialism, see D. Scott, "Colonial Governmentality." For the study of the "politics of the belly" in Africa as postcolonial governmentality, see Bayart, *L'état en Afrique*, especially the new foreword on extraversion and hegemony.

9. On the Indigenato and the organization of chieftaincies, see Hedges, "O sul e o trabalho migratório"; Meneses et al., "The Traditional Authorities"; West and Kloeck-Jenson, "Betwixt and Between." On social control and legal punishment, see Cota Gonçalves, *Projecto definitivo do Código penal dos Indígenas de Moçambique*.

10. See Mahmood Mamdani's *Citizen and Subject* for his reflections on the Indigenato and his interpretation of the failures of FRELIMO's radical centralized reform of the customary. For a supplementary critique of Mamdani's thesis with regard to the sphere of the economy and labor law, see O'Laughlin, "Class and the Customary"; as well as Mamdani's response in terms of an antireductionist view of the political that strictly separates it from the space of production and consumption, in "Indirect Rule and the Struggle for Democracy."

11. See Vail and White, *Capitalism and Colonialism in Mozambique*. The key, and magisterial, historiographic work on concessionary companies in Africa is Coquery-Vidrovitch, *Le Congo au temps des grandes companies concessionaires*. On colonial control, terror, and debt peonage in private plantation companies in South America, see Taussig, *Shamanism, Colonialism, and the Wild Man*.

12. A. Isaacman and B. Isaacman, *Slavery and Beyond*.

13. See Coissoro, "African Customary Law in the Former Portuguese Territories." On the concept of the "fiscal subject" and its relation to citizenship and sovereignty, see Roitman, *Fiscal Disobedience*.

14. For general historical contextualization of the juridico-political processes depicted in this section, see Serra, *Historia de Moçambique*, vols. 1–2; as well as Newitt, *History of Mozambique*.

15. These administrators were the so-called royal high commissioners, who explicitly admired the level of development attained by British colonial policy.

16. On colonialism as a private venture, see John Comaroff, "Reflections on the Colonial State, in South Africa and Elsewhere." For the case of the East India Company, see Dirks, *Scandal of Empire*; Sen, *Empire of Free Trade*; P. J. Marshall, "The British in Asia."

17. See Isaacman, "Mozambique."

18 Capela, *O imposto de palhota e a introdução do modo de produção capitalista nas colónias*.

19. Clarence-Smith, *The Third Portuguese Empire*.

20. See O'Laughlin, "Class and the Customary."

21. On slavery in northern Mozambique, see Capela, *Escravatura;* Medeiros, *As etapas de escravatura no Norte de Moçambique*.

22. A key text on colonial labor policy and the struggle for rights in Mozambique is Penvenne, *African Workers and Colonial Racism*. On the labor movement, see Capela, *O movimento operário em Lourenço Marques, 1898–1927*.

23. For a contextualization of settlers' and natives' rights in a broader African context, see Mamdani, "When Does a Settler Become a Native?"

24. In their treatises-reports on the colony they ruled they asserted that "assimilation is the fundamental vice of our overseas legislation" (Enes) and "a race [as inferior as the black race] does not move suddenly from a state of slavery to the full use of all its rights and prerogatives. It would be lacking in the passage through an intermediate stage—servilism—although in this case it is much tamed by the state of civilization of the dominant Europeans" (Mouzinho). See Antonio Enes, "Moçambique: Relatório apresentado ao governo," Agenca Geral das Colonias, 1946 (1893).

25. See Mamdani's elaboration of the figure of the *assimilado* in *Citizen and Subject*, but also note how this liminal juridical category helps begin a deconstruction of the binary opposition between citizen and subject as well. For a large-scale comparison, vis-à-vis British and especially French colonial policy on the association of native citizens and labor, see Cooper, *Decolonization and African Society*.

26. Chiefs were called *autoridades gentilicas*, a Portuguese term (its Latin root refers to *gens*, "family") that denotes belonging to the place where one is born.

27. On the colonial state's reshaping and "modernization" of the local and the customary, see Mamdani, *Citizen and Subject*. For Tanzania, see Pels, "The Pidginization of Luguru Politics." For India, see Cohn, *Colonialism and Its Forms of Knowledge*; and, most recently, Dirks, *Castes of Mind*.

28. For a broad comparative view on the situation in the continent at that moment, see Cooper, *Decolonization and African Society*.

29. See West and Kloeck-Jenson, "Betwixt and Between."

30. Borges Coelho, "State Resettlement Policies in Postcolonial Rural Mozambique."

31. See West, "Creative Destruction and Sorcery of Construction"; and West, "This Neighbor Is Not My Uncle!"

32. Myers, "Competitive Rights, Competitive Claims."

33. See Geffray, *La cause des armes au Mozambique*; Vines, *RENAMO*.

34. Lei de terras 19/97 de 1 de Outobro; Decreto no. 66/98—Regulamento da lei de terras, approved by Council of Ministers, 15 July 1998; Diploma ministerial no. 29-A/2000 de 17 de Marco; Anexo tecnico ao regulamento da lei de terras, Ministério de Agricultura e Desenvolvimento Rural, 2001. For a thorough history and analysis of the law, see Tanner, "Law-Making in an African Context"; and *Mozambique Peace Process Bulletin* 17 (November 1996), available at http://www.geocities.com/Paris/1661/mozpeace962.html.

35. For a contextualization in terms of continental trends, see Berry, "Debating the Land Question in Africa"; Ribot and Larson, *Democratic Decentralisation through a Natural Resource Lens*. For Mozambique, see Hanlon, "Renewed Land Debate and the 'Cargo Cult' in Mozambique"; West and Gregory, "A Piece of Land in a Land of Peace?"

36. Secondat, *Spirit of the Laws*.

37. "Eccentric" is here to be understood as peripheral to an alleged "center," marginal to Enlightenment philosophies of the law and the state.

38. Decreto 15/2000, Boletin da República, 20 de Junho, Maputo, Publicação oficial da República de Moçambique. On the decree, see Sousa Santos, "The Heterogenous State and Legal Pluralism in Mozambique"; and the analysis by Santos, Trindade and collaborators in Sousa Santos, Trindade, and Meneses, *Law and Justice in a Multicultural Society*. See also Lars Buur and Helene Maria Kyed, "The Legible Space between State and Community: State Recognition of Traditional Authority in Mozambique," in Buur and Kyed, *State Recognition and Democratization in Sub-Saharan Africa*, 105–30.

39. See, e.g., an article by the project's director Irae Batista Lundin, "Traditional Authority in Mozambique." I thank Irae Batista Lundin for discussing some of her views during an interview in Maputo in 2000.

40. See texts by Sousa Santos, Trindade, Buur and Kyed, West, and Mucanheia.

41. On the empty place of power in democracy, see Lefort, *Political Forms of Modern Society.*

42. See Riklin, "Montesquieu's So-Called 'Separation of Powers' in the Context of the History of Ideas."

43. Following Hegel's definition in *Phenomenology of Spirit.* The influence of Montesquieu on Hegel is well documented. See also Kojève, *Introduction to the Reading of Hegel*; and Avineri, *Hegel's Theory of the Modern State.*

44. The effect is of an infinite recursion of specular images, or the insertion of a miniature replica of the larger whole, within the literary or plastic work of art. I interpret through this rhetorical device the mirror effect between state and customary and the fact that the state's discourse on the locality presents the state itself as crowded with a multiplicity of other, minor states that mime its own structure. For the field of poetics, the original reference is Gide's *Journal, 1889–1938.* See Morrissette, "Un héritage d'André Gide." See Jacques Derrida's critique of the concept in terms of the metaphysics of presence in "Living On: Border Lines."

45. Lopez, *Subsidios para urn código de usos e costumes indígenas nos territorios da Companhia de Moçambique*; Cota Gonçalves, *Mitologia e direito consuetudinario dos indígenas de Moçambique.*

## Notes to Chapter Three

1 Weber, *Politics as a Vocation.*

2. For a remarkable theoretical analysis of the postcolonial state in Africa, see Young, *African Colonial State.*

3. Ekeh, "Colonialism and the Two Publics in Africa."

4. See Ake, *Democracy and Development in Africa*; Mazrui, *Nationalism and New States in Africa from About 1935 to the Present*; Shivji, *State and Constitutionalism.* For a poignant critique of this literature, see Mbembe, "African Modes of Self-Writing"; and a reply to his critics in "On the Power of the False."

5. Ranger and Olufemi, *Legitimacy and the State in Twentieth-Century Africa.*

6. Mamdani, *Citizen and Subject.* See also his conceptualization on ethnic citizenship in Mamdani, *When Victims Become Killers.*

7. Bayart, "Foucault au Congo"; Bayart, *The State in Africa.* See R. Marshall's thorough critique of this argument in *Political Spiritualities.*

8. Bayart, Ellis, and Hibou, *Criminalization of the State in Africa.*

9. See Mitchell's essay on the state effect: "Society, Economy, and the State Effect."

10. Harvey, *A Brief History of Neoliberalism*; Harvey, *Spaces of Global Capitalism*; Jean Comaroff and John Comaroff, *Millennial Capitalism and the Culture of Neoliberalism*; Ong, *Neoliberalism as Exception.*

11. The reference is to the work of the German ordo-liberals as opposed to that of, for instance, Hans Kelsen.

12. For Africa, see Harrison, *Neoliberal Africa.*

13. Rose and Valverde, "Governed by Law?"

14. Foucault, *Birth of Biopolitics.*

15. Wacquant, "Crafting the Neoliberal State"; Rose, *Powers of Freedom*; Barry, Osborne, and Rose, *Foucault and Political Reason.*

16. Foucault, *Security, Territory, Population.*

17. On norm and normalization in Foucault's work, see Ewald, "Norms, Discipline, and the Law."

18. Mozambique adopted structural adjustment programs in 1987, under stern conditions and impositions from the IMF, in a situation of open warfare and calamity. See the program developed by the Mozambican government under advice from the World Bank, *Action Plan for the Reduction of Absolute Poverty, 2006–2009* (final version approved by the Council of Ministers, Maputo, 2 May 2006), esp. secs. V and VIII (on macroeconomics and fiscality and governance/economic development), available at the World Bank website, http://www.worldbank.org /en/country/mozambique. On structural adjustment in Mozambique, see the various publications by Joseph Hanlon, such as *Mozambique: Who Calls the Shots?* On Africa in general, see Mkandawire and Soludo, *Our Continent, Our Future.* On privatization of the state in Mozambique, see Pitcher, *The Politics of Privatization.*

19. See Hibou, *Privatizing the State.* On Mozambique's economy and structural adjustment, see Luis Landau's assessment report *Rebuilding the Mozambique Economy.* See Silva Francisco, "Economic Development from 1960s to 2000."

20. Reno, *Warfare in Independent Africa*; Reno, *Warlord Politics and African States*; Chabal and Daloz, *Africa Works.*

21. My conceptualization of the political field in contemporary Africa references this early etymological sense of the state apparatus. On the early modern conception of the state as condition, or "status" (from *res publica* to commonwealth to *lo stato del principe*), see the important genealogy traced by Skinner, "Genealogy of the Modern State." Asad quotes this conception in "Where Are the Margins of the State?," in Das and Poole, *Anthropology in the Margins of the State*, 279–89. On the territorial dimension of the state apparatus in Africa, see Boone, *Political Topographies of the African State.*

22. On Naparama, Mungoi, and other spiritual phenomena linked to the civil war, see Serra, *Combates pela mentalidade sociológica.*

23. "A administração da justiça em Moçambique," Universidade de Coimbra e Universidade Eduardo Mondlane, 2002.

24. I gratefully acknowledge conversations with Sara Berry and Mahmood Mamdani regarding their work on, respectively, "customary rights" and "ethnic citizenship," which has paved the way for what I try to develop here. I also have been influenced by exchanges with Achille Mbembe on the poetics of the resilience of the customary.

25. Batista Lundin, "A pesquisa piloto sobre autoridade/poder tradicional em Moçambique." For a thorough critical analysis of the project and its main conclusions, see West, "'This Neighbor Is Not My Uncle!'"; West, "Creative Destruction and Sorcery of Construction"; West and Kloeck-Jenson, "Betwixt and Between."

26. Batista Lundin, "A pesquisa piloto sobre autoridade/poder tradicional em Moçambique." On these categories as crucial loci of neoliberal governmentality, see Rose, *Powers of Freedom.*

27. For the southern province of Inhambane, see Goncalves, "Local Democracy and the Politics of Recognition."

28. On the state as fetish and its theatricality, see Michael Taussig's "Maleficium: State Fetishism," in *Nervous System,* 111–40, and the expansion of the argument in his *Magic of the State.* On power as a fetish in postcolonial Africa, see Mbembe, *On the Postcolony.*

29. Geffray, *La cause des armes au Mozambique.*

30. The legal category of jurisdiction must be contextualized through reference to its definition in Western juridico-political practice and thought. Jurisdiction amounts to the delimitation of a realm, which can be spatial (territories, seas, terrains, etc.), generic (competence over subject matters), or temporal (the past, specific time frames, etc.). See Cormack, *A Power to Do Justice.*

31. These definitions have been derived, respectively, from Roman law and medieval Western European concepts of sovereignty and justice. With regard to the first meaning, Roman law established a magistracy of private law stating jurisdictional rights for proliferating courts and created rules for the demarcation of competence and practices of disentanglement for conflict resolution. With regard to the second meaning, while at present in liberal democracies jurisdictional authority is derived from constitutional mandate, its genealogy relates it back to proprietary rights. In the Middle Ages legal jurisdiction was related to land tenure and was one of the bonds linking a tenant to a lord. The lord could claim jurisdiction, and to solve conflicts, he could "hold a court" for a community of his tenants.

32. Nancy, "The Jurisdiction of the Hegelian Monarch."

**Notes to Chapter Four**

1. Manning, *Politics of Peace in Mozambique.*

2. See Chan and Moisés, *War and Peace in Mozambique*; Chingano, *The State, Violence and Development*; Finnegan, *A Complicated War*; Hanlon, *Mozambique*; Minter, *Apartheid's Contras.*

3. See Vines, *RENAMO.*

4. Mahmood Mamdani recalled this slogan during a conversation we had on his experiences circa the 1970s in Dar es Salaam and Maputo.

5. A minor state unfolds as a modality of micropolitics. It is predicated, not

upon questions of scale or space as in the administrative "local state," but rather along the textures and materialities of the minor. Deleuze and Guattari defined "minority" in terms of national languages and literatures. Located within a national language, a minor literature is a decayed, fragmented version of the hegemonic discourse. It is a diminished version of a dominant grammar. It can be a mixed language spoken at a crossroads or border area, combining elements from different traditions and sanctioned models. State discourse operates at the level of scale, defining the alleged jurisdictions of "central," "regional," and "local" states. While the state establishes itself within public space through the distinctions between public and private, a minor state is deterritorialized, articulating different agents working along the borderlines between the law and its alterity. See Deleuze and Guattari, *Kafka*.

6. The names of people and places in Nampula Province have been changed.

7. On micropolitical struggles and ethnography, see "Micropolitics and Segmentarity," in Deleuze and Guattari, *A Thousand Plateaus*, 208–32.

8. I thank Valeria Procupez for inspiring me, through her own work, to think about life stories, memories, and histories embedded in buildings as lived space.

9. This argument was developed by Ferguson and Gupta, in "Spatializing States."

10. On the urban-rural divide in terms of political citizenship and legal rights, see Mamdani, *Citizen and Subject*. Also see, for a historico-political development, Ferguson, *Expectations of Modernity*; Geschiere and Gugler, "Introduction: The Urban-Rural Connection."

11. On this point, see Chanock, *Law, Custom and Social Order*.

12. On "planes of historicity," see Koselleck, *Futures Past*.

13. See the contributions to Hibou, "L'état en voie de privatisation."

14. See Schmitt's definition of the political in terms of a dialectics of enmity in *The Concept of the Political*.

15. The Chupasangue (literally, Bloodsucker) was a vampire-like figure whose myth emerged in the region of Nampula for the first time around 1977 or 1978, accompanying the full-fledged establishment of the DGs and their campaigns in the northern rural countryside. The legend or belief about beings that attacked the rural population at night and sucked people's blood had seemingly started in Zambezia Province at the end of 1974, coinciding with the formation of the DGs there. These legends, propagated by means of rumor and gossip, were collectively sustained by large segments of the rural population. Sociologists and journalists have underlined the connections between the legend, related to vampirism and extraction of blood, and the beginning of primary-care medical services and blood donation campaigns implemented by FRELIMO in the rural localities. Variations of the legend are found in different regions; in some versions, strangers are alleged to attack the local people at night and extract their blood with syringes through their heads. See Serra, *Cólera e catarse*.

16. The name of the district has been changed.

17. On AMETRAMO and FRELIMO, see West, *Kupilikula*. On relations between sorcery and politics in northern Mozambique, see West, "Govern Yourselves!"

18. Meneses, "Toward Inter-legality?"; West, "Working the Borders to Beneficial Effect."

19. I found this chief's name in secret reports of the Portuguese police, which revealed that he had been imprisoned in 1966 for supporting the FRELIMO insurgency.

20. See Geffray, *Ni père ni mère.*

## Notes to Chapter Five

1. The term "case" derives from the Latin noun *casus*, from the verb *cadere*, "to fall."

2. See Nancy, *Finite Thinking*, 156.

3. See Trindade's analysis of the Mozambican system of justice in *Conflicto e transformacão social.*

4. See Centro de Formação Juridica e Judiciaria, *O papel dos tribunais comunitarios na resolução de conflitos.*

5. On justice, democracy, and the political-temporal condition of the "yet to come," see Derrida, *Specters of Marx.*

6. On this dialectics, see Kojève, *Introduction to the Reading of Hegel*. On Hegelian dialectics and Africa, see Mudimbe, *Invention of Africa, Gnosis, Philosophy, and the Order of Knowledge.*

7. For spatial dynamics at community courts in recent years, see Sousa Santos, Trindade, and Meneses, *Law and Justice in a Multicultural Society*. For the courts implemented after independence, see Sachs and Welch, *Liberating the Law.*

8. Fitzpatrick, "Impossibility of Popular Justice"; Shivji, "Rule of Law and Ujamaa in the Ideological Formation of Tanzania"; Norrie, "From Law to Popular Justice." For Mozambique, see Gundersen, "Popular Justice in Mozambique."

9. For a parallel study, see Merry, "Courts as Performances."

10. On writing and the juridical order, see Messick, *Calligraphic State.*

11. See Das and Poole, introduction to *Anthropology in the Margins of the State.*

12. See Hawkins, *Writing and Colonialism in Northern Ghana.*

13. Michel Foucault famously refers the origin of his *The Order of Things* to a reading of a story by Borges on absurd taxonomic classifications in an apocryphal Chinese encyclopedia.

14. See Derrida, *Archive Fever.* On the archive and the colonial state, see Dirks, *Castes of Mind.*

15. In Hegel's *Phenomenology of Spirit*, *Sittlichkeit* (from *sittlich*, "customary") is an ethical substance, or custom, the matter of sociability, embodied in individuals, forms of life, or various citizens.

16. See Geffray, *Ni père ni mère.*

17. See João Carlos Trindade, "Rupture and Continuity in Political and Legal Processes"; and Conceição Gomes Joaquim Fumo, Guilherme Mbilana, João Carlos Trindade, and Boaventura de Sousa Santos, "Community Courts"; both in Sousa Santos, Trindade, and Meneses, *Law and Justice in a Multicultural Society.*

18. Messick, "L'écriture en procès."

## Notes to Chapter Six

1. Geffray, *Ni père ni mère*; Rita-Ferreyra, *Povos de Moçambique.*

2. This logic of kinship as credit was already noted by Geffray (*Ni père ni mère*).

3. Through an ethnographic study of law, gift, and debt, this chapter delineates an argument on social, moral, and economic value. For a postcolonial perspective on the value form, see Spivak, *Critique of Postcolonial Reason.* In anthropology, see the seminal essay by Appadurai, "Commodities and the Politics of Value," in his edited volume *The Social Life of Things*, 3–63. For a compendium of anthropological theory of value, see Graeber, *Toward an Anthropological Theory of Value*; and the ethnographic essays in Parry, *Money and the Morality of Exchange.* On West Africa, see Guyer, *Money Matters.* On debt, gift, contract, and social relatedness, see Mauss, *The Gift*; and the essays on Mauss in Schrift, *Logic of the Gift.*

4. Wiredu, *Person and Community*; Appiah, *In My Father's House.*

5. See Mbembe's thoughts on the "intimacy of tyranny" in his *On the Postcolony.*

6. See Sahlins, "The Spirit of the Gift," in *Stone Age Economics*, 149–85, a political reading of Mauss's classical analysis of the spirit of the gift in terms of social contracts and the avoidance of war.

7. On the gift as presence/present, see Derrida, *Given Time.* On justice as gift, see Jennings, *Reading Derrida / Thinking Paul.*

8. On urban life, economic exchange, and spirituality, see Simone, *For the City Yet to Come.*

9. See Laclau and Mouffe, *Hegemony and Socialist Strategy.*

10. See Ferguson, *Anti-politics Machine.*

11. I base these remarks on information that I collected through interviews and observation in Nampula. See also Geffray, *Ni père ni mère.*

12. On filiation and the political, see Derrida, *Politics of Friendship.*

13. On the register of the genealogical as underlying the liberal democratic postcolony, see Povinelli, *Empire of Love.* On the genealogical in terms of

historical formations and political economy in West Africa, see Berry, *Fathers Work for Their Sons.*

14. *Confuso* is a term from the heyday of Socialist rule, meaning "confused" and denoting social deviants or people opposing the FRELIMO regime.

15. See Diouf, "African Historiography."

16. Poulantzas, *State, Power, Socialism.*

17. For a parallel problematization of these issues in terms of filiation, nature, and the social contract, see Das, "Secularism and the Argument from Nature."

18. See Foucault, *Naissance de la biopolitique*; Foucault, "'Omnes et Singulatim.'"

19. As proposed by Christian Geffray in his study of kinship among Makhuwa people in Nampula (*Ni père ni mère*).

20. On a few occasions during my fieldwork, I accompanied the five judges on these rare excursions.

21. On intimacy and the corporeal in relation to law and rights, see Povinelli, *Empire of Love*. On desire, see Deleuze, *Expressionism in Philosophy.*

22. Foucault, *Naissance de la biopolitique.*

## Notes to Chapter Seven

1. On naming and belonging among Makhuwa people in Nampula Province, see Geffray, *Ni père ni mère*. Also see, in terms of a political philosophy, Lazarus, *L'anthropologie du nom*; and vom Bruck, *An Anthropology of Names and Naming.*

2. See Butler, *Giving an Account of Oneself*; Butler, *Psychic Life of Power.*

3. Foucault, "What Is Enlightenment?" For the unfolding of this problematic with regard to postcolonial Africa, see Mbembe's *On the Postcolony.*

4. See Foucault, "Truth and Juridical Forms."

5. See Macaire, *L'heritage Makhuwa à Mozambique.*

6. Macpherson, *Political Theory of Possessive Individualism.*

7. On citizenship and subjectivation in the light of Enlightenment tradition, see Balibar, "Subjection and Subjectivation." On subjectivation in Africa, see, e.g., Bayart, *L'état en Afrique*. On the postcolonial subject—between state, law, and desire—see the classic works of Fanon, *Black Skin, White Mask*; Bhabha, *The Location of Culture*; and Spivak, *Critique of Postcolonial Reason*. For Africa, see Mbembe, *On the Postcolony.*

8. See Mamdani, *Citizen and Subject*; also Diawara, "Reading Africa through Foucault."

9. See Foucault, *Technologies of the Self*. See also the classic Mauss, "Techniques of the Body." For West Africa, see Marshall, *Political Spiritualities.*

10. See Jewsiewicki, "The Subject in Africa."

11. See Monga, *Anthropology of Anger*; John Comaroff and Jean Comaroff, *Civil Society and the Political Imagination in Africa*; Ferguson, "Transnational

Topographies of Power"; also Guyer, "Spatial Dimensions of Civil Society in Africa."

12. See Kantorowicz, *The King's Two Bodies*.

13. See Balibar, *Citoyen/Sujet*.

14. In the case of Mozambique, in between these two layers of subjectivity—colonial subject and postcolonial citizen—there also exists the legacy of Afro-Marxism, which after independence envisioned the subject as vacant matter from which to shape and construct a Socialist utopia of subjectivity: the "New Man."

15. The split is meant here in an ethnographic, not psychoanalytic, way.

# Index